The F-Word

How Our Tax Code Is *FAILING* American Taxpayers—and Why!

DOUGLAS SPIKER

ENROLLED AGENT
ADMITTED TO PRACTICE BEFORE THE INTERNAL REVENUE SERVICE

The examples contained herein, including any supporting data or information, are provided for informational purposes only, and are not intended as legal or tax advice. Accordingly, any information provided in this book is not intended or written to be used, and cannot be used, by any taxpayer for the purpose of determining individual tax liability or for avoiding paying tax or gaining relief from penalties that may be imposed on the taxpayer. Please consult an independent tax or legal advisor for any questions regarding your individual situation based on your particular circumstances.

Copyright © 2015 Douglas Spiker
All rights reserved.

ISBN: 1505521440
ISBN 13: 9781505521443

Contents

Preface v
Introduction xi

Section I Tax Chronicles 1
Chapter 1 Taxation throughout History 5
Chapter 2 Philosophy of Taxation 15
Chapter 3 US Tax Saga 37
Chapter 4 Constitutional Questions 59
Chapter 5 Complexity or Insanity? 77

Section II Every Means Necessary, Fair and Unfair 103
Chapter 6 Living on the Margin 111
Chapter 7 When Capital Gains, Income Loses 123
Chapter 8 Payroll (Can We Say Income?) Tax 143
Chapter 9 What Choice Do I Have? 155

Section III Social Engineers or Social Dilettantes? 169
Chapter 10 The American Dream
    (or Nightmare on Main Street) 177
Chapter 11 Congress's Pet Is Our Peeve 187
Chapter 12 Fair or Foul? 205
Chapter 13 No Such Thing as a Free Lunch 213

Section IV Fool's Gold in Our Golden Years 223
Chapter 14 Social (In)Security 227
Chapter 15 Plethora of Plans 245
Chapter 16 Same Peanut Butter on Different Bread................ 259

Section V The Whole Nine Yards..271
Chapter 17 Playing Hide-and-Seek 277
Chapter 18 Peeling Back the Onion... 287
Chapter 19 Just Say When 293

Section VI There Must Be a Better Way 299
Chapter 20 Buy Now and Pay 307
Chapter 21 One Size Fits All 325
Chapter 22 Tax Do-Over.. 333
Chapter 23 The Last Word 347

Extra, Extra: Read All about It 355

Preface

Out of sheer frustration, I find myself uncharacteristically muttering the *F* word more frequently these past few years. Often, my clients do more than just mutter. Typically, the *F* word is used to describe actions taken by the Internal Revenue Service (IRS) or the arbitrary, unfair result of a provision of the Internal Revenue Code (IRC).

Although the title is a not-so-subtle hint at what many feel the Internal Revenue system is doing to American taxpayers, I chose it for another reason. Yes, I wanted to grab your attention, but more importantly, I titled this book *The F-Word* because there are many adjectives that begin with the letter *F* that can be appropriately used to describe our failed tax system—frustratingly faulty and fatally flawed. In a word—our tax code is fubar. (Author's note: For those with limited exposure to the military, *fubar* is a military acronym that dates from World War II. It stands for #%#*@ (read *F* word) up beyond all recognition/repair/reason.)

The future of the American economy, weighed down by a finicky, fluctuating tax code, is frightening. Problems will continue to fester under a flaky, feckless, and fluky tax system. Maintaining the status quo is foolish, but trying to fix this snafu is futile. The

The F-Word

Internal Revenue Code is a farce and we have to start over—we have to do better.

Notwithstanding the two reasons stated before, I chose the title of this book for one very critical reason. Regardless of which adjective is applied to the Internal Revenue Code, there is one *F* word in the Internal Revenue lexicon that no taxpayer wants to hear an Internal Revenue employee use to describe a return filed by that taxpayer. As I describe in chapter 4, the IRS is quick to call constitutional challenges to our tax laws *frivolous.*

However, the best place to start a book is at the beginning. The idea to write this book initially came to mind while playing bridge—a favorite hobby.

I first encountered the term *Morton's Fork* in the fiercely competitive world of duplicate bridge. As a serious, if not skilled, player, I studied various methods to improve my play, including the Morton's Fork coup. In bridge, the term describes a tactic that forces an opponent to choose from two equally inferior, losing plays. Literally, it refers to logical reasoning in which outwardly contradictory arguments lead to the same, usually unpleasant, conclusion.

The origin of the term is generally attributed to John Morton, Archbishop of Canterbury. As Lord Chancellor of England, he was charged with the responsibility to restore the royal treasury, depleted by King Edward IV. He determined that all citizens, rich and poor alike, could afford to pay exorbitant taxes. The Lord Chancellor instructed his tax collectors as follows:

> If the subject is seen to live frugally, tell him because he is clearly a money saver of great ability, he can afford to give generously to the King. If, however,

Preface

the subject lives a life of great extravagance, tell him he, too, can afford to give largely, the proof of his opulence being evident in his expenditure.

The dilemma faced by those subjects has been named Morton's Fork. As the king's tax collector, the Lord Chancellor's philosophy reveals a government belief that all citizens, regardless of their economic condition, have an unlimited ability to pay taxes. Just as British subjects were skewered on Morton's "fork," middle-class Americans now find themselves impaled on its tines. Americans are taxed if they work hard and save and taxed if they work hard and spend. Anything earned is always minus taxes. For anything purchased with what is left over, the price paid is nearly always plus taxes.

Using relevant, straightforward examples, this book presents an up-close-and-personal look at our tax code to illustrate that America's tax system—specifically the Internal Revenue Code—is destroying much of what America was intended to be, whether by design or by unintended consequences.

Before you draw the wrong conclusion, I am not denouncing taxes in general. If we are to live in an orderly society, I support the premise that certain functions must be provided by the government. I will not argue which roles are permissible or which functions are necessary; I just accept that they exist and they have a cost.

Although I am knowledgeable on most provisions of the Internal Revenue Code related to individual income taxes, I caution every new client, "I don't know the tax code, and, in my view, no one does." It is just too complicated and changes too frequently.

This complexity was aptly described by former Treasury Secretary Paul O'Neill, who said, "Our tax code is so complicated, we've

The F-Word

made it nearly impossible for even the Internal Revenue Service to understand." For average taxpayers, there is no way they can understand what the code requires or allows, no more than they can comprehend how it truly affects them.

The growth of the tax-preparer industry and the proliferation of user friendly tax preparation software have rendered this problem largely moot for most taxpayers. They can now easily prepare and file their own returns, or they can have their returns prepared by a professional—in either case, whether correctly or not. Year after year, a majority of American taxpayers choose one or the other option to file their returns knowing little of the tax code and, worse, understanding none of its real impact. Contrary to the familiar expression, what you do not know *can* hurt you.

The truth of that last statement is clearly described in chapter 10, titled The American Dream (or Nightmare on Main Street). For me, the arbitrary, inequitable, and changing benefit of the first-time homebuyer credit was the proverbial "straw that broke the camel's back." I started writing this book during the final days that credit was in effect.

At the time, several of my clients asked me why the homebuyer credit was created and implemented the way that it was. I understood their question. Frequently, when I explain a provision of the tax code, I am asked why. After years of struggling to provide a sensible answer to a reasonable question, I finally gave up. I refuse to try to explain the logic of a system that has none. I cannot justify the rationale of a legislative body that has lost all reason. Sadly, I had no answer—no explanation—for them.

My office wall holds a framed cross-stitch given to me by my daughter several years ago. Now, if a client asks "why," I just point to the tapestry, which reads,

Preface

> I can tell you what.
> I can't tell you why.

If, while reading a section of this book, you find yourself thinking that something doesn't make any sense and wonder "Why is that?" you should return to this page for my answer.

The problems America faces are as many and diverse as the people who call the United States home. Solutions to these problems are frequently complicated and more often hard to find. If a resolution is identified, it is seldom easy to implement even if agreement is reached on the solution. It seems intuitive, however, that the simplest injury to prevent, the easiest wound to dress, is one that is self-inflicted.

Yet many of the injuries America sustains are self-inflicted by our tax system. I believe that the cause of many of our problems can be traced to the completely dysfunctional IRC. We aren't just shooting ourselves in the foot with our tax system; we are playing Russian roulette with only one chamber empty!

Already, the Preface has lent an ominous, foreboding tone to this book. Perhaps some levity is required. The word *joke* carries a variety of definitions, including "something not to be taken seriously." But, given the unbridled authority bestowed on the IRS to enforce an unenforceable tax code, the issue of tax reform must be taken seriously. Our tax code is no joke.

A second definition suggests that a joke is a story intended to cause laughter. Try as I might, I find nothing in our tax code that can be considered a laughing matter. However, I do use humor throughout the book, not to make light of a serious subject, but to make reading about this tedious topic more enjoyable. To paraphrase a line from the movie *My Best Friend's Wedding*, "Maybe there won't be a happy ending…but, by God, there'll be laughter."

The F-Word

Writing this book was important to me. But bringing about real tax reform is important—scratch that—critical for all Americans. I told one of my sons that I wrote this book for me, but I took on the task because of my children. I went on to say that I finished it for my grandchildren, so that they might have the same opportunity Americans who came before had and enjoy the same freedom my generation and preceding generations enjoyed.

Introduction

The year 2013 marked the hundred-year anniversary of a defining moment in US history, an anniversary that likely went unnoticed as Americans went about their daily lives. In 1913, the Sixteenth Amendment to the Constitution was ratified by a sufficient number of states, making income tax a permanent fixture in the United States. The amendment states this:

> The Congress shall have power to lay and collect taxes on incomes, from whatever source derived, without apportionment among the several States, and without regard to any census or enumeration.

Those thirty words led to the Frankenstein monstrosity known as U.S. Code: Title 26—Internal Revenue Code, which contains an estimated four million words and growing daily. That power and the ensuing laws implementing that power forever changed the tax landscape of the United States. The transformation of our tax structure permanently altered our nation's economic and political climate. Many have argued the results have not all been positive.

It is disturbingly clear to me and many taxpayers—indeed, to most elected officials—that our tax system is completely broken. In nearly every presidential election in the past half century, candidates of both parties have commented on the need to reform—most recently phrased "simplify"—our tax code. Each affirmed that he or she was committed to this effort. Republican and Democrat, conservative and liberal, educated and uninformed—virtually all maintain a constant clarion call for action.

In response to our collective plea, Congress acts—often. Since the passage of the Revenue Act of 1913, our income tax laws have undergone dozens of major modifications, adding or deleting one, then another, tax provision. Many of these amendments euphemistically contained the word *reform* in their title, with each arguably making our tax code even more unworkable.

In her FY2011 report to Congress, the National Taxpayer Advocate said

> Last year we noted, for example, that a search of the tax code turned up 3.8 million words and that there had been approximately 4,428 changes to the code over the preceding ten years—an average of more than one a day, including an estimated 579 changes in 2010 alone.

Despite the assurances of elected leaders and frequent congressional action, our tax system has become noticeably worse. Humorist Will Rogers is said to have commented, "The only difference between death and taxes is that death doesn't get worse every time Congress meets." This proclamation suggests that trusting Congress to repair our tax code requires circular logic. We might be better served to ask Congress to stop.

Predictably, during the time it took to write this book, a number of changes to the tax code were enacted that may render some

Introduction

examples provided in this book inaccurate or outdated. However, unless those changes brought about a complete overhaul of the tax code, those inaccuracies or that obsolescence may, in some way, make the basic point of the book.

My purpose is not to discuss how much our government spends or on what programs the government spends its revenues. Rather, this book is focused on the nature, complexity, and inequity of the Internal Revenue Code.

In order to make a point, I sometimes use absolutes when they may not be completely accurate. Given the ever-changing, confusing, sometimes arbitrary, often ambiguous, and occasionally conflicting nature of our tax code, I understand that caution must be exercised when using words such as *every, all, never,* or *always* to describe a tax situation.

For the examples provided, unless a unique taxpayer is described, the phrase "average taxpayer" refers to a married taxpayer filing jointly and claiming two dependents. Further, unless stated otherwise, taxable income is determined by taking the standard deduction and tax liability is calculated using the tax code that was in effect for the tax year 2013.

Additionally, unless defined otherwise, the terms *law* or *laws, code, IRC, tax law,* or *tax code* refer to the Internal Revenue Code, and the terms *Service, IRS,* or *commissioner* refer to the Internal Revenue Service.

The book is divided into six sections. The first section provides a historical, constitutional, and philosophical overview of taxes and tax methods. The final section describes some alternatives to our current system. Sandwiched between those two sections, individual chapters offer specific illustrations of the complexity, the inequity—indeed the insanity—that is our tax code.

The F-Word

Just as Jack Webb intended to portray realism in his TV crime drama *Dragnet*, I hope that I have painted a realistic, crystal-clear picture of the unfair, illogical, and incomprehensible nature of our tax system. To paraphrase that show's opening narrative, "Ladies and gentlemen: the tax inequities you are about to read are true. The names, places, and amounts have been changed to protect innocent taxpayers."

At a sales seminar I attended years ago, it was suggested that if someone has a problem and is not doing anything about it, he is either unaware of the problem or not sufficiently disturbed to take action. Therefore, a salesperson's challenge was simple—make that person aware of the problem or bothered enough to do something. This book is my attempt to make you aware of the clear and present threat posed by our tax system and troubled enough to act.

Typically, a nonfiction book is meant to educate, enlighten, and inform. This book may more closely resemble a Stephen King novel. Prepare to be frightened. On reflection, perhaps *horrified* is a better word. Regardless, if after reading this book, you conclude that our future is in danger, and you are sufficiently disturbed to take action, I will have accomplished my goal.

Section I

Tax Chronicles

Overview

> Government's view of the economy could be
> summed up in a few short phrases:
> If it moves, tax it. If it keeps moving, regulate it.
> And if it stops moving, subsidize it.
> President Ronald Reagan

> We don't seem to be able to check crime,
> so why not legalize it and then tax it out of
> business?
> Will Rogers, Humorist

> In this world nothing can be said to be certain,
> except death and taxes.
> Benjamin Franklin, Founding Father

> We contend that for a nation to try to
> tax itself into prosperity
> is like a man standing in a bucket
> and trying to lift himself up by the handle.
> Prime Minister Winston Churchill

THE F-WORD

At one time or another, most of us have heard these or similar remarks regarding taxes. As a society, we laugh at late-night comedians poking fun at the Internal Revenue Service and ridiculing our tax code. However, the well-documented problems with our current tax system beg the question: should we really be laughing—or crying?

Taxes are required for an orderly society. They are omnipresent, though often hidden. Few people enjoy paying them, yet most agree they are a necessary evil. But any agreement is superficial at best and usually falls apart when the discussion turns to what kind of tax is implemented, how much tax is assessed, and on whom the tax is levied. We all know taxes exist, but do we truly understand them?

Beginning with the first organized civilization, governments of every kind, secular or theocratic, despotic or democratic, have imposed taxes of one sort or another. Recorded history is replete with lengthy narratives of taxes and taxation and their impact on the evolution of nations. Indeed, seeds of many historically significant events, including the American Revolution, were sown by a dispute over taxation.

Taxes understandably exist to raise revenues. In historical times, that need was most closely associated with the costs of war and as stated by Adam Smith, in *Wealth of Nations*, "of maintaining the dignity of the sovereign." Undeniably, many of the most significant changes in the kinds of taxes levied and the largest increases in the level of taxes occurred immediately prior to, during, or directly after a time of war.

In practice, however, taxes have been used as much to control populations, to affect trade, to punish losers in a war, to prevent or compel individual actions, to change behavior, and, in short,

Section I – Tax Chronicles

to socially engineer society, as they were used to raise revenue. In the latter part of the nineteenth century, New Zealand imposed a poll tax on Chinese immigrants after which annual immigration dropped from well over ten thousand to less than a hundred. In many Southern states, poll taxes, since declared to be unconstitutional, were often enacted to prevent African-Americans from voting. Throughout this book, I repeatedly demonstrate that our income tax laws are now designed as much to affect behavior as to raise revenue.

It is an economic reality that if you can affect someone's pocketbook, you can influence their actions and impact their lives. The reality of human nature is that the greater the impact, the more likely behavior will change. Governments have long known that truth, and the tax methods they employ reflect that knowledge.

For Americans, the evolution of taxes and tax methods produced the Internal Revenue Code, creating a tax system that, as you will see, can drive a man like me to drink.

Chapter 1

Taxation throughout History

> No government can exist without taxation.
> King Frederick the Great

> Every tax, however, is, to the person who pays it,
> a badge, not of slavery, but of liberty.
> Adam Smith, Author and Philosopher

> Taxes are what we pay for a civilized society.
> Hon. Oliver Wendell Holmes, Associate Justice of
> the Supreme Court

> The power of taxing people and their property
> is essential to the very existence of government.
> President James Madison

In order to understand where we are today and recognize pitfalls as we move forward, we must remember the road taken previously. Almost a decade before passage of the Sixteenth Amendment, Spanish-American philosopher George Santayana wrote: "Those who cannot remember the past are condemned to repeat it." As currently written, the Internal Revenue Code is one mistake we should not repeat.

The F-Word

But what is it that constitutes a *tax?* Throughout human history, in every country and culture, that word, and questions surrounding it, have been the subject of discussions around dinner tables, as well as great debates in halls of Parliament, and the precursor to wars and rebellion, leading to the creation of new nations and the demise of others.

In a general sense, a *tax* is any assessment imposed by government upon individuals for the use and service of the state, whether under the name of tax, toll, tribute, tithe, tariff, tallage, gabel, impost, duty, custom, excise, subsidy, aid, or supply. *Black's Law Dictionary* defines *tax* as a "pecuniary burden laid upon individuals or property owners to support the government…a payment exacted by legislative or executive authority…not a voluntary payment or donation, but an enforced contribution, exacted pursuant to legislative authority."

The word *tax* has other meanings. While these definitions may be derivatives of the financial levy imposed by a government, they imply a subtler, more insidious affect. As defined in *Merriam-Webster*, tax can mean "make onerous and rigorous demands on." Synonyms include *demand, pressure, aggravate, agitate, annoy, bother, harass, hassle, irritate, nettle, peeve,* and *pester*. The Internal Revenue Code, as enforced by the Internal Revenue Service, is "taxing" Americans in ways we may not even realize.

As I suggested before, governments impose taxes for one of two reasons: to raise revenue or to control behavior. Regardless of which of these two fundamental goals a government seeks to achieve, the same questions arise when devising a specific tax to be assessed. Who should pay the tax? What should be taxed? How much should the tax be? How can the collection of the tax be done most effectively and efficiently?

Section I – Tax Chronicles

What should be taxed is often the first issue addressed. Although variations exist for each, the "what" generally falls into one of the following categories.

> **People**—This could include everyone or some collective of persons (households, family units, or members of a race, ethnicity, or religion, for example); often it includes only a specific subset of people (such as males, adults, property owners, or noncitizens). Through time, a tax levied specifically on individuals has been referred to as a poll tax, capitation tax, head tax, or census tax.
>
> **Property**—This may include real property (such as land, buildings, and fixtures), personal property (sometimes defined as moveable property, such as a car), or investment property. This tax is typically called property tax or land tax.
>
> **Commerce**—Business and trade of all types have nearly always been subject to tax. International trade has been subject to customs, duties, and tariffs. Local commerce has often been the target of sales and value added taxes. Specific behaviors and actions have often been subject to narrowly defined excise taxes, sometimes referred to as "sin" taxes, such as a tax on distilled spirits.
>
> **Wealth**—The accumulation of wealth has also fallen prey to the tax collector, both during the life of the wealth holder and at time of death. Under Islamic law, Muslims have been subject to the Zakat, or wealth tax, levied at 2.5% of a person's wealth. The French imposed an *impôt sur la fortune* or simply

"tax on wealth." This levy is generally referred to as a wealth tax. In many countries, this tax is assessed at the point wealth is transferred, usually upon the death of the wealthy individual. In this case, the tax is predictably named an estate tax. Those opposed to taxing wealth pejoratively refer to an estate tax as death taxes. If wealth is given away, it may be subject to a gift tax.

Income—Since the nineteenth century, income has been increasingly subjected to a tax, referred to as just that: income tax. However, what constitutes income, and whether all forms of income are taxed the same way, has varied over time.

Once "what" to tax has been determined, the question of "whom" to tax then takes center stage. The legislature must set its sights on which of its citizens it must loot. Governments must decide who is covered by the tax. To answer this question, elected officials must ascertain whether the primary purpose of the tax is to raise revenue or affect societal behavior in some way.

If the intent is to impose a restriction on a specific element of the population, a capitation tax can be imposed on that segment of the population. Recall the poll tax utilized by many Southern states as well as the tax assessed against Chinese immigrants in New Zealand. Property and commerce can be taxed in one area and exempted in another. If the intent is to redistribute wealth, those earning less than a specified amount may be exempt from paying the taxes.

After decisions have been made regarding what to plunder and whom to loot, tax rates must be considered. It must finally be determined to what degree it is necessary to pillage the designated target. At this juncture, the issue of fairness arises, generating an argument for or against a progressive tax system. More progressive tax systems endeavor to shift much of the total tax burden onto those more able to pay, including those with accumulated wealth or higher incomes. More conservative or regressive systems attempt to create a uniform assessment including all members of society.

This question is not a new one. Throughout history, this issue has played a significant role when developing and implementing a tax. Some individuals have been exempted from paying a tax while tax rates have been raised or lowered for others based upon their ability to pay the tax.

Rates can be fixed—the same percentage for all taxpayers—or they can vary, increasing or decreasing based on some predetermined criteria. Graduated tax rates tend to apply only to income or wealth taxes. Rates can be subject to thresholds, amounts below which tax is not assessed, or ceilings, amounts above which tax ceases. Activities that the government wishes to curtail or eliminate can be assessed higher rates. Alternatively, lower rates can be levied on those activities that the government wishes to encourage.

Once the basic tax itself has been established—the what, who, and how much—the infrastructure must then be created—the how, when, and where—allowing for the collection of the tax. Just as with taxes themselves, collection methods have also varied from place to place and over time. In the Roman Empire, tax farming was employed. Under that methodology, local citizens were allowed to bid for the right to collect taxes.

In other times and other cultures, tax collectors were often hired to do the work of the sovereign and collect the appropriate tribute. Generally, this method served to create a class of citizens held in low regard, even contempt, by the general populace. In the United States, this infrastructure is the Internal Revenue Service. Need more be said?

History offers no finite borders and no definitive time periods when one type of tax—income tax, property tax, or poll tax for example—existed at the exclusion of all others. However, the evolution of tax methods can be shown to have followed a pattern. As a particular society progressed from a homogeneous, agrarian culture to one more dependent on tradesmen and craftsmen, taxes and tax systems also changed.

In the early stages of a nation's economic development, during which little or no differentiation or specialization existed, a tax on individuals—a poll or capitation tax—was most often used as the tax was easy to administer—just count noses, assess the appropriate tribute, and collect payment. As societies became more stable and developed, and as members of society began to accumulate wealth, taxing that which most nearly defined wealth—real property—began to occur more frequently.

As a nation's economy continued to grow and evolve, and as manufacturing and trade expanded, taxes on commerce became more prevalent. From the middle of the seventeenth through the middle of the nineteenth centuries, an era during which much of this change occurred, vast fortunes were accumulated by captains of commerce.

As a result, government leaders began to recognize that a tax levied on commerce comprised an indirect tax, and, because it was ultimately paid by the consumer rather than the merchant, it unfairly shifted the tax burden on those least able to pay. As a consequence of this realization, income tax and wealth tax began making their way into political discourse.

Section I – Tax Chronicles

Conventional wisdom holds that levying a tax on income is a recent development. Contrary to that view, however, recorded accounts suggest that income taxes have existed for many centuries. One record indicates that an income tax was established in China in the year AD 10. An unprecedented income tax, levied at 10% of profits, was assessed on skilled laborers and professionals.

Another of the earliest recorded uses of an income tax was the Saladin tithe, established by Henry II in AD 1188. Necessitated by the expenses of the Third Crusade, the tithe taxed each layperson a tenth of their personal income and moveable property.

These examples of an income tax notwithstanding, a tax system based on income carries a number of prerequisites in order to be effectively and efficiently administered. These requirements include a stable economy using generally accepted currency; accurate and consistent accounting; commonly understood and agreed upon definitions of receipts, expenses, and profits; and an orderly society with reliable records and consistent rules. These are all relatively recent human innovations.

Most modern financial records are maintained using the double-entry accounting system developed in the thirteenth and fourteenth centuries. The invention of the printing press, enabling the storage, communication, and exchange of large volumes of data, also occurred about that same time. Credit for this invention is given to various inventors in China as early as the eleventh century, in Korea during the thirteenth century, and, more familiarly to most Americans, to printer Johannes Gutenberg in AD 1450. These advances in accounting and in printing contributed to a greater ability to establish, assess, calculate, and administer a tax on incomes.

As a result of those two developments, and the more progressive political views which appeared during the eighteenth and nineteenth centuries, taxes assessed on income emerged as a core component of modern tax systems. The late eighteenth century is generally regarded as the era in which the first modern income tax was established.

In 1799, William Pitt the Younger introduced an income tax in England in preparation for the Napoleonic wars. Tax rates varied from two pennies on the pound for incomes under sixty pounds to two shillings per pound for incomes over two hundred pounds. In a precedent nearly incomprehensible today, the tax was repealed in 1816.

Today, virtually every country has implemented a tax on individual income. One notable exception includes many Middle Eastern nations, which receive adequate revenue from the sale of oil. Another exception includes several Caribbean island states that derive sufficient revenues from tourism and finance to fund government needs.

In addition to individual income tax, most countries, including the United States, utilize a mix of taxes, both direct and indirect, on property, on wealth, and on commerce. Many nations also impose a tax on the net profits of businesses—an issue subject to great debate.

Historically, only vertical distribution of the tax burden among socioeconomic groups differentiated by income was considered when assessing the relative progressivity of a particular tax. While that limitation may be appropriate when evaluating a specific tax, this narrow examination falls short when attempting to comprehend the progressive or regressive nature of an entire tax system—at least under our tax code.

Section I – Tax Chronicles

In order to fully understand the impact of our tax system on individual taxpayers, both taxes paid by and tax payments made to specific taxpayers must be examined. Under US law, tax expenditures are described in the Congressional Budget and Impoundment Control Act of 1974 as "revenue losses attributable to provisions of the Federal tax laws which allow a special exclusion, exemption, or deduction from gross income or which provide a special credit, a preferential rate of tax, or a deferral of tax liability." They blur the picture concerning the progressivity of our tax structure. Although a tax may be regressive in itself, tax expenditures paid to a household may mitigate or, in some cases, completely offset such tax.

Simply stated, the statutory tax burden is not necessarily equal to the actual tax liability incurred by a taxpayer. Deductions can reduce the income subject to tax, and tax credits can reduce the tax paid. Refundable credits such as the earned income tax credit, education credits, or child tax credits can actually result in net payments "to" a taxpayer rather than taxes paid "by" that same taxpayer.

It is likely that income tax will remain a cornerstone of our tax structure. Whether that statement is true or false, the who and what are taxed, and the when and how much they are taxed, as mandated by our tax code, will remain a subject of heated arguments. And that disagreement is apt to be magnified when, in a free society, implementation and enforcement tactics arguably abridge our constitutional freedoms.

When the Sixteenth Amendment was implemented by the Revenue Act of 1913, income taxes affected very few Americans. That statement is no longer even remotely true. And the growth of the reach and influence of the IRS has become stressful to many Americans.

The F-Word

But the stress caused by IRS and the increase in the tax burden can be alleviated by a readily available anodyne—bourbon. Even though that solace was temporarily taken away during prohibition, fear not, that relief has since been restored.

Chapter 2

Philosophy of Taxation

> Whoever hopes a faultless tax to see,
> hopes what ne'er was, is not, and ne'er shall be.
> Alexander Pope, Poet

> 'Tis true that governments cannot be supported without great charge,
> and it is fit everyone who enjoys a share of protection
> should pay out of his estate his proportion of the maintenance of it.
> John Locke, Philosopher

> What reason is there that he which laboreth much…
> should be more charged than he that, living idly…
> seeing the one hath no more protection from the commonwealth than the other?
> Thomas Hobbes, Philosopher

> When there is an income tax,
> the just man will pay more
> and the unjust less on the same amount of income.
> Plato, Philosopher

The F-Word

Well-intended politicians and well-reasoned citizens have forever hotly contested different tax methods. Disputes over taxes have been the precipitant of rebellion, and the cause of the rise and fall of political fortunes and of empires. Those quarrels continue today and embrace social, political, economic, and philosophical arguments. Just as before, controversy exists regarding how much to tax, what kind of tax to levy, who pays the tax, and how to collect the tax. But that argument has at no time, and in no place, been as heated as when the debate includes discussion of a tax on income.

Frequently, debates on tax methods are muddied with dialogue concerning expenditures. Politicians simultaneously argue how to raise revenues and how the money should be used. When the debate links taxes and government expenditures, the result is often a complex, arbitrary, and inefficient tax system. How and how much tax is assessed should, at least in some small measure, have a rational basis. The tax system should make some sense regardless of how the revenue is spent.

Children are often told that two wrongs don't make a right. That adage should be clearly explained to Congress. Even if our government spends too much, or spends tax dollars on the wrong things, doing so cannot be corrected by implementing a tax system that makes no sense. It just makes a bad situation worse.

Very little can long survive without a strong foundation. In the movie *The Bridge on the River Kwai*, the Japanese were compelled to relocate the construction site because, in the words of British Engineer Reeves, "It's utter folly to build the bridge on this bit of ground. It's a quagmire…I'm willing to bet, Sir, that the bridge will collapse the first time a train goes over it."

The bottom line is just that. Everything needs a solid foundation. Analogies regarding the necessity of building on firm, solid

Section I – Tax Chronicles

footing exist everywhere. In the New Testament, the foolishness of building a house on sand is contrasted with the wisdom of building on solid rock. The US Constitution was built on a solid foundation—individual freedom, limited government. So too was the resulting tax structure. The fact that changing times may necessitate a change to the tax system does not negate the wisdom of building that system on a solid, logical, and philosophical basis.

If the Internal Revenue Code were a bridge, we would all be swimming in the river.

In 1776, Adam Smith, a Scottish philosopher, wrote *An Inquiry into the Nature and Causes of the Wealth of Nations*, routinely shortened to *Wealth of Nations*, in which he expounds on taxation.

However, before evaluating different prerequisites for a rational tax system, Smith believed it appropriate to consider the need for taxes in the first place. He offers commentary in Book V, Chapter 1, on the necessity of governments and resulting expenses incurred by the sovereign or commonwealth.

> THE FIRST DUTY of the sovereign, that of protecting the society from the violence and invasion of other independent societies, can be performed only by means of a military force. But the expense both of preparing this military force in time of peace, and of employing it in time of war, is very different in the different states of society, in the different periods of improvement.
>
> THE SECOND DUTY of the sovereign, that of protecting, as far as possible, every member of the society from the injustice or oppression of every other member of it, or the duty of establishing an

exact administration of justice, requires two very different degrees of expense in the different periods of society.

THE THIRD AND LAST DUTY of the sovereign or commonwealth, is that of erecting and maintaining those public institutions and those public works, which though they may be in the highest degree advantageous to a great society, are, however, of such a nature, that the profit could never repay the expense to any individual, or small number of individuals; and which it, therefore, cannot be expected that any individual, or small number of individuals, should erect or maintain. The performance of this duty requires, too, very different degrees of expense in the different periods of society.

Language contained in the preamble to the US Constitution makes for an interesting comparison with Smith's statements regarding necessary expenses of the sovereign. The wording is strikingly similar; the implication telling.

> We the People of the United States, in Order to form a more perfect Union, establish Justice, insure domestic Tranquility, provide for the common defence, promote the general Welfare, and secure the Blessings of Liberty to ourselves and our Posterity, do ordain and establish this Constitution for the United States of America.

Smith's first stated duty of the sovereign, "protecting the society from the violence and invasion," sounds a lot like "provide for the common defence." Further, "protecting, as far as possible, every member of the society from the injustice or oppression of every other member of it" seems remarkably similar to "establish Justice, insure domestic Tranquility." None can argue that Smith's final duty, "erecting and maintaining those public institutions and those public works," can be determined to be any different from "promote the general Welfare."

In short, one can logically infer that Smith's beliefs regarding functions provided by a central government were in large measure incorporated by our founding fathers into the basic framework of our Constitution.

In concluding his discussion of necessary expenses, Smith wrote:

> The expense of defending the society, and that of supporting the dignity of the chief magistrate, are both laid out for the general benefit of the whole society. It is reasonable, therefore, that they should be defrayed by the general contribution of the whole society; all the different members contributing, as nearly as possible, in proportion to their respective abilities.
>
> The expense of the administration of justice, too, may no doubt be considered as laid out for the benefit of the whole society…expense of maintaining good roads and communications is, no doubt, beneficial to the whole society…expense of the institutions for education…is likewise, no doubt, beneficial to the whole society.

For each, he concluded that they may, therefore, "without any injustice…or impropriety…be defrayed by the general contribution of all members of the society."

While this discourse seemingly strays from the main focus of the book—individual income taxes—it demonstrates that an ordered society necessarily incurs expenses for the greater good, and those expenses must be borne by the entire society. I accept as a precondition of this book the notion that those expenses exist and the existence of a greater good.

However, I recognize that legitimate differences exist regarding which expenses and how much expense reasonably fall within this concept. The rise of social welfare has changed, perhaps forever, the role of government and its impact on, and influence over, the lives of its citizens.

Assuming the existence of some form of government raises the question, "Where does the money come from to pay its expenses?" Finding a reasonable and acceptable solution to that riddle has perplexed governments from ancient Rome to modern societies. There is never an easy answer to the question and certainly not one on which everyone agrees. History is awash with details of different taxes assessed, different populations and activities taxed, and different collection methods used.

In Book V, Chapter 2, Smith proposes four maxims for a rational tax system, although he does not necessarily argue for or against any specific type of tax. He maintained, simply, that money necessary to run the government had to come from some fund under control of the government or "from the revenue of the people."

I agree with his premise that a tax system must be built on a logical framework. I believe Smith's four maxims to be on point and the implications so critical that they merit significant examination.

Balancing the Load

His first maxim addressed the requirement to pay taxes and how the tax burden should be shared.

Section I – Tax Chronicles

> The subjects of every state ought to contribute towards the support of the government, as nearly as possible, in proportion to their respective abilities; that is, in proportion to the revenue which they respectively enjoy under the protection of the state.

Considerable debate has been generated regarding the true intent of Smith's first maxim, particularly surrounding the phrase, "contribute towards the support of the government, as nearly as possible, in proportion to their respective abilities."

Conservatives and liberals alike take this maxim as evidence that Smith supported their view of taxation. Claiming him as one of their own, conservatives affirm that Smith believed everyone should pay tax. Liberals argue for Smith's progressivity, focusing on the term *in proportion* embedded in Smith's maxim.

I subscribe to the idea that Smith was arguing both points of view—that each member of society should contribute to the support of society as a whole, but such payments should be proportional to the benefit derived from being a member of that society. The debate over income taxes is often waged over these two questions: whether everyone should be required to pay, and how much they should be taxed.

Smith begins his first maxim by asserting, "The subjects of every state ought to contribute." He does not write "some subjects" or "wealthy subjects" or any other subset of subjects. It can only be understood that he meant all subjects—everyone.

Today, some conservatives decry the fact that many in our country effectively pay no income tax. In fact, given specific provisions of the tax code, it can be demonstrated that certain households with income approximating $37,800, comprised solely of earned wages, effectively pay neither federal income tax nor payroll taxes.

The F-Word

Equally irksome to liberals, however, is the idea that, under the 2013 tax code, a married taxpayer with two dependents, whose sole source of income is capital gains, could earn as much as $110,000 and pay no federal income or payroll tax.

Those who support a progressive tax argue that the least among us economically should not be obligated to pay any taxes, and, as a household climbs up the socioeconomic ladder, effective tax rates should be lower than for those much more well-off. Many who hold this belief see our current system as a violation of Smith's assertion that one should "contribute…as nearly as possible, in proportion to their respective abilities." They maintain that wealthy individuals should pay a much higher percentage of income than those in lower-income brackets.

Some religious faiths, including most Judeo-Christian sects, advocate that those who have the means should assist those who do not. We read in Deuteronomy, "If among you, one of your brothers should become poor…you shall open your hand to him and lend him sufficient for his need, whatever it may be." It is important to note, however, that this mandate is directed at individuals, not at governments. Nonetheless, members of that faith are also told that "the rich are not to give more than a half shekel and the poor are not to give less."

In the human experience, sociologists have posited that people do not value those things that for them have no cost. Thomas Paine wrote, "What we obtain too cheap, we esteem too lightly; it is dearness only that gives everything its value." Literal interpretation of Paine's assertion would render the benefits of society, of the common good, to be insignificant, even worthless in those households that pay no taxes. In this event, one possible outcome is that these households would become disconnected from society as a whole.

It is also reasonable to argue that should too much of the tax burden be shifted onto the wealthy, they will seek ways to protect their wealth from being taxed (such as moving out of the society or moving their wealth out of the economy). Examples abound of wealthy citizens moving from one state to another to avoid high state taxes. Efforts used by those well-off to shield their wealth from the inquisitive eyes of the IRS are frequently reported.

Again, I think the truth and, hence, the solution lie somewhere between these two logical extremes. To hold some households exempt from taxation can possibly create a malaise, a disinterest in the betterment of society as a whole. Taxing households at a rate that takes them below a living wage also serves no useful societal purpose.

However, taxing the wealthy at much higher, even punitive rates can create a divide among economic classes. To the contrary, implementation of a tax system that effectively taxes the very wealthy at lower effective rates than those earning much less serves two dysfunctional ends. First, this upward redistribution of wealth accelerates the shrinking of the middle class and, second, creates distrust, even animus, toward the system as a whole.

In the Sure and Certain Belief

Regardless of how the system treats taxpayers from different economic classes, Smith's second maxim is, in my view, the most critical of the four when assessing the problems inherent in our tax structure. The following maxim expresses his certainty principle:

> The tax which each individual is bound to pay, ought to be certain and not arbitrary. The time of payment, the manner of payment, the quantity to be paid,

ought all to be clear and plain to the contributor, and to every other person.

He stressed that a tax should be clear and certain, not only to the taxpayer but to his friends and neighbors. In this respect, our system falls well short of Smith's desired end. Woefully short. I place certainty at the top of the list with respect to its importance in the design of a rational tax system. Under our confused and confusing tax code, addressing this issue is critical.

Sadly, we are never likely to satisfy Smith's first maxim, which implied that all members of society pay their proportionate share. We are unlikely to agree on the definition of the term *fair share* much less develop a structure that could achieve such a result. However, we should be able to develop a system that is far less complex and far more certain as to manner, time, and amount of tax to be paid than the existing tax code.

The uncertainty of our tax code reminds me of the extraordinary difference in the ticket price often paid by two individuals sitting next to one another on an airplane. One may have purchased his ticket months before and the other only days before the flight. Either passenger may have purchased the ticket through a travel agent or directly from the airline. Often, a difference of hundreds, even thousands of dollars, exists between the prices each passenger paid for a ticket.

So is it true with our tax system. It cannot be said that anything is certain about it. The fact that a provision calling for the calculation and payment of an alternative tax is embedded within our tax code denies the existence of this certainty principle, no less its importance.

In chapter 10, I tell the story of two brothers. Briefly, you will read that both households earn essentially the same income and both

Section I – Tax Chronicles

submit an offer to buy a home within days of one another. Both close their home purchase within weeks of each other, under the same law in effect when they closed. Yet, one family receives a $7,500 loan while the other receives an $8,000 grant. Certainty, therefore, is not a component of a tax system so structured.

In the event that calculation of tax is uncertain, Smith predicted that every person subject to the tax is put in the power of the tax collector "who can either aggravate the tax upon any obnoxious contributor, or extort, by the terror of such aggravation, some present or perquisite to himself." I have participated in enough examinations—the current IRS euphemism for an audit—to recognize the result Smith forecast should his certainty maxim be disregarded.

When preparing a client for an IRS audit, I suggest that the pragmatic implementation of our tax code is based on a philosophical conundrum. In one respect, even though compliance with our tax laws is voluntary (Author's note: "Voluntary" in this respect has been determined to mean that the initial reporting of income and calculation of tax due is done by the taxpayer as opposed to the government.), I advise that, with few exceptions, the IRS accepts as truthful everything a taxpayer reports when completing and filing a return.

Conversely, I caution that the IRS believes absolutely nothing the taxpayer says during an audit. The taxpayer must prove all claims, and the proof must be in a form acceptable to the examiner. Notwithstanding the rights stated in the IRS publication, "Your Rights as a Taxpayer—Publication 1," during an audit, the examining officer is the accuser, the investigating detective, the witness for the government, the bailiff, the court recorder, the prosecuting attorney, the victim, the judge, the jury, and the executioner. Don't be fooled. It is his ballpark. He writes the rules. The referees are his. The ball is his.

The only saving grace to the examination process is that IRS guidelines are clear. Clear, that is, if you can determine which ones are applicable to you. For example, the IRS recently released Revenue Procedure 2014-63, "to update Revenue Procedure 2009-44, 2009-2 C.B. 462, incorporating provisions of Announcements 2008-111 and 2011-6 relating to mediation, to expand and clarify the types of examination and collection cases and issues in the appeals administrative process that are eligible for mediation pursuant to section 7123(b)(1) of the Internal Revenue Code. Revenue Procedure 2014-63 will be in IRB 2014-53, dated December 29, 2014." That's clear enough isn't it?

I once assisted a client during an audit that resulted in a proposed increase in taxable income. The examining officer disallowed some expenses that had been claimed, producing an increase in self-employment income reported on Schedule C. Although this change increased taxable income, the result also yielded an unintended consequence—eligibility for the earned income tax credit (EITC). However, calculation of the EITC was not included in the proposed changes offered by the IRS. Had this credit been properly calculated and included, the result would have been an increase to the original refund. As proposed by the IRS, however, the taxpayer had to pay a small tax liability.

When I reviewed this issue with my client, I was directed to just drop it because she was afraid the IRS would amend its findings to increase the amount owed. I understood her apprehension. The fact is many Americans have a deep-seated fear of the IRS. Just as Smith suggested, many taxpayers worry that the IRS will "aggravate the tax…or extort, by the terror of such aggravation."

Smith's prophecy has proven to be true. The uncertainty inherent in our tax code subjects taxpayers to the whim of the revenue agent. But Smith also predicted the effect that failure to embrace his certainty principle would have on an individual's character. He wrote, "The uncertainty of taxation encourages the insolence, and favours the corruption, of an order of men...even where they are neither insolent nor corrupt."

Many scholars appropriately contend that his prediction only applied to the tax collector (in other words, IRS employees). While recognizing the validity of that position, I maintain that Smith was more prescient than he knew, and I take the liberty to include taxpayers in his prediction.

The IRS, like many other federal agencies, consistently refers to a problem known as the *tax gap*. That term is used to describe the difference between tax revenue actually collected and the revenue that was estimated to be collected. This problem is not trivial. As of 2008, estimates of the size of the tax gap approach $350 billion annually. To put this in perspective, the federal deficit for 2008 approximated $390 billion. Eliminate the tax gap—eliminate the deficit.

The tax gap exists for a variety of reasons other than simple, honest mistakes. These include deliberately underreporting income or overstating deductions, failure to file returns, and failure to pay calculated tax. Considering just the first factor, the implication is that our tax system has created a class of thieves—those who deliberately misrepresent their true income picture. It has been alleged that a well-known novelist recently commented, "Income tax returns are the most imaginative fiction being written today."

Regardless of the origin of that statement, it is a thought-provoking observation. Our tax code has made honest men dishonest. I remind you of Plato's quote at the beginning of this chapter, "the just man will pay more and the unjust less."

The IRS describes taxpayer efforts to understate income as "gaming." The tax profession promotes this practice because there is nothing legally or ethically wrong in doing so. In *Gregory v. Helvering* (1935), Judge Learned Hand opined, "Anyone may arrange his affairs so that his taxes shall be as low as possible; he is not bound to choose that pattern which best pays the treasury. There is not even a patriotic duty to increase one's taxes."

Many use the judge's opinion to justify their efforts to game tax laws—especially if doing so reduces their taxes. However, this was not the end of Judge Hand's comment. He continued, "Everyone does it, rich and poor alike and all do right, for nobody owes any public duty to pay more than the law demands." Note particularly, "more than the law demands." It seems a perversion of his comment to game the system such that one pays less than "the law demands."

When playing the game, scrupulous tax professionals advise clients to avoid moves that would result in the use of either of two *F* words—*fraudulent* or *frivolous*—by the IRS. The use of either of these words can lead to the use of still another *F* word—*felony*—followed by frequent exclamations of the more commonly understood *F* word by the taxpayer.

However, the nature of the tax profession is to use the vagueness, complexity, and inconsistency of the tax code to reduce total tax paid. Indeed, many tax advisors and their clients believe that, in the event of an audit, should the examining officer not disallow any deduction, the tax preparer did not push the envelope far enough. As stated, it is hard to picture this environment and at the same time visualize the word *certain* as Smith intended.

Smith's second maxim referred not only to the calculation of the amount of tax to be paid but also addressed the certainty of the timing and manner of payment. In one respect, our tax system, described as a pay-as-you-go system, attempts to implement certainty for the timing of payment. One problem, however, is that existing methodology is only effective for income tax assessed on and withheld from wage income. Even in this respect, a recognized problem with the current system is the cash economy in which a significant percentage of wages is paid as cash, whether with intent to avoid taxes or simply as the easiest method. It is acknowledged that much of this cash income goes unreported—and untaxed.

This problem is compounded by the fact that most types of income are currently exempt from withholding. Ordinarily, neither investment income, including interest, dividends, and capital gains, nor self-employment income is subject to withholding. Investors and self-employed individuals are obligated to make quarterly estimated payments.

It is also interesting to note the uncertainty surrounding eligibility for refunds inherent in our tax structure. Given the severe penalties assessed if a taxpayer is under withheld, many taxpayers deliberately choose to have too much tax withheld from their paycheck. As a result, many are entitled to receive a refund—frequently a large one.

This phenomenon reminds me of a word attributed to Greg Oetjen, in an entry to a *Washington Post* wordplay contest: "*Intaxication*: euphoria at getting a refund from the IRS, which lasts until you realize it was your money to start with."

The IRS subtly supports and encourages large tax refunds. In my experience, tax refunds are the dirty little secret of our tax system. One of the first things you notice when visiting the IRS website is a link that reads, "Get Your Refund Status" or a large icon that reads, "Where's my Refund?"

Most local tax preparation agencies display oversized signs in office windows suggesting that they get taxpayers the largest, the quickest refunds. During the two tax seasons prior to publication of this book, one national company blasted television viewers with the message, "get your billions back America!" To the contrary, I admonish my clients that the fastest way to get a refund is to keep their money in the first place.

I educate my clients that, unless an extraordinary event occurred during the year, deliberately getting a large refund is nothing more than making an interest-free loan to the government. It is surprising how many taxpayers resist that notion, not out of any financial consideration but out of apprehension about our tax system and out of fear of IRS reprisal. This seemingly irrational fear is understandable and can be best demonstrated by recent IRS language regarding a little-known, even less understood, change to the tax code.

For tax year 2013, a new tax—net investment income tax (NIIT)—was added to an already confusing tax code. This tax is calculated separately from both ordinary income tax and alternative minimum tax (AMT). (Author's note: Both AMT and NIIT are discussed in greater detail in later chapters.)

For the moment, suffice to say that many Americans were unaware of the NIIT until they completed their 2013 tax return. Let me quote the IRS on one possible implication of this new tax: "If you had too little tax withheld or did not pay enough estimated taxes, you may have to pay an estimated tax penalty."

Stated simply, a new, unheralded tax was added to the tax code. If the impact on an uninformed, unsuspecting taxpayer was a large tax payment due, the taxpayer would also be subject to penalties and interest. Is it any wonder that many Americans would rather get a large refund than face the wrath and, worse, suffer the retribution of the tax collector?

Section I – Tax Chronicles

Regardless, the point of this discussion is the uncertainty that exists within our code. This uncertainty not only occurs when calculating tax but also when determining eligibility for a refund. If you fail to file a return and remember to do so several years later, or you are prompted to do so by IRS notification, you are obligated to pay any tax due plus accrued penalty and interest. Essentially, no statute of limitations exists for the requirement to file a return and pay the tax due.

Conversely, a statute of limitations does apply to refund eligibility. A taxpayer has until the later of three years from the original due date of the return, including extensions, or two years from the date the tax was actually paid to claim a refund of overpaid taxes. A claim for a refund based on a tax credit is limited to three years from the original due date of the return, excluding extensions.

If a taxpayer is entitled to a refund based solely on overpaid taxes (for example, withheld tax), or on refundable credits for which, based on the complexity of the law, he was unaware, the clock is ticking. Should he elect to file a late or amended return just as before, he may discover that he is no longer eligible for a refund.

An unintended consequence of the uncertainty created by our tax code is that the resulting apprehension creates taxpayer distrust in the system, threatening voluntary compliance. The real-life impact of all of this is well documented. Remember the TV advertisement mentioned just before, that claims American taxpayers who prepare their own returns mistakenly overpay their taxes by $1 billion annually.

This ad is not based on the premise that taxpayers are not filing returns, but on the belief that taxpayers who prepare their own returns or, more subtly implied, those who utilize tax preparation services other than the company airing the advertisement, do not take all legitimate deductions. Is anyone ever happy having paid $925 for a seat on an airplane while sitting next to someone who paid $225?

The F-Word

One edict taught to young army officers is to "keep it simple, stupid" (KISS). The simplest plans are generally the most effective and result in the highest probability of success. Personal experience demonstrated that applying this principle normally produced favorable results.

The need for simplicity was asserted by Thomas Paine in his pamphlet, "Common Sense." In this he wrote, "Draw my idea of the form of government from a principle in nature which no art can overturn, viz. that the more simple any thing is, the less liable it is to be disordered, and the easier repaired when disordered."

In developing a rational tax code, we could benefit by applying Paine's belief about simplicity to Smith's principle of certainty. Regrettably, nothing about our tax code is simple. It is difficult, if not impossible, to ensure that a system that has become so complex can, in any significant way, include a reasonable measure of certainty. Smith believed that uncertainty in the tax code would cause problems. Paine felt the absence of simplicity would preclude an easy fix to those problems. It turns out that they both were right. Perhaps we should just start over.

Again, my view is not a minority one. Even the Taxpayer Advocate, a senior IRS official appointed by the Commissioner and charged with identifying the most significant problems within our tax structure, agrees. For almost two decades, she has consistently reported to Congress that complexity, with its resulting errors, distrust, and noncompliance, is the single greatest problem with our tax system.

User [Un]Friendly

In his third maxim, Smith makes a strong argument that the tax system should be structured so that any tax can be conveniently paid:

Section I – Tax Chronicles

> Every tax ought to be levied at the time, or in the manner, in which it is most likely to be convenient for the contributor to pay it.

The requirement to withhold income tax as mandated by existing tax laws offers limited compliance with this edict. The withholding mandate also applies to payroll taxes except that an employee does not need to complete Form W-4 or any other form. All that is required is for an employer to pay wages to an employee. The tax is automatically calculated, withheld, and paid to the IRS without any intervention or action by the employee.

Payroll taxes are paid in a way that follows Smith's prescription. It seems logical that we could improve and expand our current withholding system so that, whenever any income is paid, the payment is reported, and some portion of that income is calculated, retained, and paid over as income tax. Regardless, convenience does matter when considering ease of compliance. Think sales tax. When a purchase subject to a sales tax is made, the tax is calculated and paid right then.

But, even if all income were subject to withholding, significant problems would still exist because actual tax liability cannot be determined until such time as a return is filed. Only then is all income reported, deductions and adjustments subtracted, and credits applied. Only after these steps are taken can the actual tax liability be determined. In truth, under a code as complex as the IRC, no easy or convenient method can be implemented to withhold a materially accurate tax amount at the time income is paid.

The Onus Is on You

Smith concludes his general discussion of an ideal tax system with his fourth maxim in which he admonishes:

The F-Word

> Every tax ought to be so contrived, as both to take out and to keep out of the pockets of the people as little as possible, over and above what it brings into the public treasury of the state.

This admonishment is not so much directed at the level of government spending as it is at the nature of taxation, particularly the impact of the implementation and enforcement on individuals and the economy as a whole.

If this last missive were ignored, Smith worried that the tax system "may require a great number of officers, whose salaries may eat up the greater part of the produce of the tax, and whose perquisites may impose another additional tax upon the people."

Can anyone argue that the complex, burdensome bureaucracy we call the IRS has not fulfilled his worst fear? As explained later, compliance costs necessitated by the Internal Revenue Code drain such significant resources from our economy that its implementation is counterproductive.

It is easy to find a variety of studies—a multitude of different statistics to quantify the compliance burden created by our tax code. What is also easy to find is that, while there may be disagreement on the size of the problem, there is virtual unanimity on its existence. Estimates have been offered that suggest individual American taxpayers invest almost six billion man-hours preparing tax returns at a cost of over $100 billion. Over half of all taxpayers now pay a tax professional to prepare their tax return. More than half of those who do not purchase tax preparation software.

Smith warned of the inefficiency of a poorly designed tax system. He believed that violation of this principle would create a system that worked against itself and would "contrary to all the ordinary

Section I – Tax Chronicles

principles of justice, first create[s] the temptation, and then punishes those who yield to it; and it commonly enhances the punishment, too, in proportion to the very circumstance which ought certainly to alleviate it, the temptation to commit the crime."

This conundrum was noted by the Taxpayer Advocate in her 2005 report to Congress. In this report, she acknowledges the truth of Smith's prediction: "Thus begins an endless cycle—complexity drives inadvertent error and fraud, which drive increased enforcement or new legislation, which drives additional complexity."

In his last maxim, Smith also expressed worry that an overly burdensome and intrusive tax system would discourage individuals from pursuing certain business opportunities that might create economic growth. He wrote: "It may obstruct the industry of the people, and discourage them from applying to certain branches of business which might give maintenance and employment to great multitudes."

I have seen firsthand the truth of his prediction. I am often asked, "If I _____ (fill in the blank: buy, spend, invest or do, for example), is it tax deductible?" I always respond that the question is flawed; the answer irrelevant. Rather, I suggest to my client that he should be asking, "Do I need to _____ (fill in the blank: buy, spend, invest or do, for example).

Bottom line, Smith's foresight was spot-on. Our tax code is so confusing that individuals and businesses alike evaluate alternative actions based on tax implications rather than on personal values, sound life choices, or expected investment outcomes.

President Kennedy referenced this phenomenon in 1963 in a special message to Congress on tax reduction and reform. He said, "The present tax codes…add complexities and inequities which undermine the morale of the taxpayer, and make tax avoidance rather than market factors a prime consideration in too many economic decisions."

If the president were concerned then, shouldn't we be even more worried now? Our tax code is far more intrusive and significantly more complex today than it was in 1963.

Many modern economists believe that the real tax burden on an economy exceeds the amount of tax revenues collected. It is generally accepted that even the best-designed tax system reduces market efficiency by distorting prices, wages, and incomes. These inefficiencies, referred to as excess burdens, are nearly impossible to accurately identify yet represent an unwarranted and excessive drain on the economy. None have argued that our tax code is well designed, or even that it is a good design. What then must be the cumulative effect of those excess burdens weighing on our economy?

Our tax code has no philosophical basis and no rational foundation. At present, few if any of our elected leaders, regardless of political persuasion, argue that the Internal Revenue Code makes any sense. We should completely revamp our system, building one based on the four principles contained in Adam Smith's maxims, written almost three hundred years ago—fairness, certainty, convenience, and efficiency.

Finally, and perhaps most importantly, we should ensure our tax system is designed to raise revenue and enact other legislation to deal with social issues. That one straightforward concept should be the underlying philosophical foundation on which our tax code is based.

Should Congress ever propose a simple, logical tax system, taxpayers across America can raise a glass and wholeheartedly shout, "I'll drink to that!"

Chapter 3

US Tax Saga

> Therefore, I believe in a graduated income tax…
> and in another tax which is far more easily
> collected and far more effective—
> a graduated inheritance tax on big fortunes.
> President Theodore Roosevelt
>
> Taxes shall be levied according to ability to pay.
> That is the only American principle.
> President Franklin D Roosevelt
>
> People try to live within their income so they can
> afford to pay taxes
> to a government that can't live within its income.
> Robert Half, Businessman and Entrepreneur

In the first chapter, I quoted Oliver Wendell Holmes, "Taxes are what we pay for a civilized society." Activities necessitated by maintaining a civilized society serve as the rationale behind the need for government in the first place.

The signers of the Declaration of Independence set out to establish a new form of government, designed to protect the rights of all to "life, liberty and the pursuit of happiness." When the founding fathers drafted the Constitution, the power to levy taxes was just one necessary function given to the federal government to provide that protection.

In "Federalist 12" of the *Federalist Papers*, Alexander Hamilton wrote, "A nation cannot long exist without revenues. Destitute of this essential support, it must resign its independence, and sink into the degraded condition of a province. This is an extremity to which no government will of choice accede. Revenue, therefore, must be had at all events."

It seems clear that a majority of the delegates to the Constitutional Convention determined that our central government must have the power to tax, so they wrote that authority into the Constitution. Over time, taxes created by the federal government have evolved into the income tax system we now have.

But before analyzing our current tax code, it may be enlightening to take a trip down US tax memory lane. Americans' collective view regarding arbitrary taxes was expressed even before we were a nation.

On the evening of December 16, 1773, about one hundred American colonialists, several of whom belonged to a group called the Sons of Liberty, boarded three ships anchored in the port of Boston. Many were dressed as Indians, both to disguise themselves and to make the point that they identified more with America than with Great Britain. They intended to dump the tea those ships carried into the harbor, thereby eliminating the requirement to pay the duty on that tea.

Their action was the culmination of years of bitter disagreement between the colonies and the British over the issue of taxation. With the passage of the Stamp Act in 1765, many of the colonials

Section I – Tax Chronicles

banded together in separate yet like-minded groups to oppose British taxes. A number of these factions merged to form the Sons of Liberty who adopted the catchphrase, "No taxation without representation," attributed to noted Bostonian James Otis Jr., as their battle cry.

The first century of American history established that opposition to taxes was as American as apple pie—maybe more so—demonstrated by the Shays' Rebellion (1786), the Whiskey Rebellion (1794), the Fries Rebellion (1799), and, more dramatically, by South Carolina's attempt to nullify the Tariff of 1828 and the Tariff of 1832.

The genesis of the United States was rooted in resistance to taxation. Among the architects of the Declaration of Independence, there was virtually unanimous concern regarding the level of taxing authority to be given to the national government. In 1773, Benjamin Franklin wrote a satirical essay titled "Rules by which a Great Empire may be reduced to a Small One." In two paragraphs of that essay—excerpted here—he lampoons taxes and tax administration. (Author's note: I added *italics* for emphasis.)

> IX But remember to make your *arbitrary tax* more grievous to your provinces by public declarations importing that your *power* of taxing them *has no limits*, so that when you take from them without their consent one shilling in the pound, you have a clear right to the other nineteen. This will probably weaken every idea of security in their property and convince them that under such a government they have nothing they can call their own, which can scarce fail of producing the happiest consequences!
>
> XI To make your taxes more odious and more likely to procure resistance, send from the capital a *board of officers* to

> superintend the collection, composed of the most *indiscreet*, *ill-bred*, and *insolent* you can find. Let these have large salaries out of the extorted revenue and live in open grating luxury upon the sweat and blood of the industrious, whom they are to worry continually with groundless and expensive prosecutions...If any revenue officers are *suspected* of the least *tenderness* for the people, discard them. If others are justly complained of, protect and reward them. If any of the under-officers behave so as to provoke the people to drub [criticize harshly] them, promote those to better offices: this will encourage others to procure for themselves such profitable drubbings by multiplying and enlarging such provocations, and all will work towards the end you aim at.

Since the marginal income tax rate has previously risen as high as 94%, perhaps Mr. Franklin's observation that the government would have "a clear right to the other nineteen" is not so much satire as foresight. Considering the issues surrounding enforcement tactics used by the IRS over the past half century, it may be that the commissioner of the Internal Revenue Service failed to notice the title of the essay. Rather than recognizing the satire dripping from the nib of Mr. Franklin's pen, the commissioner perhaps believed he was following prescriptive doctrine.

Think about Franklin's comment, "Let these have large salaries out of the extorted revenue." You might not be aware of the controversy over the issue of bonuses paid to IRS employees. A number of print, broadcast, and Internet news sources have reported that the IRS paid more than a million dollars in bonuses between October 2010 and December 2012 to approximately one thousand employees who owed back taxes. Talk about large salaries!

How about the news reports regarding IRS conferences? Huge sums paid for free drinks and for hotel rooms upgraded to suites.

Section I – Tax Chronicles

Could that be what Franklin meant when he referred to "grating luxury"? Adding insult to injury, the IRS acknowledged that it allowed violation of IRS rules for employees attending such conferences.

Comedian and *The Tonight Show* host Jay Leno had the right idea: "Forget Gitmo. How about closing the IRS? Why don't we do that?"

Throughout our history, our federal tax system has undergone frequent, sometimes dramatic, changes in response to fluctuating economic, social, and political circumstances. The types of taxes levied, the magnitude of revenue collected, and their proportion to the economy are all vastly different now than they were in the early years of US history. Many of these differences were brought about by specific events, such as the Civil War or the passage of the Sixteenth Amendment.

It has been argued that the changing role of government has brought about modifications of our tax system. While that argument carries some truth, many contend the larger truth lies in the reverse of that assertion. They maintain that alterations to our basic tax structure, specifically the imposition of an income tax, resulting in a dramatic increase in available revenues, led to the escalation of government's role in society.

This last point is supported by the following observation. In 1917, only four years after the ratification of the Sixteenth Amendment, the federal budget exceeded the total budget for all years since 1789. Although expenses were elevated as a result of World War I, it is more telling that tax revenue was greater than the total tax revenue collected for all prior years.

While the Revolutionary War was being fought, the Articles of Confederation were adopted. These articles reflected the newly formed nation's fear of a strong central government and reserved the lion's share of political power for the states. The central government had no taxing authority, relying instead on the states for its revenue. Under the articles, each state was a sovereign entity and could levy taxes as it pleased.

This one factor was arguably the greatest single weakness leading to the failure of the Confederacy to survive. This failure led to a call for a Constitutional Convention and the drafting of our Constitution, which conferred taxing authority on the central government.

Agreement on giving the federal government the authority to tax did not come easily. Final language required a compromise on the kind of taxes Congress could levy. The Constitution gave Congress the ability to levy direct and indirect taxes but required direct taxes to be apportioned. In order to better comprehend our tax methods therefore, it is important to understand the difference between the two.

Direct taxes are commonly understood to be taxes paid by the individual against whom the tax is levied. Examples of a direct tax include poll taxes and property taxes. Indirect taxes, on the other hand, are assessed on one entity and paid by another. They comprise sales taxes, levied on the retailer but paid by the consumer, and customs duties, levied on the importer yet ultimately paid by the individual end user of the goods.

The question of whether income taxes are a direct tax, and must therefore be apportioned, or are an indirect tax is complicated. Under US law, as interpreted by the Supreme Court, income taxes are indirect if applied to income from labor, and direct if levied on income from property. As discussed later, the Sixteenth Amendment eliminated the necessity to apportion income taxes, regardless of whether that income derived from rents (property) or labor.

The issue of a direct tax versus an indirect tax also arises when considering income taxes, payroll taxes, or any other type of tax assessed against a business. Considerable disagreement exists on whether corporate taxes constitute a direct or indirect tax. I offer examples later to demonstrate that all business taxes are indirect taxes. Ultimately, indirect taxes are paid by consumers through higher prices, by employees with lower wages, or by owners realizing lower profits.

Early Americana

In "Federalist 12," Hamilton wrote this:

> It is evident from the state of the country, from the habits of the people, from the experience we have had on the point itself, that it is impracticable to raise any very considerable sums by direct taxation. Tax laws have in vain been multiplied; new methods to enforce the collection have in vain been tried; the public expectation has been uniformly disappointed, and the treasuries of the States have remained empty.

Having just recently severed political ties with Great Britain, the founding fathers looked to the British system as they crafted the Constitution. As a consequence of that assessment, Hamilton continued:

> In so opulent a nation as that of Britain, where direct taxes from superior wealth must be much more tolerable, and, from the vigor of the government, much more practicable, than in America, far the

> greatest part of the national revenue is derived from taxes of the indirect kind, from imposts, and from excises. Duties on imported articles form a large branch of this latter description.

While Hamilton believed in the absolute necessity of unlimited taxing authority, he determined that direct taxes, including income taxes, would be difficult to levy and enforce. He further concluded that they were not needed in any event, as sufficient revenues could be derived from indirect taxes such as customs duties.

He also expressed support for specific excise taxes, in particular a tax on whiskey. He did so both because of the potential for large sums of revenue as well as for the social benefit to be gained: "If it should tend to diminish the consumption of it, such an effect would be equally favorable…to the morals, and to the health of the society." This tax offers an example of a tax levied with a revenue purpose as well as a social engineering purpose.

Hamilton's conclusion about duties and tariffs proved correct. For most of our history, taxpayers had little contact with federal tax authorities as most federal taxes were derived from excise taxes, tariffs, and customs duties. Despite his supposition, he opposed any limitation on the taxing authority of the federal government. If any restrictions were suggested, he pointed out the failure of the Confederation as the result of such limitation as contrary logic.

In *The Federalist Papers,* Hamilton addressed a concern held by many delegates that the central government would have the ability to usurp the taxing authority of the states. Substantial disagreement existed regarding which entity could levy internal taxes, including direct or indirect assessments, and which could impose external taxes, generally comprised of indirect taxes. Opponents of a strong central government argued that authority to levy internal taxes should be reserved solely to the states. Disagreeing with the final language in the Constitution, they held that the central government should be limited to external taxes.

Hamilton argued that limiting the taxing authority of the federal government to duties and imposts would ultimately be insufficient to the needs of the government and would ensure the failure of the fledgling United States. He summarized this view in "Federalist 30":

> We could not reasonably flatter ourselves that this resource alone, upon the most improved scale, would even suffice for its present necessities. Its future necessities admit not of calculation or limitation; and upon the principle, more than once adverted to, the power of making provision for them as they arise ought to be equally unconfined.

Thus, when the Constitution was adopted in 1789, the federal government was granted the authority to raise taxes. The Constitution gave Congress the power to "lay and collect taxes, duties, imposts, and excises." Other than the requirement to apportion any direct taxes, the taxing authority of Congress had no limitations.

Initially, Congress levied excise taxes on distilled spirits, tobacco, and other items. Even then, social purposes influenced tax policy throughout the states. As an example, Pennsylvania imposed an excise tax on liquor "to restrain persons in low circumstances from an immoderate use thereof." Such practice continues to the present with tax preferences given to desired actions, such as savings, and taxes levied on unwanted behavior such as smoking.

Following the ratification of the Constitution and the establishment of the United States, many Americans maintained the tradition of opposing taxes they believed to be unfair. In 1794, President Washington was forced to send troops to suppress Pennsylvania farmers who had taken up arms to oppose the whiskey tax. This event served to affirm two ideas. First, Washington's response established the precedent that the federal government was able and determined to enforce its laws. Second, the rebellion confirmed that resistance to taxes had not disappeared from the political consciousness with the adoption of the Constitution.

In 1798, Congress imposed the first direct tax through a levy on owners of houses, land, slaves, and estates. President Jefferson abolished this tax during his first term in office. In his second inaugural address on March 4, 1805, he stated,

> The suppression of unnecessary offices, of useless establishments and expenses, enabled us to discontinue our internal taxes. These, covering our land with officers and opening our doors to their intrusions, had already begun that process of domiciliary vexation which once entered is scarcely to be restrained from reaching successively every article of property and produce...it may be the pleasure and the pride of an American to ask, What farmer, what mechanic, what laborer ever sees a tax gatherer of the United States?

Those words conveyed a portent that has since gone unheeded. Today, the Internal Revenue Code looks with prying eyes into every facet of the lives of all Americans and touches "every article of property and produce." We can now scarcely imagine a time similar to that described by Jefferson in which no American "ever sees a tax gatherer of the United States."

To raise money for the War of 1812, Congress imposed additional excise taxes and raised customs duties. These taxes were repealed in 1817. From then until the beginning of the Civil War, the federal government levied no internal taxes. Instead, the government raised needed revenue from customs duties and from the sale of public land.

A Pox on Their Incomes

With the onset of the Civil War, Congress passed the Revenue Act of 1861 that, for the first time in America, imposed a tax on personal incomes. The income tax was levied at 3% on all incomes higher than $800 a year. The following year, this law was replaced by the Revenue Act of 1862.

The 1862 act contained three significant provisions that presaged major components of our present-day income tax system. First, this measure provided for the first progressive tax. A two-tiered rate structure was mandated with taxable incomes up to $10,000 taxed at 3% and higher incomes taxed at 5%. A standard deduction of $600 was allowed, essentially exempting incomes below $600 from the tax. Second, to assure timely collection, taxes were "withheld at the source" by employers. Finally, this act created the office of the Commissioner of Internal Revenue, the predecessor of today's Internal Revenue Service.

The tax rates established by the 1862 act quickly proved insufficient to meet revenue demands caused by the war. As a result, this law was replaced by the Revenue Act of 1864, which added a third tax bracket and increased overall tax rates. Section 116 of this act levied an income tax beginning in 1864 and "in each year until and including the year eighteen hundred and seventy and no longer." From the time this tax expired until the Sixteenth Amendment was ratified, substantially all federal tax revenue was collected from excise taxes.

During the last half of the nineteenth century, progressive political movements began to appear in Europe and in the United

States. The Socialist Labor Party advocated a graduated income tax in 1887. The Populist Party "demanded a graduated income tax" in its 1892 platform. William Jennings Bryan, a three-time Democratic candidate for president, advocated an income tax and wrote that plank into the Democrats' platform in 1908.

With growing political support for an income tax, Congress passed the Wilson-Gorman Tariff of 1894. Under this measure, many tariffs were reduced, and, in exchange, the first peacetime income tax was created. During the debate over this measure, many traditional arguments against taxes in general and income taxes in particular were again raised. While Ohio Congressman Tom Johnson supported an income tax, he did so as the lesser of two evils, stating his support "for an income tax as against a tariff tax but…it was un-Democratic, inquisitorial, and wrong in principle."

Implementation of Wilson-Gorman led to a lawsuit in which the plaintiff argued that income taxes were unconstitutional. Under the Constitution, Congress could only impose direct taxes if they were levied in proportion to the population of each state. The Supreme Court ruled Wilson-Gorman to be unconstitutional because the income tax provisions were a direct tax and were not apportioned according to the population of each state.

After the Supreme Court's ruling, debate on different tax sources, including a tax on income, remained lively. Lacking necessary revenues and unable to implement an income tax, the federal government relied increasingly on higher tariffs for its revenues. But it was becoming ever more apparent that high tariffs and excise taxes were not sound economic policy and often fell disproportionately on those less able to pay.

Eventually, the debate over income tax pitted congressmen from the agricultural and rural areas of the Southern and Western states

Section I – Tax Chronicles

against those representing the industrial Northeast. Pragmatic politics ultimately produced an accord calling for imposition of a tax on business income and passage of a constitutional amendment granting Congress the ability to levy an individual income tax.

By 1913, the required number of states had ratified the Sixteenth Amendment, thereby making income taxes levied without apportionment constitutional. In October of that year, Congress passed the Revenue Act of 1913, establishing an income tax. The normal tax rate was set at 1% and a surtax—from 1% to a high of 6%—was added. Less than 1% of the population paid income tax under this act. This law also introduced Form 1040, which, although drastically changed and expanded, remains the standard individual income tax form used today.

This first levy of an income tax included the word *lawful* in the definition of income subject to tax. This resulted in a problem of how to define *lawful*. Congress eliminated this problem by amending the law in 1916 and deleting the word from the definition.

Hence, from 1916 until the present, all income, even income earned illegally, has been subject to income tax. Several years after the law was changed, the Supreme Court declared the Fifth Amendment could not be used by bootleggers and others who earned income through illegal activities to avoid paying taxes. Consequently, many who were able to escape punishment for their criminal enterprises were subsequently arrested, tried, and convicted on tax evasion charges for failure to report the income derived from those efforts. Al Capone was perhaps the most notable of these offenders.

The beginning of World War I increased the demand for revenue. Congress responded by passing the 1916 Revenue Act, which raised the lowest tax rate from 1% to 2% and raised the top rate to 15% on incomes over $1.5 million. This measure also imposed taxes on estates and excess business profits.

Driven by the war and funded by the new income tax, the 1917 federal budget approximated the total budget for all the years between 1791 and 1916. But needing still more tax revenue, Congress passed the War Revenue Act of 1917, which lowered exemptions and significantly increased tax rates. In 1916, a taxpayer needed taxable income of $1.5 million to incur a 15% rate. By 1917, a taxpayer with only $40,000 faced a 16% rate, and an individual with $1.5 million in income paid 67%.

Yet another revenue act was passed in 1918, this time raising the bottom rate to 6% and the top rate to 77%. These changes increased revenue from $761 million in 1916 to $3.6 billion in 1918. Even in 1918, however, only one of every twenty Americans paid income tax.

Congress reduced taxes five times during the 1920s, ultimately returning the bottom tax rate to 1% and lowering the top rate to 25%. In October 1929, the stock market crashed, thus marking the beginning of the Great Depression. In 1932, the federal government collected only $1.9 billion, compared to $6.6 billion in 1920.

In the face of rising budget deficits that reached $2.7 billion in 1931, Congress followed the prevailing economic wisdom of the time and passed the Tax Act of 1932, which increased tax rates significantly. This was followed by another tax increase in 1936 that improved the government's finances, but further weakened the economy. Under this latest increase, the top and bottom tax rates were set at 79% and 4%, respectively.

Even prior to the United States entering World War II, increased defense spending led to the enactment of two tax laws in 1940 that increased individual and corporate income tax rates. These were closely followed by another tax hike in 1941.

By the end of the war, provisions affecting federal income tax had fundamentally changed. Reductions in exemption thresholds meant that taxpayers with taxable income of only $500 incurred a tax rate of 23%, while taxpayers with income exceeding $1 million faced a top rate of 94%. The result of these changes was an increase in tax receipts from $8.7 billion in 1941 to $45.2 billion in 1945. More significantly, however, these changes increased the number of taxpayers from four million in 1939 to forty-three million in 1945.

Another important change to our tax system enacted during WWII was the return to income tax withholding as initially required during the Civil War. While significantly easing tax collection for both the taxpayer and the government, it also reduced taxpayers' awareness of the tax. Politicians understood that tax withholding would make it easier to raise taxes in the future—out of sight, out of mind.

In 1953, the Bureau of Internal Revenue was renamed the Internal Revenue Service (IRS) to stress the service aspect of its mission. Some may suggest that this was and remains a misnomer. By the time John and Jackie Kennedy arrived in Washington—ushering in a modern-day Camelot—the IRS had become the world's largest accounting, collection, and forms-processing organization. Beginning in 1961, Americans were required to provide their Social Security numbers when filing their tax return.

From the late 1960s through the 1970s, runaway inflation became the norm for the American economy, surpassing 13% by 1979. At the time, fixed amounts established under income tax laws—such as income brackets, exemptions, deductions, and credits—were not indexed for inflation. It became obvious, even to the most casual observer, that if tax provisions were not adjusted for inflation, the growing tax burden created by graduated income tax rates would wreak havoc on middle-income taxpayers.

Due in part to the high tax burden caused by inflation, the economy dramatically underperformed. This led to the passage of the Economic Recovery Tax Act of 1981—commonly called the Reagan tax cut—which featured a 25% reduction in individual tax rates. This reduction was phased in over three years and indexed for inflation thereafter, lowering the top tax bracket to 50%.

Following the enactment of additional tax changes in 1982 and 1984, growing political sentiment favoring a deeper, fundamental overhaul of income tax laws took hold in Washington. In his 1984 State of the Union speech, President Reagan called for sweeping tax reforms to broaden the tax base, lower overall tax rates, and provide a fairer, simpler tax system.

His determination culminated in the Tax Reform Act of 1986 that lowered the top individual tax rate from 50% to 28% and the highest corporate rate from 50% to 35%. The number of tax brackets was reduced while the personal exemption and standard deduction amounts were increased and indexed for inflation. These changes shrank the tax base, relieving millions of taxpayers from paying any federal income tax.

However, this change also modified a tax provision initially created under the Nixon administration designed to establish a minimum tax to be paid by wealthy taxpayers. Renamed the alternative minimum tax (AMT), this tax was assessed against individual and business taxpayers. Given the mood of the times, provisions of the AMT were not originally indexed for inflation. This failure would ultimately make this section of the code punitive to

Section I – Tax Chronicles

many middle-class taxpayers. Since the change brought by the Tax Reform Act of 1986, the AMT has proved to be overly complicated and arbitrary.

The 1986 Tax Reform Act was meant to be revenue neutral—that is, it was not designed to either increase or reduce total tax revenue. Rather, it was intended to shift part of the tax burden from individuals to businesses. Viewed through a wide-angle lens, the tax reform enacted in 1986 represented the final step in a twenty-two-year period of extraordinary tax rate reductions. From 1964 through 1986, the highest individual tax rate was reduced from 91% to 28%.

However, lower tax rates linked with increased government spending led to persistent budget deficits that created unrelenting pressure to again raise taxes. In 1990, Congress approved a tax measure that increased the top tax rate to 31%. Shortly after his election, President Clinton insisted on a second tax increase, enacted by Congress in 1993, that raised the top rate to 36% with a 10% surcharge, making the top tax rate 39.6%. These two laws reversed the decades-long trend of lowering tax rates.

The Taxpayer Relief Act of 1997 made additional changes to the tax code including a modest tax cut. The centerpiece of this act was a new tax benefit named the child tax credit. The most significant feature of this credit was that it was refundable. In many cases, an eligible taxpayer received a credit in the form of a tax expenditure or payment in excess of his tax liability before the credit was applied. As an example, if a taxpayer had a tax liability of $1,000 and a nonrefundable credit of $1,200, he would end up at zero. He would pay no tax and receive no refund. However, if the $1,200 credit were refundable, this same taxpayer would get a $200 check.

Although refundable tax credits, such as the earned income tax credit, had been in existence for many years, the child tax credit began a new trend in federal tax policy. Previously, tax relief was generally bestowed through lower tax rates or increased deductions or exemptions. The 1997 act effectively launched the modern proliferation of individual tax payments that essentially implement government assistance programs via the tax system.

By 2001, total tax revenues produced a projected annual budget surplus estimated at $281 billion, with a ten-year surplus predicted to exceed $5.5 trillion. Consequently, under President George W. Bush, Congress passed the Economic Growth and Tax Relief and Reconciliation Act of 2001. The centerpiece of this measure was lower marginal tax rates. Future tax increases were rescinded, and the top tax rate was lowered from 39.6% to 33%. This measure also put estate and gift taxes on a path to eventual repeal.

It is noteworthy that the tax reductions implemented under President Bush represented the first time in American history that Congress lowered taxes while the nation was at war.

Changes to the IRC continue to this day. During the Obama administration, no less than five major tax laws have been passed, including the Housing and Economic Recovery Act of 2008; the American Recovery and Reinvestment Act of 2009; the Worker, Homeownership, and Business Assistance Act of 2009; the American Taxpayer Relief Act of 2012; and the Patient Protection and Affordable Care Act. While these laws addressed issues other than taxes, each included significant provisions that had considerable impact on taxpayers by creating, eliminating, or modifying taxes, tax preferences, or tax credits.

What's in a Name?

Finally, a historical overview of the US tax system would be incomplete without considering payroll taxes. It is not clear to me why

Section I – Tax Chronicles

they are not typically included in discourse on income tax because Social Security and Medicare taxes are, in reality, a tax assessed on income, specifically against earned income.

Merriam-Webster defines income tax as "a tax paid on the money that a person or business receives as income." An income tax is generally understood to be the product of a tax rate multiplied by taxable income. Don't both of those statements accurately describe payroll taxes?

The impact of the Great Depression on America led to passage of the Social Security Act in 1935. Contrary to a commonly held belief, this act was not limited to Social Security payments to retired persons. This measure also provided support for widows and fatherless children, providing a safety net for Americans facing an economic threat whether due to old age, poverty, or unemployment. The original law contained the first-ever federal aid program to provide aid to the states for various health and welfare programs including the Aid to Dependent Children program.

These programs were financed by a 2% payroll tax, one-half of which was subtracted directly from an employee's paycheck and one-half collected from employers. The tax was levied on the first $3,000 of an employee's salary or wage. The original law excluded many wage earners from coverage.

Self-employed taxpayers became subject to a similar tax by the enactment of the Self-Employment Contributions Act (SECA) of 1954, which is codified as part of the Internal Revenue Code. Otherwise, the Social Security system remained essentially unchanged until 1956.

Beginning that year, Social Security began a continuous evolution as more and more benefits were added, beginning with the addition of disability benefits. In 1958, benefits were extended to dependents of disabled workers, and benefits were later extended to surviving spouses. In 1965, Congress enacted the Medicare program, which was designed to meet the medical needs of persons aged sixty-five or older, regardless of income. Automatic cost-of-living increases to benefits were established under the 1972 amendments.

The increase in benefits from the trifling payments authorized in 1936, together with the advent of Medicare, necessitated significant additional payroll tax revenue. Thus, the basic payroll tax rate was repeatedly increased. By 1962, the payroll tax rate had risen from 2% to 6%.

Consequently, the maximum Social Security tax burden rose from a modest $60 in 1949 to $3,175 in 1980. Annual wages of $3,000 earned in 1949 incurred a Social Security tax liability of $30. That income, roughly equivalent to $30,000 in inflation-adjusted dollars, would produce $2,295 in payroll tax paid by the employee. This equates to a tenfold increase in payroll taxes paid by wage earners, after allowance for inflation.

In the early 1980s, Congress mandated future increases that would, by 1990, raise the payroll tax rate to 15.3%. Between 1980 and 1990, the maximum Social Security payroll tax burden on an individual more than doubled to $3,924. As of 2013, that amount has more than doubled yet again. The Center on Budget and Policy Priorities has reported that a substantial number of taxpayers now pay more in payroll taxes than they do in income tax.

Many Americans do not believe payroll taxes are part of the Internal Revenue Code. That disbelief, while understandable, is not correct. The taxing provisions of Social Security—assessment and collection—were taken out of the Social Security Act and inserted into the Internal Revenue Code as part of the 1939 amendments. This section was renamed the Federal Insurance Contributions Act (FICA). Thus, FICA, a phrase familiar to most Americans, is nothing more than the tax provisions of the Social Security Act as written within the Internal Revenue Code.

In summary, our federal income tax system, which realistically began in 1913, affecting less than 1% of all eligible taxpayers, has today grown to the tax behemoth created by the Internal Revenue Code. Every American is affected in one way or another by the IRC. In the 2013 edition of the *Projections of Federal Tax Return Filings*, the IRS predicted that a total of 245.7 million returns would be filed.

This number includes 194.6 million individual returns (all versions of Form 1040), 3.1 million fiduciary returns (Form 1041), 4.3 million partnership returns, 7.5 million corporate returns, 0.3 million gift and estate returns, 31.3 million employment tax returns, and 1.2 million exempt organization returns. Additionally, the IRS projected that more than seventeen million extensions would be requested, and almost six million amended returns would be filed.

The total number of returns and documents filed is expected to increase to more than 275 million by 2020. The IRS now employs approximately a hundred thousand people and collects over $2.4 trillion annually in taxes.

Hamilton's belief that Americans "will ill brook the inquisitive and peremptory spirit" of taxes and tax authority has clearly not held true. Under current law, little can be done about the intrusion or the access and control of private information held by the government vis-à-vis the IRS—something to ponder.

The F-Word

As I close this chapter on the evolution and growth of our tax code, I am reminded of a lasting legacy of Alexander Hamilton embedded within our tax code—an excise tax on distilled whiskey. But, as much as I admire Hamilton, I think I must again contribute to the government's coffers and enjoy a mint julep.

Chapter 4

Constitutional Questions

> The people made the Constitution,
> and the people can unmake it.
> It is the creature of their will, and lives
> only by their will.
> Hon. John Marshall, Chief Justice of the
> Supreme Court

> One thing is clear: The Founding Fathers
> never intended a nation
> where citizens would pay nearly half
> of everything they earn to the government.
> Hon. Ron Paul, Congressman

> If Patrick Henry thought that taxation without
> representation was bad,
> he should see how bad it is with representation.
> *Farmer's Almanac*

> What has made the Constitution durable is the
> same as what makes it demanding:
> the fact that so much was left out.
> Professor Jill Lepore, Author and Historian

The F-Word

Taxes and the delegation and use of the power to tax dominated many debates during the drafting and adoption of the US Constitution. Seven of *The Federalist Papers* specifically address the question of taxes and taxing authority. Many others include substantive references to the topic. Not surprising, considering the dawn of the American Revolution arose over the issue of taxation.

Indeed, at the time of the Revolutionary War, much of Europe wrestled with a rising tax burden and the concurrent question of tax fairness, largely due to the length and frequency of wars during the seventeenth and eighteenth centuries.

The Articles of Confederation, ratified during the Revolutionary War, created a union of thirteen individual colonies rather than a single nation. The articles allowed the central government to prosecute the war and to negotiate with foreign powers, but, while it could print money, it could not raise money—Congress was denied the power to levy any tax. Congress essentially went hat in hand to request money from the individual colonies—requests that, absent any enforcement powers, were generally ignored by the various colonies.

To pay its bills, Congress printed money. As more money was printed, the Continental dollar depreciated giving birth to the phrase, "Not worth a Continental." In 1779, George Washington wrote to John Jay, "A wagon load of money will scarcely purchase a wagon load of provisions." In an appeal to the states for funds, Jay wrote, "Taxes were the price of liberty, the peace, and the safety of yourselves and posterity." Yet once again, the states failed to provide requested funds.

This lesson was well learned by those chosen to draft the Constitution. In "Federalist 30," Hamilton wrote:

Section I – Tax Chronicles

> IT HAS been already observed that the federal government ought to possess the power of providing for the support of the national forces…But these are not the only objects to which the jurisdiction of the Union, in respect to revenue, must necessarily be empowered to extend. It must embrace a provision for the support of the national civil list; for the payment of the national debts…in general, for all those matters which will call for disbursements out of the national treasury. The conclusion is that there must be interwoven, in the frame of the government, a general power of taxation, in one shape or another.

The following sections regarding the power to tax were ultimately included in the Constitution. However, this language generated significant discussion and debate during the Constitutional Convention. The dispute over the meaning of this language continued even after the Constitution was ratified and endures today.

> Article I. Section. 8—The Congress shall have Power To lay and collect Taxes, Duties, Imposts and Excises, to pay the Debts and provide for the common Defence and general Welfare of the United States; but all Duties, Imposts and Excises shall be uniform throughout the United States.

> Article I. Section. 9—No Capitation, or other direct, Tax shall be laid, unless in Proportion to the Census or enumeration herein before directed to be taken.

This language is not the final word on taxes in the United States. Just as with all of our laws, final authority ultimately rests on the Supreme Court's interpretation of any tax law enacted.

Many constitutional scholars agree that the original architects of the Constitution believed that the judiciary would be the weakest branch of the national government. That view has not been borne out in practice. In fact, the Supreme Court has come to wield enormous power, with decisions that have reached inside the homes and into the lives of every citizen.

Decisions of the Supreme Court are final, so overturning its rulings generally requires an amendment to the Constitution or a revision to federal law. This was the case with respect to income taxes because of one of those decisions. The result of the court's ruling in *Pollock v. Farmers' Loan and Trust Company* was passage of the Sixteenth Amendment to the US Constitution.

AMENDMENT XVI Passed by Congress July 2, 1909. Ratified February 3, 1913.

> The Congress shall have power to lay and collect taxes on incomes, from whatever source derived, without apportionment among the several States, and without regard to any census or enumeration.

Our federal tax system, now based primarily on income taxes, effectively began with this amendment. But the Sixteenth Amendment, implemented by the Revenue Act of 1913, also called the Tariff Act of 1913, was not the federal government's first attempt to create an income tax. It was actually the third bite at the apple.

As stated, passage of the Sixteenth Amendment was necessitated by a Supreme Court ruling that held the Revenue Act of 1894 (Wilson-Gorman Tariff Act) to be unconstitutional. This act imposed the first peacetime income tax, but this was also not the first attempt to implement a federal income tax. This was the second bite at the apple.

Section I – Tax Chronicles

The first bite at the apple occurred with passage of the Revenue Act of 1861 that levied the first-ever federal income tax on American citizens. The law assessed a 3% tax on all individuals with annual incomes above $800. This tax was levied due to the costs resulting from the onset of the Civil War.

However, by 1862, Congress realized the war would continue and that the revenue produced by the 1861 act would not be sufficient. As a result, the Revenue Act of 1862 was passed, which stated, "Duties on incomes herein imposed shall be due and payable in 1863 and each year thereafter until and including 1866 'and no longer.'"

The Internal Revenue Act of 1864 imposed an income tax on "the gains, profits, and income of every person residing in the United States, or of any citizen of the United States residing abroad, whether derived from any kind of property, rents, interest, dividends, or salaries, or from any profession, trade, employment, or vocation, carried on in the United States or elsewhere, or from any other source whatever." The measure created a third tax bracket and increased overall rates from those set in 1862.

This last statute led to the first constitutional challenge of an income tax in *Springer v. United States*. In this case, William M. Springer challenged the constitutionality of the 1864 act. Springer had filed an income tax return for 1865 reflecting income of $50,798 and income tax of $4,799, which he refused to pay. In *Springer*, the Supreme Court upheld the law and rejected Springer's argument that income tax was a "direct tax" within the meaning of Article I of the US Constitution.

The constitutionality of a federal income tax was again challenged following passage of the Wilson-Gorman Tariff Act of 1894, which required that "gains, profits and incomes" in excess of $4,000 would be taxed at 2%. When the Farmers' Loan & Trust Company announced to its shareholders that it would pay the tax, Charles Pollock, a shareholder, sued the company to prevent the company from paying the tax.

Pollock lost his suit but appealed to the Supreme Court, which agreed to hear the case. In *Pollock v. Farmers' Loan and Trust Company*, Pollock argued that the tax was paid on income from land, and since a tax on real estate is a direct tax, then a tax on the income from such property must be a direct tax as well. Pollock claimed that the income tax should be declared unconstitutional because the Constitution prohibited a direct tax "unless in Proportion to the Census."

In *Pollock*, the court agreed with the plaintiff that a tax on real estate was a direct tax and, therefore, it followed that a tax levied on the income derived from real estate was necessarily a direct tax. As a result, the court ruled as follows:

> The tax imposed by...the act of 1894, so far as it falls on the income of real estate...being a direct tax, within the meaning of the constitution, and therefore unconstitutional and void, because not apportioned according to representation, all those sections, constituting one entire scheme of taxation, are necessarily invalid.

A fundamental difference between *Pollock* and the earlier *Springer* case is that, in *Pollock*, the court held that the income that was being taxed was attributable to property, hence, a direct tax. In *Springer*, the issue related to tax derived from income produced by labor, which the court has held to be an excise, or indirect, tax. Given that determination, the court had no choice but to rule Wilson-Gorman unconstitutional.

Section I – Tax Chronicles

Faced with the "no can do" ruling of the court on Wilson-Gorman, Congress was forced to go back to the drawing board.

Since the passage of the Sixteenth Amendment and the enactment of various laws implementing our current tax system, arguments over the constitutionality of an income tax, particularly as it exists under the IRC, continue to arise. Indeed, with the growth of the Internet, taxpayers can find dozens of sites urging noncompliance with federal income tax laws based on the premise that they are unconstitutional.

As one example, some income tax opponents have used the Supreme Court ruling from *Brushaber v. Union Pacific Railroad* (1916) to support the argument that our income tax is unconstitutional if applied to American citizens. *Brushaber* was the first major constitutional test of the Sixteenth Amendment and its enabling legislation, the Revenue Act of 1913.

The belief that income tax is unconstitutional, and that this belief is supported by Supreme Court rulings, is often referred to as the simple truth about our income tax. You can find this logic, taken from *Brushaber*, reproduced on a number of websites and written up in several books. I find that rationale and those arguments unpersuasive.

The court summarized *Brushaber* by affirming that Article I, Section 8 gave Congress the ability to levy taxes of any kind including an income tax. The Sixteenth Amendment did not grant Congress that power; it already had that power. What the Sixteenth Amendment did was to relieve Congress from the requirement to apportion income taxes.

I am neither a constitutional scholar nor an attorney, but I believe income taxes are constitutional. I do question whether some provisions of our tax code and the enforcement of that code might reasonably be considered unconstitutional. For me, the constitutionality of many provisions of the IRC, and of the enforcement methods employed by the IRS, is less straightforward than simply whether Congress has the right to levy a tax on income. Constitutional concerns do exist.

Frivolity

In one respect, I chose the title for this book simply to garner attention. However, a serious implication relates to one *F* word—*frivolous*—at least if used by the IRS. It is not a word you want to hear from the IRS when speaking about your return or any claim you made on that return. While not part of this constitutional discussion, you also do not want to hear the word *fraudulent* spoken by an IRS employee. Should you hear either word, it is possible, even likely, that a different *F* word may escape your lips.

It is generally understood that our legal system is grounded in the rule of law; that the Constitution is the supreme law of the land; and that our legal system is based, first, on the Constitution and, second, on black letter law (that is, specific language within a piece of legislation) and, third, on precedent (which includes prior judicial interpretation and application of black letter law) and, finally, on common law.

I take no issue with the ability of Congress to lay and collect income taxes. I agree with court rulings rejecting arguments that the Sixteenth Amendment was not properly ratified. I also concur with the court's dismissal of the notion that income tax laws are unenforceable, as some contend, because the amendment fails to contain the language, "Congress shall have power to enforce this article by appropriate legislation." While some amendments contain this language, others, including the Sixteenth Amendment, do not.

Nonetheless, considering the precedent cornerstone of our legal system, particularly since judicial rulings change over time,

Section I – Tax Chronicles

including those handed down by the Supreme Court, preventing a taxpayer from making any constitutional argument against implementation and enforcement of our income tax laws makes a mockery of our Constitution.

To demonstrate this point, consider court-approved segregation. Had Americans been unable to challenge a law because of a prior Supreme Court ruling, we might still be living in a country where "separate but equal" was legal and appropriate as ruled by the Supreme Court in *Plessy v. Ferguson*. That decision was overturned, belatedly but correctly, almost sixty years later in *Brown v. Board of Education*.

But such is now the terrible and omnipotent power of our tax code that constitutional arguments against filing or paying taxes are discounted and dismissed. Worse still, even making such an argument can command a steep price. Any attempt to do so may result in assessment of civil or criminal penalties. The IRS has issued a number of rulings on this issue, including Revenue Ruling 2005-19, excerpted here.

> The Sixteenth Amendment to the U.S. Constitution was properly ratified and authorizes the federal income tax. Filing a federal income tax return and paying federal income tax does not constitute the taking of property without due process of law under the Fifth Amendment to the U.S. Constitution. Filing a federal income tax return, paying federal income tax, and incarceration for failure to comply with federal income tax obligations is not involuntary servitude or slavery prohibited by the Thirteenth Amendment to the U.S. Constitution. A taxpayer may not properly refuse to file a federal income tax return based on the claim that the requirement to do

so violates the prohibition against self-incrimination of the Fifth Amendment to the U.S. Constitution. Arguments to the contrary are frivolous.

If a taxpayer attempts to make such an argument, the IRS states, "In addition to liability for tax due…individuals who claim…these and other frivolous arguments face substantial civil and criminal penalties."

I understand the dilemma. On one hand, as the enforcement arm of our tax system, the IRS must be allowed to calculate, assess, and collect taxes efficiently. To allow any challenge, regardless of its merit, irrespective of prior judicial precedent, is contrary to that end. However, to essentially ban any constitutional argument, and to assess significant penalties for attempts to do so, seems contrary to our basic freedom.

It is not my intent to write a constitutional treatise. My concern is that, under existing law, including IRS rulings, it is difficult if not impossible to protest any aspect of the Internal Revenue Code on constitutional grounds. Given that our law, based on changing interpretations handed down by the Supreme Court, is a living, evolving construct, such limitations would appear to be, as a doctor might say, contraindicated.

I believe using the word *frivolous* in a sentence describing legitimate discussion and debate about the constitutional impact of our tax code to be, in a word, *unconstitutional.*

Constitutional Conundrums

The inconsistencies within our tax code and potential contradictions between that code and the protections found within our constitution do make for some interesting theoretical legal discussion questions. Previously, some taxpayers have claimed that the requirements to file a return and to report all income violate their constitutional right against self-incrimination. Others have argued that enforcement of our tax code violates our right to privacy.

Whether or not you agree that the Constitution guarantees a right to privacy, given various Supreme Court rulings, particularly *Griswold v. Connecticut*, in which the Supreme Court ruled that the Constitution protected a right to privacy, such a right does exist under the Constitution. In the ruling, Justice Douglas, writing for the majority, explained that, although the Bill of Rights does not explicitly mention *privacy*, the right to privacy was to be found in the *penumbras* [implied right] of other constitutional protections. He further wrote that the right to privacy is seen as a right to "protect[ion] from governmental intrusion."

In light of the *Griswold* ruling, the far-reaching scope of our tax code gives the lie to any thought that implementation of the IRC is not a government intrusion into Americans' private matters. This truism has been recognized by Congress, and attempts have been made to limit the potential harm. However, any old farmer will tell you closing the barn door once the horse has fled to the pasture does little good.

Big Brother is Watching

In an effort to limit damage to individual taxpayers, Congress included a nondisclosure provision in the Tax Reform Act of 1976 relating to federal tax return information. Prior to the passage of this act, abuses of personal information obtained from tax returns had been well documented, up to and including abuses by the office of the president. Given recent revelations of deliberate and inadvertent disclosures of private information held by the IRS, it might be argued that the safety provisions of that measure have yet to be fully realized.

During the debate on this bill, the Joint Task Force stated, "The IRS has more information about more people than any other agency in this country." If Congress thought the IRS had a lot of information in 1976, what must its members think now? And here's an even better question. How is it that Congress can express this concern, yet an American taxpayer cannot raise a similar argument?

In 1985, President Reagan alluded to the intrusive nature of our tax system in a speech delivered to high school students in Atlanta, Georgia. He suggested that the lyrics, "Every breath you take, every move you make, I'll be watching you," taken from a song written by Sting, made an appropriate motto for the IRS. The lyrics are even more revealing as they continue to warn that you will be watched every day—every word and every move. That's a scary thought. It seems the president might have been onto something.

The constitutional protection against self-incrimination is, of necessity, linked to the right to privacy. While it is well-established that a taxpayer cannot raise the Fifth Amendment as a legal defense against properly completing and filing an income tax return, how the IRS uses the information provided is a different matter and is a frightening possibility.

One of the most notable rulings on the use of the Fifth Amendment to support failure to file a return was issued in *The United States v. Sullivan* (1927). Justice Holmes, writing the majority opinion, asserted:

> The defendant's gains were subject to the tax...gross income includes gains, profits, and income derived from...any source whatever...As the defendant's

Section I – Tax Chronicles

income was taxed, the statute, of course, required a return. In the decision that this was contrary to the Constitution, we are of opinion that the protection of the Fifth Amendment was pressed too far. If the form of return provided called for answers that the defendant was privileged from making, he could have raised the objection in the return, but could not on that account refuse to make any return at all.

One Toke Over the Line

In this case, the question of claiming deductions tied to illegal gains was also raised. On this issue, Justice Holmes deferred, stating, "It is urged that, if a return were made, the defendant would be entitled to deduct illegal expenses, such as bribery. This by no means follows, but it will be time enough to consider the question when a taxpayer has the temerity to raise it." Temerity—I appreciate his sarcasm.

Holmes's opinion notwithstanding, a taxpayer demonstrating the temerity to argue the legitimacy of claiming a deduction of an "illegal expense" or expenses tied to the production of illegal income will likely soon occur. In the past several years, the issue of medicinal marijuana has moved to the forefront of national consciousness, and the use of marijuana to treat certain health problems has been approved in a number of states. In the past two years, recreational use of marijuana has also been approved in some states, which brings us to a constitutional enigma.

Section 280E of the Internal Revenue Code states, "No deduction or credit shall be allowed for any amount paid or incurred during the taxable year in carrying on any trade or business if such trade or business (or the activities which comprise such trade or business) consists of trafficking in controlled substances (within the meaning of schedule I and II of the Controlled Substances Act) which is prohibited by Federal law or the law of any State in which such trade or business is conducted."

You guessed it. Marijuana is specifically named as a controlled substance. The legality of deducting expenses incurred to produce legal marijuana will likely rise to the Supreme Court to decide. Judging whether a taxpayer, engaged in producing and selling marijuana, whether for medicinal or recreational purposes, in any state(s) allowing that activity, can legitimately deduct the expenses for production of the controlled substance for federal income tax purposes, seems a waste of the court's time.

Walls Come Tumbling Down

I believe other reasonable and legitimate questions can be raised concerning the constitutionality of our tax code. As one example, the First Amendment to the Constitution includes the following: "Congress shall make no law respecting an establishment of religion, or prohibiting the free exercise thereof." Thomas Jefferson declared that this language effectively built "a wall of separation between Church and State."

This section of the First Amendment, often referred to as the freedom of religion clause, has spawned a number of Supreme Court rulings. In *Everson v. Board of Education* (1947), notably, Justice Hugo Black wrote in the majority opinion, "The 'establishment of religion' clause of the First Amendment means at least this: Neither a state nor the federal government can set up a church. Neither can pass laws which aid one religion, aid all religions, or prefer one religion to another. We could not approve the slightest breach."

It is clear, however, that our tax code breaches Jefferson's wall, at least in light of Justice Black's opinion. I will leave it to you to decide whether that breach is a good or bad thing, but it is the truth. Our tax code does "aid one religion, aid all religions." If the code permits contributions made to religious organizations to be taken as deductions to reduce taxable income, the result is to aid that religion. And it can be logically inferred that this provision of the tax code compels others, even those who would oppose that particular religion, to indirectly support that religion.

Under our tax code, an individual can make a donation of a religious artifact, with a sizable value determined solely by that faith, to a religious organization designated as tax exempt by the IRS. Even if the intent of the donation—indeed a restriction assigned to it—is that the artifact will ultimately be sent to a religious institution of that faith outside the United States, that donation is fully deductible. (Author's note: *Fully* is an absolute term and, as noted before, cannot be used when describing a tax provision. The deduction could only be taken if the taxpayer itemized and would be limited to 50% of AGI, or, under certain…never mind. You get the idea.)

By Your Leave

Despite the constitutional conundrums already described, an even more heinous potential outcome exists under current law. The IRC delegates to the IRS the authority to grant or withhold tax-exempt status to various organizations, including religious orders. It can be logically inferred that discretionary—someone less kind might say indiscreet—use of that authority could ultimately serve to "prefer one religion to another."

Recall the recent uproar regarding the IRS's handling of tax-exempt status for various political groups that included the words *Tea Party* in their name. Depending on those involved, could this same arbitrary consideration also be applied to a religious order?

While one may not agree with the specific beliefs of an individual religious order or, for that matter, a spiritual or secular group of any kind, to the extent that a particular group does not violate any law, permitting, or even worse, directing the IRS to flex its muscle against that group is not only unconstitutional, but undercuts our most basic freedoms.

The documented abuse of IRS power is not restricted to one or another political party. Because such abuses have occurred under both Republican and Democrat administrations, arguing which party is the more irresponsible is counterproductive. The solution is to rein in the unbridled power of the IRS. And that can only be done by changing the underlying code that gives it that power.

All Are Punished

In a speech to the British House of Commons, Edmund Burke summed up the problem best, "Because the greater the power, the more dangerous the abuse." Can there be any doubt that the Internal Revenue Service possesses virtually limitless power—thus the potential for unlimited abuse?

There are so many other issues, so many questions that remain unanswered. Under our system of laws, if it is alleged that you have broken a law or caused harm, the government—in a criminal proceeding—or plaintiff—in a civil case—is charged with the responsibility to prove the allegation. Not so under our tax laws. If the IRS declares that your return is wrong, then your return is wrong. It is that simple. If the IRS says you owe additional tax, including penalties, and you do not believe that you do, you have to prove the IRS wrong. The burden of proof is on you.

Our legal system is complex. Civil law is different than criminal law, but one facet of these two distinct legal arenas is similar—a

Section I – Tax Chronicles

criminal act or civil tort can result in punishment, including fines. Ask any taxpayer who has had to pay back taxes whether he felt he had been punished. For those subjected to the wrath of the IRS, just as were the Capulets and the Montagues, "all are punished."

I do not claim that the legal requirement to file a tax return violates the Fifth Amendment. My worry is something quite different. If the IRS thinks a taxpayer has filed an improper return, an examination is initiated. During the course of that examination, the examining agent may require the taxpayer to document everything on the return.

Assume a taxpayer provides a bank statement to the examiner to substantiate a business deduction (for example, an electronic payment to a vendor). While reviewing the statement, the examiner notices an unusually large deposit. In response to the examiner's question about it, the taxpayer replies that it was a gift, or a repayment of a loan—in other words, anything other than income.

The examiner may then demand that the taxpayer, "Prove it!" Absent satisfactory proof, the examiner can include the amount as income and assess a penalty for underreporting income and another penalty for late payment of tax. An accuracy-related penalty may also be assessed. Finally, if the amount is substantial, it may also lead to a civil or criminal sanction for filing a fraudulent—another one of those pesky *F* words—return.

How about double jeopardy? Consider an individual accused of a white-collar crime, convicted and sentenced. Would you care to guess who is waiting when that large steel door we have all seen on television opens to let the newly freed convict out of prison? So much for the idea that this individual has paid her debt to society! If the crime involved money, the IRS will be waiting for her release to demand their ounce of flesh, with penalties to boot.

For those of you who may think that's appropriate, let me be clear. I am not arguing whether those convicted of a money crime should or should not be free from worry about paying taxes once they have served their sentences. I am concerned that many provisions of our tax code run up against protections found within our Constitution, if they do not comprise an outright violation.

These are complex issues and they are serious enough to merit something other than an IRS ruling that essentially asserts "our way or the highway." Under our Constitution, we should not have an agency of the federal government wielding the unchecked authority to dismiss constitutional concerns as frivolous.

In a larger sense, the idea of equal treatment under the law, which has never existed in its purest form, seems to be under serious attack from the disparate treatment dictated by our income tax laws.

Legal theorists might argue that my view is naïve and demonstrates ignorance of the proper application of that concept. They may contend that we are all subject to the same laws, properly and fairly passed by duly elected representatives, subjected to judicial scrutiny, and that process inherently results in equal treatment.

Considering our tax laws, I would have to respond to anyone making such arguments, "We shall just have to agree to disagree."

In the movie *Caddyshack*, when an argument develops between Judge Smails and Al Czervik, laid-back lothario Ty Webb suggests the group adjourn to the judge's office for a drink. As I close this chapter on the constitutional conundrums created by our illogical tax code, I confess this effort has left a bitter taste in my mouth. No bourbon sour for me this day. I must adjourn and enjoy a bourbon-spiked, lemonade sweet-tea.

Chapter 5

Complexity or Insanity?

> The way I look at this, we essentially
> have a tax system that's held together
> by chewing gum and chicken wire.
> Pamela Olsen, Assistant Treasury Secretary
> for Tax Policy

> The most dangerous thing you can do to any
> businessman in America
> is to keep him in doubt,
> and to keep him guessing on what our tax policy is.
> President Lyndon B Johnson

> Allow Americans to file their tax returns
> without the help of a lawyer or accountant, or both.
> Hon. Robert Dole, Senator

Left, right, and center, pundits and politicians, comedians and citizens—for over half a century, all have placed tax code complexity at the forefront of our collective political consciousness.

Merriam-Webster defines *verbose* as "containing more words than necessary or impaired by wordiness." Had Noah Webster lived a century later, *verbose* might have been defined as "containing more words than necessary; impaired by wordiness; *see the Internal Revenue Code.*"

Form over Substance

U.S. Individual Income Tax Return is the name given to Form 1040, the basic form for a federal tax return. Forget for the moment that this form now has three variations (Form 1040A, Form 1040EZ, and Form 1040PR). Forget also that data required to complete this form are not limited to information about an individual, but rather include family or, even more correctly stated, household data. The title seems simple enough, but reality reveals a different truth about our individual income tax—one that is not so simple.

Form 1040 requires income from fifteen specific sources to be listed and described. That number increases to twenty if a discrete subset is added for taxable and tax-exempt variations of many of those categories. Detailed line instructions require even more parsing of income categories. When sundry definitions are included (for example, farming income and fishing income reported on Schedule F), this number increases to over twenty-five. Line 17 lists so many special income categories that it closes with the catchall "etc." Line 21—listed simply as "Other Income"—requires the Other Income Statement to be attached in order to detail forty distinct types of income.

How do you think an average taxpayer defines income? It is likely defined as a dollar in his pocket, regardless of where it came from.

Segregating income as required might even make sense, but distinctions created by the IRC do not stop with just income. There is not sufficient space in this book to enumerate the different deductions from, adjustments to, and exclusions of income. And each of those deductions, adjustments, and exclusions comes with its own

Section I – Tax Chronicles

set of definitions, exceptions, calculations, and variations. Income can be passively or actively earned, as if that should matter.

Let's consider again the title of the form itself, Individual Income Tax Return. Do we think that the form is designed to calculate income tax? Perhaps, but not exclusively! How is it that a form titled Individual Income Tax Return is not restricted to individual data or limited to computing income tax?

Once a taxpayer has listed and totaled all income earned, it is then a straightforward exercise to calculate the tax, right? If you said yes, wrong again! Form 1040 provides for more than a dozen separate schedules or forms to calculate several different taxes. These include the alternative minimum tax (AMT), self-employment tax (SECA), and household taxes. Since passage of the Affordable Care Act, taxpayers must now calculate and include other taxes, reported on one of three separate lines on Form 1040.

Taxpayers must separately compute income tax two ways in order to determine whether they owe AMT. They must also decide whether income exceeded various thresholds to determine if they owe one or more taxes other than AMT.

Receipt of other kinds of income, such as unreported tips, excess benefits, or early distributions, or making excess contributions, all of which are subject to special taxes, must also be considered. Taxpayers must decide if they are required to repay any previous credits they received. As a final insult, taxpayers must ascertain whether they incurred any penalties for engaging in actions Congress deems inappropriate, exemplified by the tax levied for refusing to purchase health insurance.

Finally, before total tax liability can be determined, an array of refundable and nonrefundable credits must also be evaluated.

The F-Word

Our tax code even allows for "partially refundable" tax credits. If a taxpayer is eligible for a credit, one or more separate forms must be selected from over a dozen and properly completed to claim the credit(s). Only after all of this effort can a taxpayer sit back, relax, and enjoy an adult beverage.

If a Tree Falls, Does Anyone Hear It?

The Office of the National Taxpayer Advocate, established in 1996 by the Taxpayer Bill of Rights 2, is required to provide an annual report to Congress in which it must "identify areas of the tax law that impose significant compliance burdens on taxpayers or the Internal Revenue Service, including specific recommendations for remedying these problems." The most compelling comments from prior annual reports are excerpted here. (Author's note: I added *italics* for emphasis.)

The FY2000 report stated, "*Complexity* of tax law remains the number one problem facing taxpayers, and is the root-cause of many of the other problems on the Top 20 list. Our respondents reported so many issues relating to *complexity*, we decided this year to list it as two problems."

The FY2001 report stated, "In the 2000 Annual Report to Congress, tax code *complexity* was identified as the top problem...This year's Report adopts that concept as a truism and incorporates it into every aspect of the report."

The FY2004 report stated, "The most serious problem facing taxpayers and the IRS alike is the *complexity* of the Internal Revenue Code. Without a doubt, the largest source of compliance burdens for taxpayers and the IRS alike is the overwhelming *complexity* of the tax code."

Section I – Tax Chronicles

The FY2005 report stated, "Our tax code has grown so *complex* it creates opportunities for taxpayers to make inadvertent mistakes as well as to game the system…Thus begins an endless cycle—*complexity* drives inadvertent error and fraud, which drive increased enforcement or new legislation, which drives additional *complexity*. In short, *complexity* begets more *complexity*."

More recent reports reaffirmed this concern.

The FY2011 report stated, "The Internal Revenue Code has been growing longer and more *complicated* by the year—and sometimes by the day. In prior reports, I have identified tax code *complexity* as the most serious problem facing taxpayers and the IRS alike."

The FY2012 report stated, "In this report, we identify tax *complexity* as the #1 most serious problem facing taxpayers, and we recommend (as we have in prior reports) that Congress vastly simplify the tax code."

I could have included identical comments from every report, but you get the idea—our tax code is exceedingly and unnecessarily complex. And we know that, or at least those experts appointed to evaluate our tax system know it. Over fourteen consecutive years, each individual report expressed this singular alarm. Many elected officials, scholars, economists, and political pundits have expressed similar frustration. But Congress can't seem to see the forest for the trees. And they seem to be unable to hear the warnings being shouted all around them.

Even the IRS acknowledges the dilemma inherent in a tax code that is virtually incomprehensible to the average taxpayer. While the phrase "IRS Guidance in Plain English" might appear to be a contradiction in terms, the IRS has made an attempt to provide such

The F-Word

guidance on their website: "For anyone not familiar with the inner workings of tax administration, the array of IRS guidance may seem, well, a little puzzling at first glance." Puzzling? A little puzzling?

Judge Learned Hand, a well-respected and oft-cited legal philosopher and jurist, wrote regarding our income tax laws:

> [The] words of...the Income Tax...merely dance before my eyes in a meaningless procession: cross-reference to cross-reference, exception upon exception—couched in abstract terms that offer [me] no handle to seize hold of [and that] leave in my mind only a confused sense of some vitally important, but successfully concealed, purport, which it is my duty to extract, but which is within my power, if at all, only after the most inordinate expenditure of time.

Despite the ongoing, consistent trepidation expressed by the National Taxpayer Advocate and the agreement on both sides of the political aisle, Congress has either done nothing or has made the problem worse. Since the Revenue Act of 1913 was enacted, Congress has passed more than fifty major tax laws, several of which specifically include the word *reform* in their title, yet our tax code continues to get more ruinous.

In the years immediately following passage of the Sixteenth Amendment, the title given to tax laws was typically short and to the point (such as the Revenue Act of 1950). Recently, naming conventions reflect other politically motivated goals: providing relief, creating jobs, addressing some perceived calamity (for example, the Tax Relief, Unemployment Insurance Reauthorization, and Job Creation Act of 2010). Laws such as the Patient Protection and Affordable Care Act, passed in 2010, are promoted as legislation to address social issues but which, in reality, bring significant changes to our tax code. And, at the risk of being redundant, with the passage of each new law, whether titled reform or otherwise, our tax system continues to deteriorate.

President Reagan summed it up neatly: "Most tax revisions didn't improve the system, they made it more like Washington itself, complicated, unfair, cluttered with gobbledygook and loopholes designed for those with the power and influence to hire high-priced legal and tax advisers."

If you ever wondered why Reagan was called "the great communicator", this statement explains it. One word—gobbledygook! The right word!

Madness

You may fairly and reasonably ask why this is so. The answer is hard to take because, in large measure, the answer is ourselves, each and every one of us. Senator Russell Long is often credited with a succinct, humorous explanation of the reason that meaningful tax reform never truly occurs. He said that tax reform meant, "Don't tax thee, don't tax me, tax that fellow behind the tree."

And therein lies the problem. Many argue, as I do, that to realize real reform, we have to eliminate the myriad tax treatments, tax preferences, schedules, allowances, deductions, and tax credits, not to mention the ever-popular AMT. Almost everyone agrees with the need for simplification and reform, at least up to the point that any proposed change affects an individually favored tax preference. It is then that any real progress on reform ceases and the unending debate continues.

The F-Word

The result: American taxpayers get more of the same. This process calls to mind the last words in the movie *The Bridge on the River Kwai*: "Madness...madness."

In addition to the natural, popular resistance to any real reform effort, we are faced with the vagaries of politics and the caprice of politicians. In this respect, I believe the tax reform debate is often centered on the wrong issue regarding simplification of our tax code. The argument frequently evolves into a discussion of the number of tax brackets, and range of tax rates, often by those in favor of a flat tax.

In my view, neither the number of tax brackets nor the degree to which tax rates are flattened has a significant bearing on complexity. Far from creating a complicated equation, the math required by using multiple tax brackets is easily understood. Rather than the number of brackets, complexity within our tax system primarily results from the use of the tax code to legislate social policy.

For the past several decades, income tax laws have been used by Congress to encourage activities deemed socially useful—getting health insurance, sponsoring employee health care and retirement, raising children, owning a home, developing alternative energy or driving alternative energy cars, getting an advanced education, and so on.

And with each election, with every new malady, with any injustice, real or perceived, policy preferences change. Changing social policy thus results in frequent, often hidden, and sometimes contradictory modifications to the tax code. Regardless of merits of the social intent or the success or failure of the tax code to drive behavior, taxes created for any purpose other than raising revenue necessarily increase complexity. And given the disparate treatment that often occurs solely from the timing of these changes, this approach encroaches on the fundamental American principle of equal treatment under the law.

Fixing this problem requires an act of Congress, no pun intended. Article 1, Section 7, of the US Constitution states, "All bills for raising Revenue shall originate in the House of Representatives." Isn't it ironical that we are compelled to rely on Congress, the same body that got us here in the first place, to repair our tax code? I am reminded of an observation credited to Mark Twain: "Suppose you were an idiot, and suppose you were a member of Congress; but I repeat myself."

You have to applaud members of Congress in one respect. They don't give up trying. It has been said that our tax code is rewritten so often that it should be drafted in pencil.

Congress's Tinkertoy

It is true that many factors contribute to the complexity now firmly embedded in our tax code. But the primary reason is that our tax laws are now enacted more to drive specific behavior or to effect income distribution—in short, to implement social engineering—than to raise revenues sufficient to support necessary government functions. As newly elected officials strive to fulfill their social views, the easiest method, and often the first tried, is to tinker with the tax code.

Given the state of our national politics, using the tax code to change behavior may be a practical way to enact social policy, but it is an extraordinarily inefficient way to write a tax code. The code now has a deep and wide reach into all aspects of Americans' lives—and that reach is growing.

I acknowledge that any form of tax will have some effect on behavior, and any tax will raise revenue. Nonetheless, because our tax code is now used more as a social engineering tool than as a method to raise revenue, the multiplicity of tax preferences, the different income treatments, the confusing definitions, the host of income ceilings limiting eligibility for various deductions, and the multitude of thresholds restricting a taxpayer's claim for a specific credit make our tax code incomprehensibly, irrationally complex.

Before we consider some examples of the complexity buried within the individual income tax provisions of the code, let me offer a disclaimer. The IRC directs and controls individual income tax, business income tax, trust and estate taxes, and gift taxes. While the management of retirement plans generally falls under the Employee Retirement Income Security Act of 1974 (ERISA), the IRC weighs in with reporting requirements, limits, definitions, penalties, and more.

The IRC also controls the assessment and collection provisions of Social Security. You cannot even imagine the complexity created with the various "tax-exempt" provisions of our tax code. And the list goes on. Each of these sections is at least as complex, if not more so, than provisions relating to individual income tax. I point out these facts to acknowledge that the complexity of the code is not limited to individual income taxes. Demonstrating this would take several volumes.

Suffer the Little Children to Come

A child is a child is a child, correct? To most of us, maybe, but not according to our tax code. While it has been suggested that it takes a village to raise a child, it takes a bevy of tax attorneys and accountants to understand what constitutes a child viewed through the prism of the IRC. To complicate matters further, the assistance of those same lawyers and accountants is needed to determine which taxpayer may claim that child and the impact claiming that child may or may not have on that taxpayer.

Section I – Tax Chronicles

Most taxpayers understand the basic concept that a minor—an adjective that may not actually apply—child may be claimed as a dependent. However, to be relevant for a specific income tax return, a child must be a "qualifying" child. Current IRS guidelines state, "A 'qualifying child' may enable a taxpayer to claim several tax benefits."

Possible benefits include the ability to file as head of household (HOH), offering an increased standard deduction and tax brackets that provide lower effective marginal rates. Taxpayers can also lower their tax liability by claiming the dependent exemption, and/or claiming child tax credit, and/or claiming the child and dependent care credit. Finally, claiming a qualifying child on a tax return can result in eligibility for a tax payment—money paid to the taxpayer regardless of their tax liability—from refundable credits based on either the earned income tax credit or additional child tax credit or both.

The IRS previously acknowledged that, prior to 2005, each potential tax benefit was linked to different definitions of a qualifying child, leaving many taxpayers confused. Really! But help was on the way through enactment of the Working Families Tax Relief Act of 2004. That law created a uniform definition of a qualifying child that took effect in 2005.

I must caution you against getting your hopes up too high. IRS guidance states, "This standard definition applies to all five of the tax benefits, with each benefit having some additional rules." My interpretation of "some additional rules" is inconsistent with my understanding of "uniform." So much for the promise of a uniform definition for a qualifying child.

According to Internal Revenue Publication 501, "In general, to be a taxpayer's qualifying child, a person must satisfy four tests." But again, use of the term "in general," which is inherently imprecise, also conflicts with "uniform."

- **Relationship**—the taxpayer's child or stepchild (whether by blood or adoption), foster child, sibling or stepsibling, or a descendant of one of these. (Author's note: Niece, nephew, grandson, granddaughter, grandniece—you get the picture.)
- **Residence**—has the same principal residence as the taxpayer for more than half the tax year. Exceptions may apply for children of divorced or separated parents, kidnapped children, temporary absences, and for children who were born or died during the year.
- **Age**—must be under the age of nineteen at the end of the tax year, or under the age of twenty-four if a full-time student for at least five months of the year, or be permanently and totally disabled at any time during the year.
- **Support**—did not provide more than one-half of his/her own support for the year.

Consider that each test has its own definition and, in some cases, unique exceptions or exclusions. As an example, the test for age seems simple enough. However, as the Genie said to Aladdin, "Uh, ah, almost. There are a few, uh, provisos." To be a qualifying child, the child must also be younger than the taxpayer or younger than the taxpayer's spouse, if married filing jointly. Two of the five benefits also set a different age than that specified in the uniform definition.

In order to move this example along, let's assume these four tests can be understood and properly applied. But before a taxpayer actually prepares the return, the question, "For which taxpayer is this child a 'qualifying' child?" must be answered. The IRS weighs in on this question with some tie-breaker rules:

If a child is claimed as a qualifying child by two or more taxpayers in a given year, the child will be the qualifying child of

- The parent;
- If more than one taxpayer is the child's parent, the one with whom the child lived for the longest time during the year;
- If the time spent with each parent was equal, the parent with the highest adjusted gross income;
- If neither taxpayer is the child's parent, the taxpayer with the highest adjusted gross income.

Confused yet? Stay with me here. Let's assume we understand what a qualifying child is and who can claim that child. In that case, we are sufficiently armed and dangerous enough to examine each of the tax benefits and apply the "uniform definition for a 'qualifying child'" provided under the Tax Relief Act of 2004.

Following the outline of Form 1040, let's first determine the impact on filing status. As noted, a taxpayer with a qualifying child may be able to file as HOH, gaining a larger standard deduction and lower marginal tax rates.

The last of three requirements needed to file as HOH as stated by the IRS on Form 1040 instructions is that "a qualifying person lived with you in the home for more than half the year (except for temporary absences, such as school)." Note that this requirement specifies a qualifying "person" not child. Form 1040 instructions further state:

To qualify you for head of household filing status, the qualifying person must be one of the following:

- Your qualifying child or qualifying relative who lived with you for more than half the part of the year he or she was alive.
- Your parent for whom you paid, for the entire part of the year he or she was alive, more than half the cost of keeping up the home he or she lived in.

That clears that up. This rule clarifies that a qualifying child is a qualifying person. I will limit this discussion to a qualifying child because a qualifying relative does not actually have to be related.

Before I get carried away, is this qualifying child the same as defined earlier? Previously, a qualifying child included your child or stepchild (whether by blood or adoption), foster child, sibling or stepsibling, or a descendant of one of these. This would include nieces or nephews. To the contrary, to file as HOH, a qualifying child *does not* include nieces or nephews. IRS guidance states "qualifying child (such as a son, daughter, or grandchild)." Note the absence of progeny from a sibling relationship.

Again, however, IRS rules eliminate inconsistencies among different definitions. They direct that nieces and nephews may be claimed as a qualifying relative, not as a qualifying child. Again, I will refrain from commenting on this as a person does not have to be related to meet the test as a qualifying relative. You can't make this stuff up.

Returning to HOH filing requirements, a taxpayer is told that he must generally—here we go with that word *generally* again—be able to claim a qualifying child as a dependent. To be claimed as a dependent, a qualifying child must also meet both of these tests:

- Nationality—be a US citizen or national, or a resident of the United States, Canada, or Mexico. There is an exception for certain adopted children.
- Marital status—if married, did not file a joint return for that year, unless the return is filed only as a claim for refund and no tax liability would exist for either spouse if they had filed separate returns.

Whether correct or not, let's assume we have finally determined which filing status to use. We must then decide which, if any, of the available credits we can claim based on our qualifying children.

The language defining eligibility for the credit for child and dependent care expenses is also confusing. If you pay someone to care for a child, or other dependent—a qualifying person—you may be eligible for this credit. A qualifying person includes a qualifying child who is your dependent under age thirteen when the care was provided, or was permanently and totally disabled.

Unlike the HOH requirement that a qualifying child must be your dependent, if you cannot claim your child as a dependent, he or she is treated as your qualifying person if the child received over half of his or her support during the calendar year from one or both parents who are divorced or legally separated and "the child was in the custody of one or both parents for more than half the year…you were the child's custodial parent."

In an effort to leave no word undefined, the IRS defines custodial parent as the parent with whom the child lived for the greater number of nights. Keep in mind, the instructions now call for a test based on the number of nights compared with a test based on more than half the year for dependent exemptions, with exceptions.

Regardless of whether you can claim the credit for child and dependent care expenses, you should evaluate the first of two refundable credits: the child tax credit. This credit can reduce your tax liability or can be paid to you as a refundable credit if your income falls below a certain threshold.

The qualifying child tests used for the child tax credit follow closely those listed for the uniform definition of a qualifying child. But the child tax credit has an absolute requirement that the child must be claimed as a dependent on the return. Thus the dependent tests are applicable as well. One notable difference is that of age. To receive the child tax credit, the child must be under the age of seventeen—not ages thirteen, nineteen, or twenty-four, as prescribed elsewhere. Further, there are no exceptions to the age requirement for the child tax credit for a disabled child.

The second refundable credit available to a taxpayer with a qualifying child is the earned income tax credit (EITC). This credit increases as the number of qualifying children increases. The number of children that can be claimed has changed over the years, and, presently, the maximum credit can be received by claiming three children. Claiming a higher number does not affect the credit under current rules.

Unlike the child tax credit, the EITC does not require that a taxpayer claim the qualifying child as a dependent. But determining a qualifying child for EITC uses all of the same tests listed in the uniform definition. Also, a qualifying child for the EITC must have lived with the taxpayer in the United States for more than half the year and must have a valid Social Security number.

Section I – Tax Chronicles

Earlier, I provided a list of IRS tie-breaker rules to determine dependent status for those qualifying children who could be claimed by more than one taxpayer. For the purposes of the EITC, that list includes two additional rules:

- The person with the highest AGI if no parent can claim the child as a qualifying child; or
- A person with the higher AGI than any parent who can also claim the child as a qualifying child but does not.

The IRS estimates that up to 20% of eligible taxpayers fail to claim the EITC. It is easy to understand how this might happen. Despite the recent addition of a uniform definition, the criteria used to determine a qualifying child remain inconsistent among different tax provisions.

The IRS has published a three-page table listing the criteria to establish a qualifying child for the EITC, child tax credit, dependent exemption, head of household filing status, and the child and dependent care credit. Three pages! It seems reasonable to ask, is that really necessary?

Most taxpayers with children take advantage of two or more of these tax provisions. Yet confusion is unavoidable when a child may be a qualifying child under one provision but not another, a qualifying child for one taxpayer, not another. Regardless of whether one agrees with these provisions or not, if they are to be included in our tax code, it should not be that difficult to determine eligibility and calculate the tax benefit.

There's a Hydra in Our Tax Code

My second example summarizes the explosion of income limits affecting deductions or credits. Anytime Congress removes one limit, two more appear in its place. Lest this discussion become overly lengthy, I will restrict examples to those applicable to a married couple filing a joint return.

The easiest to list, in terms of number of instances, are income thresholds that trigger either a higher or alternative tax. The first is the threshold above which Social Security retirement benefits begin to be taxed. Should a retired taxpayer's modified adjusted gross income exceed $32,000, part of the Social Security received becomes subject to income tax. (Author's note: Modified adjusted gross income is different from the adjusted gross income most taxpayers are familiar with.)

A second threshold applies to a new tax, added for 2013, unknown to most Americans. It is the additional Medicare tax levied on wage income above $250,000, but withheld by the employer if wage income exceeds $200,000. It is likely that many wage earners are aware of the third limit, $113,700, above which Social Security tax ceases.

A fourth threshold comes from another tax that began in 2013, the net investment income tax, assessed on earnings from investment (interest, dividends, capital gains) when adjusted gross income exceeds $250,000. Finally, if modified adjusted gross income exceeds $153,900, the taxpayer becomes subject to the alternative minimum tax.

Our tax code has also experienced an explosion of income thresholds above which certain benefits, deductions, or credits are limited or eliminated. What follows is a brief listing of a few of these.

The percentage used to calculate child care credit decreases when earned income exceeds $15,000. Once earned income rises above $43,000, the percentage is capped at 20%. To calculate this credit for a married couple filing jointly, the income of the spouse with the higher earned income is used.

Section I – Tax Chronicles

The child tax credit is reduced when adjusted gross income surpasses $110,000. The upper limit for elimination of the credit varies with the number of children for whom the credit is claimed. For two children, the credit ceases entirely when AGI exceeds $149,000.

The American Opportunity Credit is lowered when AGI tops $160,000. It is eliminated when AGI exceeds $180,000.

The ability to deduct all itemized expenses is limited when AGI exceeds $300,000 while deductibility of student loan interest is phased out when modified adjusted gross income falls between $125,000 and $155,000.

Deductibility of IRA contributions is limited by income if one or both spouses are covered by a retirement plan with their employer. In that event, deductibility of contributions is reduced when modified adjusted gross income is between $115,000 and $188,000.

Tax Preference	Threshold	Impact if Threshold is Exceeded
Social Security Benefits	MAGI[1]—$32,000	Up to 85% of benefits are subject to tax.
Additional Medicare Tax	Wage Income—$250,000	A .09% additional Medicare tax is assessed on excess.
Social Security Tax	Wage Income—$106,800	Social Security tax is not assessed on additional wage income.
Net Investment Income Tax	AGI—$250,000	Net investment income is subject to additional tax of 3.8%.
Alternative Minimum Tax	MAGI[2]—$153,900	The taxpayer could be subject to alternative minimum tax.
Deduction for Exemptions	AGI—$300,000	The deduction for dependents may be limited.
Child Care Credit	Earned Income—$15,000	The amount of credit is reduced.
Child Care Credit	Earned Income—$43,000	The amount of credit is capped at 20% of eligible costs.
Child Tax Credit	AGI[3]—$110,000	The amount of credit is reduced.
Child Tax Credit	AGI[3]—$149,000	The credit is eliminated
Education Credits	AGI—$160,000	The amount of credit is reduced.
Education Credits	AGI—$180,000	The credit is eliminated
Student Loan Interest	MAGI—$125,000	Deductibility of the interest is limited.
Student Loan Interest	MAGI—$155,000	Deductibility of the interest ceases.
IRA Contributions[4]	MAGI—$115,000	Contribution deduction may be limited.
IRA Contributions[4]	MAGI—$188,000	Contribution deduction not allowed.
Itemized Deductions	AGI—$300,000	Total itemized deductions may be limited.

Table 1 - Listing of Income Thresholds for married taxpayers filing jointly.

[1] MAGI is a calculation most taxpayers are unfamiliar with. For this example, tax-exempt interest and one-half of Social Security must be added to income to determine MAGI.
[2] MAGI is a different calculation than the earlier example.
[3] AGI threshold is dependent on the number of qualifying children. The number shown reflects the threshold for 2 children.
[4] IRA deductions may be limited if one or both spouses are covered by a retirement plan at work.

Even if the premise that tax benefits should be limited as income increases is reasonable, it seems that the application of that philosophy should be consistent. Under the IRC, nothing could be further from reality. Five taxes together with six different deductions or credits produce sixteen different income thresholds for a married couple filing jointly. While I believe limiting deductions based on income is fair and logical under the code as it exists, using a different limit for every type of tax provision seems nonsensical.

If you also consider income limits for individual itemized deductions, on claiming certain losses, and on a host of other tax provisions, the words of Judge Hand again come to mind as the numerous forms, instructions, publications, revenue rulings, revenue procedures, and technical bulletins "merely dance before my eyes in a meaningless procession."

Frankly, the problem is more complex than can be easily shown. Attempting to fully demonstrate the complexity of the code is, in itself, a complicated task. I point again to the constant plea for simplification posited by the Taxpayer Advocate. The continual promise of reform made by candidates of both parties at all political levels also serves as evidence that our code is beyond irrational.

Bring Me Your Tired (I Can Make Them Poor)

My last example of the insane complexity of our tax code highlights the Patient Protection and Affordable Care Act (ACA). As now happens, many of our most complex tax laws no longer even refer to tax in their title. This law, often referred to as Obamacare, was enacted in 2010. This illustration is limited to the eligibility for a refundable credit for health insurance premiums as provided in section 1401, reprinted in part as follows.

Section I – Tax Chronicles

However, I should probably first apologize for inserting the text verbatim. As an experienced tax professional, even my head hurts, my eyes water and I get nauseous when I read verbatim passages from our tax code. Before you begin, perhaps it's time to make a visit to the liquor cabinet. Nonetheless, assuming you are actually able to read this excerpt, I think it clearly portrays the insane complexity of our tax code.

SEC. 1401. REFUNDABLE TAX CREDIT PROVIDING PREMIUM ASSISTANCE FOR COVERAGE UNDER A QUALIFIED HEALTH PLAN.

    (a) In General—Subpart C of part IV of subchapter A of chapter 1 of the Internal Revenue Code of 1986 (relating to refundable credits) is amended by inserting after section 36A the following new section:

SEC. 36B. REFUNDABLE CREDIT FOR COVERAGE UNDER A QUALIFIED HEALTH PLAN.

    (a) IN GENERAL.—In the case of an applicable taxpayer, there shall be allowed as a credit against the tax imposed by this subtitle for any taxable year an amount equal to the premium assistance credit amount of the taxpayer for the taxable year.

    (b) PREMIUM ASSISTANCE CREDIT AMOUNT.—For purposes of this section—

        (1) IN GENERAL.—The term 'premium assistance credit amount' means, with respect to any taxable

year, the sum of the premium assistance amounts determined under paragraph (2) with respect to all coverage months of the taxpayer occurring during the taxable year.

(2) PREMIUM ASSISTANCE AMOUNT.—The premium assistance amount determined under this subsection with respect to any coverage month is the amount equal to the lesser of—

(A) the monthly premiums for such month for 1 or more qualified health plans offered in the individual market within a State which cover the taxpayer, the taxpayer's spouse, or any dependent (as defined in section 152) of the taxpayer and which were enrolled in through an Exchange established by the State under 1311 of the Patient Protection and Affordable Care Act, or

(B) the excess (if any) of—

(i) the adjusted monthly premium for such month for the applicable second lowest

Section I – Tax Chronicles

> cost silver plan with respect to the taxpayer, over
>
> (ii) an amount equal to 1/12 of the product of the applicable percentage and the taxpayer's household income for the taxable year.

Stop already—enough! I can envision liquor cabinets opening all across the country. Can anyone explain the meaning of this section in plain English? I can't. Okay, maybe I can, but the point is neither I nor anyone else should have to.

This unnecessary complexity carries with it a far greater negative consequence. In practice, this credit is designed to offset some or all of the cost of health care premiums for those in lower income brackets. But language this obscure and convoluted makes it more difficult for those intended as beneficiaries to actually claim the credit.

Data suggest that many of the individuals who would be eligible for this credit include those less educated, those for whom English is a second language, and those with limited Internet access. While others will also be eligible, many of those listed may have to depend on the assistance of others in order to actually claim the credit. Why is that? Our tax code should not be so complicated that it is, in reality, incomprehensible to a majority of Americans.

The IRS has acknowledged that a statistically significant percentage of those eligible for some or all of the various credits based on a qualifying child has not taken advantage of them. A few years from now, it is likely that Congress will spend a lot of money—our money at that—to pay for countless studies to determine what common sense already tells us. These studies will similarly

The F-Word

conclude that many eligible taxpayers had not claimed the premium assistance credit.

Perhaps I should have inserted this excerpt prior to my earlier reference to Judge Hand's lament. I think it now likely that the true meaning of his words "cross-reference to cross-reference, exception upon exception—couched in abstract terms that offer [me] no handle to seize hold of" have now become painfully clear. Bourbon helps. If nothing else, it dulls the pain in the back of your head—at least until the next morning.

It may be impossible to imagine, but other sections of this legislation are equally confusing, perhaps even more so. Out of compassion, I have limited a verbatim example to this one excerpt.

Affordable Care advocates insisted that the cost would be paid for; they promised that the plan would be budget neutral. Proof of that assertion can only be determined over time. Clearly, however, payment of the costs incurred must come in the form of increased tax revenue—either an increase to an existing tax rate, the creation of a new tax, or the reduction or elimination of an existing tax preference.

Regardless of what the ultimate cost will be, doesn't it make sense to pick one payment method? Just increase one or more tax rates, or create one straightforward, easily understood new tax levy. Or, instead, just eliminate one tax preference. Obviously, the benefit of a simple approach was not readily apparent to Congress.

In their incomparable wisdom, members elected to continue the path of confusion and uncertainty by combining all three methods,

Section I – Tax Chronicles

including variations and exceptions for each. To make implementation of this law even more difficult and confusing, they created bewildering calculations of the various newfangled credits as well as the computation of newly added penalties.

This law adds new taxes, creates new refundable tax credits for individuals, and generates new business tax credits. It initiates tax penalties for those who choose not to obtain coverage and penalizes employers who can't or don't offer coverage to eligible employees. Despite being portrayed as health care reform, it is clearly a major piece of tax legislation, adding to the already complex, confusing tax code.

The ACA was amended only seven days after it was enacted by the Health Care and Reconciliation Act of 2010. As amended, this law specifically added the following tax provisions, listed in no particular order. Given Congress's past performance, it is likely that this list will grow lengthier over time.

> Established a penalty for taxpayers who do not obtain minimum coverage, in the amount of $95, or one percent of income, whichever is greater. By 2016, this penalty increases to $695 ($2,085 for families), or 2.5% of income, whichever is greater.
>
> Raised the deduction threshold from 7.5% to 10% of adjusted gross income for qualifying medical expenses itemized on Schedule A.
>
> Levied a new excise tax on health insurance companies based on market share. The rate gradually increases between 2014 and 2018 and thereafter increases at the rate of inflation.

> Established a $2,000 per employee penalty on employers with more than fifty employees who do not offer health insurance to their full-time workers.
>
> Implemented the first of two new taxes—the additional Medicare tax—assessed at .09%, applied to earned income above a threshold amount.
>
> Implemented the second of two new taxes—the net investment income tax—assessed at 3.8% (equal to the Medicare tax paid by employees and employers), applied to net investment income above a threshold amount.

This unnecessary complexity has removed all transparency from our tax system. Arguments about who pays and how much they pay must be limited to specific taxpayers and well-defined circumstances. The multitude of different exceptions, exclusions, and credits makes it impossible to identify how the code actually affects Americans in general, even those within a specified income bracket.

Unless taxpayers compel our elected officials to stop this nonsense, and until we require Congress to enact real tax reform, things will just get worse. Is our tax code complex or insane—or both? What is your opinion now?

To be fair, however, I should acknowledge that distilled spirits often have complex flavors. Mixers can enhance or hide the flavor. Do you prefer your bourbon in a mixed drink, neat or simply on the rocks?

Section II

Every Means Necessary, Fair and Unfair

Overview

> A democratic government is the only one in which
> those who vote for a tax
> can escape the obligation to pay it.
> Alexis de Tocqueville, Political Historian

> Get the government out of the business of picking
> winners and losers
> Dan Mitchell, Economist

> The wisdom of man never yet contrived
> a system of taxation
> that operates with perfect equality.
> President Andrew Jackson

> I apologize for the inequities…but if we should
> wait…to adjust the taxes
> upon each man in exact proportion with every other,
> we shall never collect any tax at all.
> President Abraham Lincoln

The F-Word

In the United States, as in most modern social welfare economies, disagreement over the inherent fairness of the tax code is a constant companion to everyone—politician and citizen. Discussion on taxes, whether held in the chambers of the Capitol or at the local pub, is often bitter. Some argue that, to be fair, taxpayers should be treated exactly the same—that is, they should pay the same tax, either in absolute dollars or in flat tax rates. Others suggest that tax fairness is determined by its nature—progressive or regressive.

Generally, a tax is considered to be progressive if it takes a higher percentage as income increases. Indirect taxes, including sales taxes, especially if assessed on basic necessities such as food, clothing, or medicine, are widely viewed as examples of regressive taxes. Property taxes, which can be either direct or indirect, are also widely considered to be regressive as well because they are assessed at a flat tax rate.

Determining whether a tax is progressive or regressive would be a straightforward exercise, except for the fact that individual opinions are often clouded by political persuasion. Regardless, even if agreement is reached on whether one or another tax method is progressive or regressive, the impact of that determination on actual tax reform usually creates further disagreement.

A related discussion often occurs regarding the term "income redistribution." Whether a nation engages in social welfare and thus implements some degree of income redistribution has no bearing on whether a tax is progressive or regressive. Such redistribution may mitigate the impact of a regressive tax, but it does not change the nature of that specific tax.

To the extent government undertakes any effort other than general defense, public safety, or the common good (roads, schools,

Section II – Every Means Necessary, Fair And Unfair

and the like), some degree of social welfare exists. But assuming social welfare only benefits lower-income households can lead to false conclusions, especially given the multitude of tax preferences under the IRC. As shown later, many of these tax preferences provide considerable benefits to upper-income households.

Leaving aside the questions of how much the government spends and for what, the issue of tax fairness is, like beauty, in the eye of the beholder or, in this case, the wallet of the taxpayer. In the current political environment, it appears we are not likely to reach consensus on what constitutes a fair tax. We cannot even agree on what data to use.

It is often said that statistics lie, but that is not quite true. ESPN airs a program, *Numbers Never Lie*. The title of the show implies that numbers can give us the truth. That is also not quite true. The veracity of an argument can neither be proved nor discredited simply by the data offered. Assuming they are not a figment of someone's imagination, numbers neither lie nor tell the truth.

The reality is that the truth can be, and frequently is, distorted by selective bias—which numbers are used, how they are obtained, and how they are presented. Those on either side of a debate on one or more tax provisions will use data that best support their argument. They will be biased in obtaining data, selective in what data to use, and colored in their presentation of the results.

In a speech made during the 2012 presidential election campaign, President Obama suggested, "Asking a billionaire to pay at least as much as his secretary, that's just common sense." It is just common sense. His choice of words, however, was imprecise. The wording might be interpreted as suggesting that some billionaires pay less income tax than a secretary. I suspect few billionaires, if any, pay less tax, in actual dollars, than their secretaries. However, given the complexity of our tax code and the different treatment afforded different types of income, many wealthy individuals do pay a lower percentage of their income than those who work for them.

The president might have more precisely commented, "Asking a billionaire to pay at least the same tax rate as his secretary, that's just common sense." But that phrase is not quite as emotionally charged or as compelling, is it? Nonetheless, to be fair, the president is not alone in his selective use of words. All politicians, Republican and Democrat, liberal and conservative, choose their words carefully—and intentionally.

Despite conventional wisdom, politicians seldom choose words that are patently untrue; neither are they overly concerned with precision. They use the words that best make the point they are trying to communicate. It is up to the listener to separate the wheat from the chaff.

Amid this political banter, do we even know what our real taxes are or how much we really pay? Our income tax code is even more imprecise than the politicians who created it. Our current income tax policy is generally understood to employ a progressive marginal-rate tax structure. Use of the word *progressive* implies that *marginal* tax rates increase as taxable income increases. But does that result actually occur in real life?

When most politicians talk about income taxes, they typically use marginal rates as a starting point. As you will learn, assuming you are not already aware, the use of *marginal* to suggest rates increase as income increases is not quite accurate—at least not under the Internal Revenue Code.

That imprecision causes most tax professionals to use the word *effective* when describing tax rates. Consider that, while the highest

Section II – Every Means Necessary, Fair And Unfair

marginal tax rate under present law is 39.6%, if all of a taxpayer's income is treated as capital gains, the highest applicable rate is 20%. (Author's note: With the passage of the Affordable Care Act, even this is not quite true.)

Few taxpayers pay the marginal rate their actual income would dictate. The difference is due to which tax preferences can be claimed, which deductions can be taken to reduce income, which credits can be exploited to reduce tax liability. Added together, these preferences can lower the total tax burden, thus producing an effective tax rate lower than the marginal rate that is assessed against the absolute value of the taxpayer's income.

Regardless, some believe a marginal system to be fair and that higher income should be taxed at higher rates. Conversely, others believe this method is unfair. They contend that those earning more already pay higher taxes, in absolute dollars, and that they pay the lion's share of total taxes paid. Those last two assertions are correct.

According to the Congressional Budget Office, for 2010, households in the top quintile paid 68.8% of all federal taxes collected, while those in the bottom quintile paid only 0.4% of the total collected. Those who oppose marginal tax rates further argue that their use punishes success and hard work.

To the contrary, others maintain that our tax system is unfair, not because of marginal rates, but because the highest rates are mitigated by other tax preferences. These critics insist that the highest rates are not high enough. They grudgingly concede that those earning higher income typically pay more in absolute dollars but believe they should pay even more than the current system requires.

When considering our existing tax structure, the issue of fairness is not just a function of vertical equity—whether tax rates are too high on the poorest or too low on the richest—but it is also a function of horizontal equity—whether those with the same income incur the same tax liability. Under our tax code, a parity problem exists because taxpayers with roughly the same incomes often pay shockingly different taxes depending on their circumstances. An individual's tax liability can fluctuate wildly depending on the kind of income earned, where he works, and what he does with his earnings. And, given the recent propensity for frequent changes to the law, the tax incurred can vary wildly due only to the timing of an event.

Should the wealthy pay the substantial percentage of total taxes? Should a lower percentage be assessed on their income compared to the rate levied on more modest incomes? These are hard questions. Should those on the lowest rungs of the economic ladder be compelled to pay taxes at all? This is yet another difficult question. Each of these questions speaks to the issue of fairness. Fairness is a mental construct at best. What one person perceives as fair may be incredibly inequitable, biased, and wrong to another.

Fairness is unlike equal treatment. These two philosophical concepts are similar and often related but definitely different. As demonstrated throughout this book, our tax code often treats taxpayers reporting the same income differently—sometimes dramatically so. Identical incomes frequently produce significantly different tax liability. To me, that seems not only unfair, but borders on a violation of the basic concept of equal treatment under the law.

All agree that the current system contains numerous injustices. Members of Congress, presidents, presidential candidates, and special committees appointed to review our tax code—everyone agrees. Our tax code is just plain wrong, yet no one truly addresses the problem.

Section II – Every Means Necessary, Fair And Unfair

Elected officials discuss taxes and government spending by using the word *billions*. Economists talk about quintiles of income distribution. In all of this noise, we forget real people and the real impact on them, whether fair or unfair. We overlook the truth that Santayana offered, "Injustice in this world is not something comparative; the wrong is deep, clear, and absolute."

In the movie, *Gandhi*, one scene depicts a US correspondent, on assignment to cover India's resistance to British rule, dictating a telegram regarding the harsh action taken by the British army against protesters at a salt mine. He said, "It went on and on... Stop. But still, it went on and on." So it goes with our tax code—on and on. In his wire, the correspondent concluded that Great Britain had lost her moral right to maintain control over India and that the citizens of India would no longer accept or tolerate such rule.

It has become nearly impossible to tolerate our existing tax system, even with a stiff drink.

Chapter 6

Living on the Margin

> It would be a hard government that should tax its people
> one-tenth part of their income.
> Benjamin Franklin, Founding Father

> I think that people at the high end—people like myself—
> should be paying a lot more in taxes.
> Warren Buffett, Businessman and Philanthropist

> The necessaries of life occasion the great expense
> of the poor.
> They find it difficult to get food,
> and the greater part of their little revenue is spent
> in getting it.
> Adam Smith, Author and Philosopher

As a frequent visitor to the University of Pennsylvania, founded by Benjamin Franklin, I often pass the life-sized bronze statue called "Ben on the Bench" on Locust Walk and reflect on Franklin's legacy. Considering that the *lowest* marginal income tax rate currently assessed under the IRC is 10% and the highest is 39.6%, I suspect he is turning over in his grave in light of his belief expressed in the quote at the beginning of this chapter. We can no longer even dream of a time when our government would "tax its people one-tenth part."

Our income tax system uses progressive marginal tax rates designed to tax higher income at progressively higher rates. With the myriad exceptions written into our tax code, however, the intended result is often not achieved.

Historically, the tax code has included as many as fifty-six brackets with the highest marginal rate once reaching 94%. For 2013, the IRC includes seven tax brackets as shown in table 2.

Tax Rate	Married Filing Jointly
10.0%	$0 to $17,850
15.0%	$17,850 to $72,500
25.0%	$72,500 to $146,400
28.0%	$146,400 to $223,050
33.0%	$223,050 to $398,350
35.0%	$398,350 to $450,000
39.6%	$450,000 and up

Table 2 - 2013 Tax Rate Table - Married Filing Jointly

When the modern income tax began with the Revenue Act of 1913, a normal rate of 1% was established for all taxpayers. A progressive marginal rate called an additional rate was also instituted. Table 3 reflects the rates as they existed in 1913.

Section II – Every Means Necessary, Fair And Unfair

Income	Normal Rate	Additional Rate	Combined Rate
0	1%	0	1%
$20,000	1%	1%	2%
$50,000	1%	2%	3%
$75,000	1%	3%	4%
$100,000	1%	4%	5%
$250,000	1%	5%	6%
$500,000	1%	6%	7%

Table 3 - 1913 Tax Rate Table
Only one set of rates existed because different filing statuses had not yet been created.

Note the table for 1913 does not reference any particular filing status. Prior to 1948, one set of income brackets and tax rates applied to all taxpayers. Now, however, separate brackets and rates have been established for single taxpayers, for married taxpayers—with a different set of rates based on filing jointly or separately—and for those who file as head of household.

Additionally, for the first thirty years under our tax code, all taxpayers had to calculate their tax liability. Completing a return forced a taxpayer to do the math. In 1941, the IRS began providing federal tax tables to help low-income taxpayers determine their tax liability. Those tables now provide specific tax liability for all income levels up to $100,000. Above that amount, a taxpayer must use the specific tax brackets and marginal tax rates as detailed in the tax schedules to calculate tax liability.

Thus far I have used the word *marginal* when describing tax rates. A progressive marginal tax rate system dictates that a higher percentage is applied on the marginal income received above each successive threshold. The number of thresholds determines the number of brackets.

The F-Word

To understand the use of marginal rates, table 4 demonstrates how marginal rates are applied. Using the 2013 brackets and marginal tax rates as shown in table 2, a return that reflects taxable income of $150,000 for a married couple filing jointly would incur a tax liability of something other than $42,000, the amount paid if 28% were applied to $150,000.

Tax Rate	Tax Bracket	Threshold	Ceiling	Marginal Tax Liability
10.0%	$0 to $17,850	$0	$17,850	$1,785
15.0%	$17,850 to $72,500	$17,850	$72,500	$8,198
25.0%	$72,500 to $146,400	$72,500	$146,400	$18,475
28.0%	$146,400 to $223,050	$146,400	$223,050	$1,008
33.0%	$223,050 to $398,350	$223,050	$398,350	$0
35.0%	$398,350 to $450,000	$398,350	$450,000	$0
39.6%	$450,000 and up	$450,000	NONE	$0
			Total Tax Liability	$29,466

Table 4 - 2013 tax liability calculation on taxable income of $150,000 - Married Filing Jointly
This calculation uses the tax rate tables and applies the marginal tax rates to marginal income.

This calculation results in a tax liability of $29,466 on taxable income of $150,000. That total may be reduced by eligible tax credits, lowering the actual tax liability even further. Under our existing marginal tax rate system, this taxpayer is described as being in the 28% bracket yet incurs an actual rate less than 20%.

A word of caution is warranted for anyone using marginal tax rates to argue for or against our tax code. Given the myriad tax exclusions, preferences, credits, and the like, marginal rates are, frankly, irrelevant. A more appropriate term, one that is more indicative of the actual tax burden, is the *effective rate*. This is determined by dividing net tax liability incurred by income. This calculation can be made using either taxable income or total income.

Comparing the tax liability just calculated to taxable income produces an effective tax rate of 19.6%. But this calculation tells us

Section II – Every Means Necessary, Fair And Unfair

the effective rate paid on taxable income, which is only slightly more relevant than the actual marginal tax rate. Most wage earners think about their take-home pay. So do most taxpayers. They want to know how much tax they paid compared to the income they made and, more importantly, how much they keep in their pockets. Answering this question requires an even more pragmatic calculation of the effective tax rate, one that uses total income.

The calculation of the effective rate paid on total income is much more enlightening when attempting to truly understand the impact of our tax code. The taxpayer in the previous example received total income of $170,000. Subtracting exemptions and the standard deduction produced taxable income of $150,000. In this example, therefore, the effective tax rate paid on total income is 17.3% as opposed to the 19.6% paid on taxable income. Simply, out of every dollar earned, this taxpayer paid just over seventeen cents in federal income tax.

If we compare two other taxpayers with the taxpayer in the previous example, once again disregarding payroll tax, we see some significant differences in the effective rate paid on total income if different types of income are included. Each of the three taxpayers is married and files jointly, with no dependents, and claims the standard deduction. Each taxpayer reports adjusted gross income of $170,000 and taxable income of $150,000, just as the taxpayer in the earlier case.

The first of these two comparisons contemplates a taxpayer who received total income of $200,000 including $30,000 of tax-exempt interest income. Reported total income was $170,000 resulting in taxable income of $150,000. His tax will be the same as calculated before, $29,466, but the effective tax rate paid on total income is 14.7%, which is 2.5% lower than the previous taxpayer. Assessing the same tax rates on higher total income resulted in a lower percentage paid on total income. Why did this occur? Despite the fact that interest, taxable or otherwise, comprises income, the tax-exempt interest is not included in either total income or taxable income.

Now, consider a taxpayer who earns total income of $170,000, half of which comes from capital gains. Even with total income and taxable income identical to that earned by the first taxpayer, instead of the tax liability shouldered by the two previous couples, this taxpayer incurs a lower tax liability of $20,486. The effective tax rate paid on taxable income is 13.6%. The effective rate paid on total income is 12%. Why? Tax liability for this taxpayer is calculated using the Qualified Dividends and Capital Gains Worksheet, using lower, fixed rates, rather than by using the marginal tax rate tables.

	Taxpayer #1	Taxpayer #2	Taxpayer #3
Wage Income	$170,000	$170,000	$85,000
Tax Exempt Interest		$30,000	
Capital Gains			$85,000
Actual Income	$170,000	$200,000	$170,000
Reported Income	$170,000	$170,000	$170,000
Standard Deduction	$12,200	$12,200	$12,200
Exemption	$7,800	$7,800	$7,800
Taxable Income	$150,000	$150,000	$150,000
Tax	$29,466	$29,466	$20,486
Marginal Tax Rate	28%	28%	28%
Effective Tax Rate	17%	15%	12%

Table 5 - Comparison of 2013 tax liability for three different taxpayers using the same total income reported on Form 1040.

Even these comparisons do not tell the entire story. If total income reported on separate returns is identical, it can derive from an economic benefit actually received that is markedly different due to tax preferences. Box 1 on Form W-2 can show the same income amount for one taxpayer as for another, but that amount may not

Section II – Every Means Necessary, Fair And Unfair

report total actual compensation. To illustrate, consider two taxpayers who each report $170,000 in total income. Apply the same circumstances as used before: married, with no dependents.

Our first husband and wife each works for a company that offers a 401(k) retirement plan. Nearing retirement age, they both elect to make the maximum contribution totaling $46,000 between them. Each employer also matches contributions up to 3% of income. The total contributions to their two retirement accounts approximate $52,480. Actual compensation earned, including employer-matching contributions, totaled $222,480 yet the two W-2s only report wage income totaling $170,000, producing taxable income equaling $150,000. Tax liability is the same as the first example, $29,466. The effective rate paid on taxable income is 19.6% while the effective rate paid on total compensation is 13.2%.

Our second couple is also nearing retirement and, just as conscientious as the earlier couple, likewise set aside $46,000 for retirement. Their employer did not have a retirement plan, so they received no additional funding for their retirement. Although they also report total income of $170,000, they reflect lower adjusted gross income of $157,000, producing a lower taxable income of $137,000. They incur a lower tax bill of $26,108. Their effective tax rate, calculated on taxable income is 19%, slightly lower than the earlier couple. Yet, the effective tax rate paid on total compensation is 15.3%.

Summarizing this last example, the first couple beneficially received $222,480 and incurred a tax bill of $29,466. The second couple earned $170,000, over $50,000 less, and although they paid a lower total tax of $26,108, as a percentage of their total income, their tax liability was 2% higher than the first couple.

Considered another way, the net effect is that the first couple paid tax of $3,358 on additional—marginal—income of $52,480. That equates to a marginal tax rate of 6.4% assessed on the marginal income. Referring back to table 2, you might expect that this couple would have incurred a marginal tax rate of 28% on their marginal income. You may now be asking why the discrepancy. But remember, I cautioned you in the Preface that I cannot answer "why." I can only answer "what."

You might think that this example can't be right. Perhaps the author erred, or maybe the second couple made a mistake on their return. It could even be that the second couple did not have the financial savvy of couple number one. But none of these conclusions are correct. In the infinite wisdom of those who drafted our tax code, the first couple could set aside $46,000 for retirement and receive additional contributions from their employer, and *were allowed to exclude both amounts* from taxable income. The second couple, setting aside the same $46,000, *can only exclude $13,000* from their income.

Once again you might ask why. My answer is that I don't know. If you ask what, I will answer that the IRC allows different tax-deferred retirement contributions based on employer type, kind of employment, and the category of retirement plan.

In practice, taxpayers also incur unexpected and unintended marginal rates as a result of other preferences within the tax code. The earned income tax credit (EITC) is one example. Eligibility for the EITC, discussed at greater length in the next section, is based on income received by working (W-2 wages, income from self-employment, or other earned income).

The amount of the EITC increases as income increases, up to a maximum credit amount, and then decreases as income continues to increase. In 2013, a taxpayer with three children, filing jointly, could receive a maximum credit of $6,044. The maximum credit

Section II – Every Means Necessary, Fair And Unfair

amount decreases when income exceeds $22,890 and ceases completely when income exceeds $51,568.

As an example, if a taxpayer with three children earned $22,875, a properly completed return would reflect a zero income tax liability. Even if no income tax had been withheld, this taxpayer would receive a tax refund from the IRS totaling $9,025, entirely due to refundable credits (EITC of $6,044 plus an additional child tax credit of $2,981). Thus, earned income plus refundable credits would produce income of $31,900. Even subtracting withheld Social Security tax, this taxpayer would realize after-tax income of $30,150.

Let's examine the marginal rate incurred by this taxpayer on additional earned income. Consider the financial impact if income more than doubles. In this scenario, the taxpayer reports wage income of $51,570. As a result of the increased income, eligibility for the EITC would be lost. That leads to a calculated marginal rate of 21.1% on marginal income of $28,695. As shown in table 2, marginal rates above 15% do not apply to married taxpayers filing jointly until income exceeds $72,500. Apparently that is not true in all cases.

What is the encouragement for this taxpayer to work longer or harder? With earned income of $51,570, our taxpayer realizes disposable income of $48,736 (wages of $51,570 less payroll taxes of $3,945 plus refundable child tax credit of $1,111). Gross income increased by $28,695 compared with the wages cited initially, yet disposable income only increased by $18,586. Considering income tax, payroll tax, and lost credits, the taxpayer surrendered $10,109 of the additional income. What is the effective marginal rate paid on the additional income? The answer is 35.2%! With income just above $50,000, this taxpayer incurs an effective marginal tax rate not ordinarily applicable until income exceeds $398,000. Now *that* is a marginal rate.

Surprisingly, the entire argument about whether or not to use marginal tax rates stems from a mistaken perception. Assume a tax system is defined as progressive only if it takes an increasing share of a taxpayer's income as that person's income rises. Using that definition, it is generally presumed that progressivity is necessarily synonymous with graduated, marginal tax rates.

Frankly, that is not exactly true. To illustrate, consider three families with total income of $50,000, $100,000, and $150,000. Further, assume that an income threshold of $25,000 is approved, below which no tax is assessed, calculated, or paid. The $25,000 is deducted from total income prior to calculating tax due. Then, accept as a given that there are no other deductions, exemptions, credits, or offsets. Finally, suppose the specified tax rate is a flat 25%.

Using these assumptions, the three families would incur an income tax liability of $6,250, $18,750, and $31,250, respectively. The first family pays an effective rate of 12.5% of its income; the second pays 18.8%; the third pays 20.8%. This result would satisfy the earlier definition of progressivity because families with higher incomes paid more tax in absolute dollars and paid a higher percentage of their income than those with lower incomes. This calculation is correct even though the tax rate is not graduated.

	Family #1	Family #2	Family #3
Total Income	$50,000	$100,000	$150,000
Income Threshold	$25,000	$25,000	$25,000
Taxable Income	$25,000	$75,000	$125,000
Flat Tax Rate	25%	25%	25%
Tax	$6,250	$18,750	$31,250
Effective Tax Rate	13%	19%	21%

Table 6 - Comparison of the tax liability for three different families to demonstrate that a flat tax rate produces a progressive tax liability.

Section II – Every Means Necessary, Fair And Unfair

Whether or not you believe those earning much higher incomes should be compelled to pay increasingly higher marginal rates, a flat tax rate can also create a progressive tax system.

One unintentional result of allowing certain deductions within a progressive marginal tax system is this often provides a greater benefit to taxpayers with higher incomes. What follows is one example of the combined effect of tax preferences and progressive marginal tax rates.

Consider a tax system that utilizes a marginal tax structure, and assume this system includes a tax preference for deductible home mortgage interest. In practice, a taxpayer whose income falls within the 15% marginal tax bracket receives a smaller incentive to buy a home than a taxpayer in the 25% bracket. The lower-income taxpayer only receives fifteen cents in tax benefits for every dollar of mortgage interest paid, unlike those in the higher bracket who receive twenty-five cents for each dollar. The pragmatic result of this methodology is that a taxpayer with a lower income receives a smaller subsidy than someone with a higher marginal rate.

As exists under the current tax code, the more a taxpayer earns, the larger the tax benefit he receives for various tax preferences. That seems to be an unintended consequence of a progressive tax system designed to make wealthier taxpayers pay their fair share.

I can offer many more examples that clearly exhibit the inequity that exists under our current marginal-rate structure. It seems self-evident that marginal rates do not make sense, that they often produce unfair results for taxpayers at either end of the income spectrum—even more so for taxpayers included among middle-income households. This is particularly true when the tax rate is affected by a multiplicity of preferences, deductions, and credits.

The F-Word

This is no time for a drink. Given the vagaries, complexity, inconsistencies, and inequities of our tax system, we are all living on the margin. In the movie *Shrek*, his friend shouts, "I'm a donkey on the edge!" It might be better said that, under the Internal Revenue Code, Americans are all living on the edge—of an abyss!

Chapter 7

When Capital Gains, Income Loses

> A light rate of capital gains is premised upon a well-functioning corporate income-tax system. The US corporate income tax system is anything but.
> David Frum, Journalist

> The tax on capital gains directly affects investment decisions,
> the mobility and flow of risk capital.
> President John F. Kennedy

> The biggest—one of the biggest—barriers to driving economic growth is the capital gains tax rate. I propose taking it to zero.
> Herman Cain, Businessman and Presidential Candidate

For classical economists, income made up the payment allocated to the various elements of production. Wages were payments for labor—the return to an individual for his physical or mental participation in the production of goods or services. Rent was payment for the use of real property such as land or buildings—the return to an owner of land. Profit was the return to the proprietor of capital stock such as machinery, tools, or structures.

Under our current tax structure, capital gains comprise the return to investors on their capital. Although it constitutes income to the investor, it is treated markedly different from all other income.

At first glance, the title to this chapter might seem to be a typographical error. You might assume I intended to end with the word "losses." But that assumption would be wrong. Under our tax code, income from capital wins while other income (such as wage income or self-employment income) loses.

This is precisely why a discussion of tax on capital gains is included in this section. It is examined here because income defined as capital gains by the IRC is currently taxed much more favorably than other earned and unearned income. Whether that treatment is appropriate may be a different question than whether it is fair.

Special—defined as lower—tax treatment of capital gains raises hackles on both sides of the aisle, yet politicians on either end of the political spectrum have made the argument that tax on capital gains should be lower than taxes on other types of income. It is argued that a tax on capital gains discourages investment. Those with a contrary view assert that taxing wages at a higher rate accelerates the upward redistribution of wealth.

The real-life impact of this different treatment led to the Buffett rule. Warren Buffett, a wealthy investor, earns millions of dollars each year. Most of his income is considered to be capital gains and is taxed at a fixed capital gains tax rate, which is lower than the marginal rate that would ordinarily be assessed on his level of income. It was greatly publicized that this resulted in a lower effective tax rate paid by Buffett than by his secretary. In fairness to him, he did

Section II – Every Means Necessary, Fair And Unfair

suggest that this outcome was not just. In truth, many politicians, Republican and Democrat, liberal and conservative, believe the impact of the tax on capital gains as currently levied is not fair.

Following Buffett's public remarks, President Obama suggested we add yet another tax calculation to an already complex, confusing tax code. His proposal, dubbed the Buffett rule, was this: "No household making more than $1 million each year should pay a smaller share of their income in taxes than a middle-class family pays." As an aside, remember that I commented earlier on a speech made by President Obama in which he stated that millionaires should pay at least as much as their secretary. Note here he says, "No household…should pay a smaller share." Better—much more precise.

However, even if the president's belief is correct and current political climate holds that existing capital gains tax treatment is unfair, change the treatment. Don't add yet another tax and develop another set of rules that will only serve to increase the complexity of the law.

During the 2012 presidential election, a political furor arose when Mitt Romney released his federal income tax return. In doing so, he revealed to every American that his effective tax rate was just below 15%. Public disclosure of his tax return created a firestorm of controversy with many decrying that, as a wealthy investor, he was not paying his fair share of taxes.

Just like Buffett, his relatively low effective tax rate was due to the fact that most of his income was treated as a capital gain. His tax liability was a by-product of the existing tax code. By releasing his return, it should be noted that Governor Romney was just a messenger for the IRS. We should not shoot the messenger for delivering a disturbing message.

The F-Word

Regardless, exactly what is the justification for awarding preferential tax treatment to those making money from money as opposed to those making money from their labor?

When a tax on income was introduced in 1913, capital gains were taxed just as all other income, initially up to a maximum rate of 7%. But, since the roaring twenties, capital gains have been treated more favorably than earned income. (Author's note: The IRC defines income from employment as earned and refers to capital gains and other investment income as unearned.) The Revenue Act of 1921 introduced a capital gains tax rate of 12.5% on the gain on assets held for two years or longer and, by comparison, established the highest marginal tax rate assessed on ordinary income at 73%.

From 1934 to 1941, income from capital gains could be partially excluded based on the length of time the asset was held. The code allowed up to 70% of gains to be excluded from reported income for assets held from one to ten years. In effect, taxes were not assessed on the entire gain based on the length of time the asset was held.

Beginning in 1942, taxpayers could exclude half of their capital gains from taxable income for assets held at least six months. Alternatively, they could elect a 25% tax rate on those gains if their ordinary tax rate exceeded 50%.

From 1954 to 1967, the maximum capital gains tax rate was 25%. Tax rates on capital gains were significantly increased in both the 1969 and 1976 tax reform acts. In 1978, Congress reversed this trend by reducing capital gains tax rates, eliminating the minimum tax on excluded gains and increasing the exclusion to 60%. Changes enacted in 1981 further reduced capital gains rates to a maximum of 20%.

Section II – Every Means Necessary, Fair And Unfair

Capital gains tax rates have undergone a number of changes since then, with increases and reductions included as part of various tax measures. Back and forth, to and fro, capital gains tax rates change on the ebb and flow of political tides.

Bear in mind, as our current code is structured, a 15% marginal tax rate applies to ordinary income above $17,850. Conversely, capital gains are taxed at a maximum rate of 15%, even when that income rises to the tens or hundreds of thousands of dollars. (Author's note: The maximum capital gains rate was increased to 20% for 2013, but that rate applies only when income exceeds $400,000—$450,000 for a married couple filing jointly.)

There is now one other caveat to the rate paid on capital gains. The Affordable Care Act added yet one more confusing tax to the mix—net investment income tax. This 3.8% tax is applied to all investment income, including capital gains, if modified AGI exceeds certain thresholds.

Returning to the basic issue, consider a married couple with no children, each of whom earns $15/hour for total annual income of $62,400. After taking the standard deduction and allowance for personal exemptions, their effective income tax rate is 8.8%, which seems reasonable. But after income and payroll taxes, they only keep seventy-six cents for each additional dollar they earn. The effective marginal rate assessed on that extra income approximates 24%.

If capital gains received by an investor equaled the wage of our working couple, that investor would pay no tax, keeping one hundred cents of each dollar received. The marginal rate paid on up to $30,000 of additional dividend income would also be zero. The investor pays 0% on his marginal income compared to our working couple, who pay a combined income and payroll marginal rate of 24%.

If that disparity makes sense to everyone, then I must consider myself in a minority of one. It makes no sense to me. I've got to stop making so many trips to the liquor cabinet.

A simple explanation of marginal tax rates is that, as income rises, the percentage used to calculate the amount of tax increases. Generally, a taxpayer totals his or her income, subtracts adjustments, subtracts deductions and exemptions, calculates tax liability, and applies tax credits for a total tax due. This statement excludes consideration of alternative minimum tax and net investment income tax.

Under the IRC, the major exception to this equation is the calculation of the tax on income defined as a long-term capital gain. A taxpayer uses Form 8949 to report sales and other capital transactions and calculate gain or loss. A lower tax rate may apply to a net capital gain than the tax rate that applies to ordinary income.

The term "net capital gain" means the amount by which net long-term capital gain exceeds net short-term capital loss for the year. The term "net long-term capital gain" is any long-term capital gains reduced by long-term capital losses including any long-term capital loss carried over from previous years. The tax rate on most net capital gain is no higher than 15% for most taxpayers. However, a 20% rate is applied to net capital gain for tax years 2013 and later if taxable income exceeds the thresholds set for the new 39.6% ordinary tax rate.

Short-term capital gains, although treated as a capital gain under our code and reported on Schedule D, are taxed as ordinary income. Tax on ordinary income is calculated using the tax tables. Income tax on long-term capital gains, reported on Schedule D,

Section II – Every Means Necessary, Fair And Unfair

is calculated using the Qualified Dividends and Capital Gains Worksheet or Schedule D Tax Worksheet, at rates that are lower and, as income rises, significantly lower than the marginal tax rates applied to the same level of ordinary income.

The gain received from the disposition of an asset held for investment for more than a year and receipt of qualified dividends are included as long-term capital gains. As with everything in our tax code, this statement has some exceptions. For the sake of simplicity, I will stick to these two types of income as examples of capital gains.

What does this mean in real life? We can see the impact by comparing two separate taxpayers, one of whom receives all income from investments, and the other who earns all income from working, either as an employee or as a self-employed sole proprietor. In both examples, the taxpayer is married and filing a joint return with no dependents and claiming the standard deduction.

Our first taxpayer, the scion of an old-money family, inherited a million shares of stock in a large publicly traded company. The company's board of directors declared a quarterly dividend of ten cents per share. For the year, he received qualified dividends of $400,000, reported on Form 1099-DIV.

When filing his return, he reports the $400,000 as qualified dividend income, which is treated as a long-term capital gain. Taxed at the capital gains rate of 15%, his total federal tax approximates $52,761 (income tax of $47,061 plus net investment income tax of $5,700). Effectively, after all deductions, exemptions, and additional taxes, our wealthy heir pays an effective tax rate of 13.2% of total income.

Compare this result with taxes paid by the taxpayer who earns only wage income. The result may shock you. Consider a senior executive who was paid a generous salary and, based on performance, earned a bonus equal to his salary. His total W-2 compensation is reported as $400,000 (salary of $200,000 and bonus of $200,000).

He reports total income of $400,000, all of which is taxed as ordinary income. Total federal tax equals $117,972 (income tax of $103,772, payroll tax of $12,850, and additional Medicare tax of $1,350). Thus, our hardworking executive pays 29.5% of his income, including payroll taxes and additional Medicare taxes. The same income as that reported by the wealthy heir results in more than twice the tax paid.

	Investor	Wage Earner
Wage Income	$0	$400,000
Capital Gains	$400,000	
Total Income	$400,000	$400,000
Standard Deduction	$12,200	$12,200
Exemption	$7,800	$7,800
Taxable Income	$380,000	$380,000
Income Tax	$47,061	$103,772
FICA Tax	$0	$12,850
NIIT*	$5,700	$0
Addt'l Medicare Tax	$0	$1,350
Total Federal Tax	$52,761	$117,972
Marginal Tax Rate	35%	35%
Effective Tax Rate	13%	29%

Table 7 - 2013 federal tax liability for two different taxpayers.
*NIIT is an acronym for Net Investment Income Tax.

Section II – Every Means Necessary, Fair And Unfair

I acknowledge that it may be easy for you to think, "So what?" Both couples are making so much money that it does not matter whether one or the other pays more or less tax. But I think it matters a great deal. However, consider this issue from a perspective much closer to home for many more taxpayers. Let's compare two families making far less income. As you will see, the difference in tax treatment becomes even more pronounced.

Let's evaluate the tax liability of a recently married couple. Both spouses work, earning a combined wage income of $92,000. The tax return for this husband and wife would reflect total ordinary income of $92,000. The total federal tax liability incurred is $16,949 (income tax of $9,911 and payroll tax of $7,038). The result is that our hardworking couple paid an effective tax rate of 18.4%.

For this comparison, our wealthy beneficiary, also recently married with no dependents, inherited significantly fewer shares. Rather than the million shares bequeathed to his older cousin, he only inherited 230,000 shares, for which he received the same ten-cent-per-share dividend each quarter. Qualified dividends reported on Form 1099-DIV totaled $92,000.

What is his tax liability? Our tax code considers that he has had an important impact on job creation. The significance of his contribution is such that he and his wife are assessed *no* tax. No income tax, no payroll tax, no tax at all. No AMT, no additional Medicare tax, no net investment income tax. None. Nada. Zip. Zilch.

	Investor	Wage Earner
Wage Income	$0	$92,000
Capital Gains	$92,000	$0
Total Income	$92,000	$92,000
Standard Deduction	$12,200	$12,200
Exemption	$7,800	$7,800
Taxable Income	$72,000	$72,000
Income Tax	$0	$9,911
FICA Tax	$0	$7,038
Total Federal Tax	$0	$16,949
Marginal Tax Rate	35%	35%
Effective Tax Rate	0%	18%

Table 8 - 2013 federal tax liability for two different taxpayers.

What about income that falls somewhere between these two extremes? Recently, politicians have fixated on $250,000 as some imaginary threshold below which a taxpayer should not be assessed higher taxes and above which he should be pilloried by the tax collector. I will compare two families using that level of income under the same conditions used before. The first taxpayer is a two-worker household, with each spouse earning $125,000. The second taxpayer, also a two-person household, receives only dividend income from an earlier stock inheritance.

Our heir and his wife are now beginning to pay real taxes. Dividend income of $250,000 causes their total tax bill to rise to $23,625. Wait, that can't be right, can it? That's less than 10%—9.5%

Section II – Every Means Necessary, Fair And Unfair

actually—of their income. Yes, the tax is correct—the underlying tax code is just wrong.

How about our two-income working household? They probably get some tax relief, do they not? Let's take a look. For wage income totaling $250,000, this couple incurs a total tax bill of $69,937 (income tax of $52,213 plus payroll tax of $17,724). That equates to a payment of 28% of their income, three times that of our wealthy heir.

	Investor	Wage Earner
Wage Income	$0	$250,000
Capital Gains	$250,000	$0
Total Income	$250,000	$250,000
Standard Deduction	$12,200	$12,200
Exemption	$7,800	$7,800
Taxable Income	$230,000	$230,000
Income Tax	$23,625	$52,213
FICA Tax	$0	$17,724
Total Federal Tax	$23,625	$69,937
Marginal Tax Rate	33%	33%
Effective Tax Rate	9%	28%

Table 9 - 2013 federal tax liability for two different taxpayers.

Keeping in mind that we are examining marginal rates, consider this. If the heir that received 230,000 shares receives additional dividends of $100,000, he pays 19.2% on that extra income. If our hardworking couple earns an additional $100,000, considering all federal taxes, they pay 28% of that additional income.

Doesn't seem right, does it? It's not. Whether our taxes are too high or too low, the tax code should, as nearly as possible, treat taxpayers in the same financial circumstances in generally the same way.

I acknowledge that these examples are provided in a vacuum. Few taxpayers, if any, exist in a financial environment that includes sources of income this sterile. Most middle-income taxpayers have multiple sources of income. Regardless, these examples illuminate the disparity in tax assessed, despite identical levels of income.

Capital gains treatment leads to another discrepancy that must be pointed out. It is often stated that small businesses are the engine of the US economy. Elected officials, economists, pollsters, and pundits speak glowingly of entrepreneurs and the contribution of small businesses to our collective financial health.

A fact seldom mentioned in this praise is the reality that many small businesses begin their existence as sole proprietors. An individual gets an idea and, willing to stake his or her economic future on that idea, starts a company, often in the basement or garage, and just as often in a rented storage unit. The hopeful, soon-to-be magnate typically begins with a basic capital investment—sweat equity. Often this initial investment is augmented with high finance, commonly known as credit card debt.

Considering the argument that preferential treatment of capital gains spurs investment and job growth, let's examine two types of investment income—dividends received from inherited company stock and income earned from starting a company. Using identical total income, let's examine the tax liability of our sole proprietor, an individual publicly lauded as someone growing the economy, compared with the liability levied on an investor who, by virtue

Section II – Every Means Necessary, Fair And Unfair

of inheriting stock and receiving dividends, is also considered as someone creating jobs.

This comparison speaks even more directly to the issue of capital gains tax treatment. It seems logical that the men and women who hold the beating heart of our economy in their hands will be treated equally with our wealthy investor.

For this analysis, keep in mind that the IRC regards sole proprietors as self-employed. Pay particular attention to the word *employed.* Remember that the IRC considers income from employment as earned income as opposed to capital gains, which is unearned income. This brings an additional tax into the equation. Our entrepreneur is subject to SECA (self-employment tax—think Social Security) and income tax.

Fearless, our entrepreneur has taken on significant debt, all of which he has personally guaranteed. He has hired three employees, paying total annual wages of $150,000. By the third year of operations, our entrepreneur has realized some success. He has even begun speaking with advisors about forming a corporation. During the year, this intrepid businessman strikes a bonanza. He incorporates January 1 of the following year and goes on to become the next dot-com king.

What about that last year as a sole proprietor? Schedule C, attached to his Form 1040, reflects net income of $250,000. His total federal tax liability is $81,223 (income tax of $48,954, self-employment tax of $20,794, and employer payroll tax of $11,475). Thus, our entrepreneur, who truly made a capital investment, who actually created jobs and made payroll, surrenders 32.5% of his income to the IRS. This compares rather unfavorably with the 9.5% tax rate borne by our wealthy heir.

	Investor	Entrepreneur
Self-employment Income	$0	$250,000
Capital Gains	$250,000	$0
Total Income	$250,000	$250,000
Adjusted Gross Income	$250,000	$239,603
Standard Deduction	$12,200	$12,200
Exemption	$7,800	$7,800
Taxable Income	$230,000	$219,603
Income Tax	$23,625	$48,954
Self-employment Tax	$0	$20,794
Employer FICA taxes*		$11,475
Total Federal Tax	$23,625	$81,223
Marginal Tax Rate	33%	33%
Effective Tax Rate	9%	32%

Table 10 - 2013 federal tax liability for two different taxpayers.

* As an employer, our entrepreneur must pay employer FICA taxes.

One interpretation of this comparison might be that our tax code treats the two fairly. The first, theoretically growing the economy by creating jobs because of dividends paid on his inheritance, pays 9.5% of his $250,000. The other, by investing his sweat, by taking a risk, by actually creating high-paying jobs, pays fully a third of his income. Another conclusion might be that this is a prank—or worse, cruel hoax.

Lest tax purists among you crash Twitter criticizing this comparison, I recognize that a number of legitimate questions can be asked regarding this stark comparison. If our entrepreneur converted his sole proprietorship to a corporation, he may receive some cash which might be treated as a capital gain. If he sells an

Section II – Every Means Necessary, Fair And Unfair

equity interest, proceeds of that sale might also be given favorable capital gains tax treatment. Some business professionals might argue that he should have started a corporation in the first place. True or not, those criticisms make my point. Our tax code is overly complex and, as a result, patently unfair.

Don't Rain On My Parade

Two common arguments are frequently offered in opposition to a tax on capital gains. First, such a tax serves as a disincentive to wealth creation and, second, it restricts investment and limits job growth.

Taxing capital gains serves as a disincentive to making more money—really? We expect a wage earner to report to work each day, even though, as demonstrated earlier, that employee only keeps seventy-six cents of each additional dollar. How can we then assume that someone who is allowed to keep substantially the lion's share of tens of hundreds of thousands of dollars of investment income would not want to make even more? If an entrepreneur keeps only sixty-seven cents of each dollar, after mortgaging his home, working up a sweat, and taking on credit card debt, why do Americans persist in starting a business?

The contention that a tax on capital gains discourages investment seems counterintuitive to me. Given the wealthy investors I have known, this claim flies in the face of reality. Nonetheless, if this argument is correct, it must affect all taxpayers, whether income is earned or unearned. If very wealthy investors stop investing because they can keep only 70% or 75% of their income, shouldn't it follow that wage earners would stop working because of the higher tax rate they must pay on additional income?

Finally, if higher tax rates truly serve as a disincentive to earning additional income, then what impact does the inordinately high marginal tax rate have on low-income taxpayers who receive the EITC? If the same argument is true, is it not also correct that the design of the EITC, intended to encourage people to work, actually serves as a disincentive to work, at least at some level of income?

Regardless, the second contention against taxing capital gains does create some angst. Those opposed to a tax on capital gains assert that doing so leads to a reduction in job growth, suggesting that capital gains equal job growth. That argument merits consideration.

Ask yourself whether you believe that assertion is accurate, at least as it exists under the IRC. Consider again the earlier example of dividends paid on an inheritance. Assume that the inherited shares were issued by an established computer company, say one based in upstate New York or perhaps by a younger, yet still well-established, software company in the great Northwest. Each pays a cash dividend to its shareholders. Those shareholders also buy and sell stock, sometimes making money and sometimes not.

When dividends are paid to shareholders, those payments decrease cash available to the company. If anything, it seems reasonable to conclude that paying dividends puts downward pressure on job growth because those payments are a drain on cash. A company needs cash to pay workers and more cash to pay more workers.

How about the purchase and sale of company stock? When shares are bought and sold (leaving aside an initial public offering or the purchase or sale of treasury stock), cash is neither provided to nor taken from the company. When an investor buys or sells stock—whether making or losing money—the company that issued the stock neither receives a benefit nor is adversely affected. Yet qualified dividends and the gain on the sale of stock comprise a substantial percentage of capital gains reported each year to the IRS.

Section II – Every Means Necessary, Fair And Unfair

It occurs to me that even if affording preferential tax treatment to capital gains is appropriate, its application under current tax law is entirely inappropriate. I suggest that making money buying and selling publicly traded stock, or receiving dividends on shares owned, has no more bearing on the growth or decline of the company that issued that stock than going to Atlantic City, placing a bet on boxcars, and rolling the dice. (Author's note: For those of you who do not gamble, *boxcars* is a word that refers to rolling a six on each of two die.)

An even more complex, unfair use of capital gains treatment is the carried interest rule. This provision is truly too intricate to adequately address here. The short version is that this rule allows money managers and hedge fund managers to report their income for tax purposes just as the underlying income is reported. Simply, if income earned by the underlying investment, the managed funds, is treated as a capital gain, the manager can treat his commission, his fee income, as a capital gain without actually having made any investment.

One fundamental premise of lower capital gains tax rates is that the benefit should be afforded to the owner of the asset, the actual investor. But key executives in the financial industry are given a significant tax benefit from this carried interest rule, which essentially affords nonowners the same benefit as owners.

The plain truth is this rule is utterly unjustifiable. If someone manages money invested by others, gain on the investment may be a capital gain under our code. If, under existing political reality, such gain is treated differently than ordinary income, fine. However, what a financial manager earns by managing that money is ordinary income—they are paid to do a job—and it should be taxed as such.

What about capital losses? In the event a taxpayer speculates in the market and hits it big one year, he is assessed either ordinary income tax rates (short-term gains) or capital gains rates (long-term capital gains). In either case, he will incur a substantial tax bill. On a capital gains bonanza of $250,000, the tax rate assessed could vary from 15% to 33%, and ignoring tax credits and preferences, the taxpayer might have to pay up to $80,000 to the IRS.

Consider if that same taxpayer elected to leverage his good fortune by speculating in the market the following year. Assume that he was not as successful the second time around and lost all of the prior gains and much of the original investment. Assuming he learned his lesson and ceased investing—all else being equal—the tax result is that he can deduct $3,000 from total income over the next twenty years. Under normal considerations it is possible, even likely, that he would never recover the tax originally paid, despite the fact that he actually lost money over the two-year period.

Remember Morton's Fork discussed in the Preface. On one tine, if you earn income from capital gains income, you must be able to afford taxes because of the money you are making. On the other tine, if your investments lose money, you must be able to pay taxes because you have so much money you can afford to lose it. Those who wrote our tax code learned well the lesson taught by the late Lord Chancellor of England.

Many taxpayers, particularly investors, are aware of the ongoing debate about the double taxation of dividends. When a corporation earns a profit, it must report that income and pay corporate income tax. While few corporations pay the maximum rate—just as with individuals, a myriad of preferences, deductions, and credits serve to reduce the marginal rate to some lower effective rate—all corporate profits are subject to income tax. When the corporation later distributes those profits to its owners in the form of dividends, those dividends, which derive from income already taxed, are taxed once again.

Section II – Every Means Necessary, Fair And Unfair

One provision of the code allows owners of small companies to elect treatment as an S corporation, which avoids this double taxation. If the owners of a corporation elect to be treated as an S corporation, the corporation does not pay federal income tax. This exclusion comes at a cost, however. The income of the corporation is passed through directly to the owners. They are obligated to show their percentage share of net income on their individual Form 1040. This income is then taxed at ordinary income tax rates.

I have not addressed many other capital gains transactions defined in the IRC that also demonstrate the needless complexity, and inherent unfairness, of capital gains treatment. These include like-kind exchanges and tax treatment of qualified small business stock. Calculating the basis of capital assets, whether they were purchased, received by inheritance or gift, or acquired in a like-kind exchange could take another entire book.

I can't get started on stock options. There exist so many different tax treatments for stock options, including how that expense is treated by a corporation, as to almost defy description. When you consider the tax implications of the receipt of such options, and how that income is reported by an individual taxpayer, the problem grows exponentially.

If the impact of the preferential tax treatment applied to capital gains under the present tax code seems fair to you, if it seems reasonable and appropriate, then I have either grabbed for the bourbon flask too frequently, or I must pour another drink. If, on the other hand, you agree that this treatment makes no sense, then you must decide to do something to bring about a fundamental change to our tax code.

Alternatively, we might both reach for that flask.

Chapter 8

Payroll (Can We Say Income?) Tax

> There has been a great deal of misinformation
> and, for that matter,
> pure demagoguery on the subject of Social
> Security.
> President Ronald Reagan

> Somebody who is making a million dollars a year
> should be paying more into
> the Social Security Trust Fund than someone who
> is making $113,000.
> Hon. Bernie Sanders, Senator

> The taxing power of the federal government, my
> dear; the taxing power
> is sufficient for everything you want and need.
> Hon. Harlan F. Stone, Associate Justice of the
> Supreme Court

Justice Stone whispered his comment to Frances Perkins, Secretary of Labor under President Roosevelt, during a luncheon, in response to her concern that Social Security might not get off the ground due to constitutional challenges. Ms. Perkins disclosed his comment in a speech to Social Security employees some thirty years after it was made. As it turns out, her concern was groundless, and Justice Stone was correct.

The broader implication of his comment, however, is disconcerting. I remind you of Chief Justice Marshall's view of the destructive potential of the absolute power conferred by an unlimited authority to tax.

The following comment was allegedly made by President Roosevelt, during a meeting with Luther Gulick, a frequent advisor to the president, in response to a question of whether payroll taxes would ever be abandoned.

> They are politics all the way through. We put those payroll contributions there so as to give the contributors a legal, moral, and political right to collect their pensions…With those taxes in there, no damn politician can ever scrap my social security program. Those taxes aren't a matter of economics, they're straight politics.

One has to give high marks to President Roosevelt for how he initially established and funded this program. The methodology he used to create Social Security has successfully created an insurmountable political obstacle to dissolution. I applaud his political acumen.

For elected officials and those running for office, Social Security has become the sacred cow of a federal social safety net. Not only is it seemingly untouchable, conventional political wisdom suggests we cannot even have a serious debate on the subject. To the extent that anyone attempts to do so, the response is typically

Section II – Every Means Necessary, Fair And Unfair

that described in President Reagan's quote at the start of this chapter—demagoguery.

The first payroll tax was assessed in 1937 under the Social Security Act passed in 1935. As noted earlier, this act covered more than just retirement benefits. The original title to the act was Economic Security Act. Different accounts exist regarding the actual change of the name to the Social Security Act.

In the original 1935 law, benefits were enumerated under Title II, which is why Social Security is sometimes called the Title II program. Taxing provisions were listed under Title VIII. The reason for this separate treatment was due to constitutional questions regarding the taxing provisions of the law. However, the Title VIII taxing provisions were taken out of the Social Security Act and codified within the Internal Revenue Code as part of the 1939 amendments. This new section of the Internal Revenue Code was named the Federal Insurance Contributions Act (FICA).

Thus FICA is nothing other than the payroll tax provisions of the Social Security Act as they appear in the Internal Revenue Code. The payroll taxes collected for Social Security are, of course, taxes, but they are usually described as contributions to the social insurance system. However, the amount that one pays in payroll taxes throughout one's working career is only indirectly associated with the benefits that one receives.

It is fair to ask why a discussion of payroll taxes is included in a book primarily about income tax. I included payroll taxes based on the following logic.

Payroll taxes are assessed on income—specifically earned income—whether from wages or net income from self-employment. The levy and collection of payroll taxes, just as for income taxes, is prescribed by the Internal Revenue Code. Payroll tax, just as income tax, is withheld at the point wages are paid. My decision to address payroll taxes was also influenced by the fact that many Americans pay more in payroll taxes than they do in income tax.

Finally, and perhaps most importantly, it is impossible to evaluate the fairness of income taxes without considering payroll taxes, which are assessed against the first dollar earned, making them the most regressive tax levied on income. Deductions, exemptions, tax preferences, and tax credits can serve to lower or eliminate income taxes under the IRC. Conversely, if a taxpayer only receives income from earnings, and those earnings are less than the Social Security wage base, all of that income will be subject to income tax. My bad, I meant payroll tax.

In the Introduction, I compared the Internal Revenue Code, the monstrosity Congress has created, to Frankenstein. In that vein, when Congress embedded Social Security taxes in the IRC, their action might be analogous to Frankenstein meets the Wolf Man. Remember, the Wolf Man becomes something other than what he appeared to be. But in actuality, his transformation reveals his true nature. So it is with payroll taxes—just income taxes with some facial hair and fangs, preying on the unwary.

Whether we call these wage deductions payroll taxes, retirement contributions, or something else, it seems clear that they are actually income taxes in disguise. Social Security contributions, whether paid by the employee or employer, are income taxes—pure and simple. And the government can use that tax revenue in any manner it chooses. Denial of that reality is naïve.

Section II – Every Means Necessary, Fair And Unfair

In Fed We Trust

The word *trust* is frequently associated with Social Security. When payroll taxes are paid to the IRS, they are placed in the Social Security Trust Fund, created in 1939 under an amendment to the Social Security Act. Regardless of where the funds are deposited, withheld employee Social Security tax—actually any withheld tax—is regarded differently than employer contributions and differently than corporate income tax. Failure to pay withheld taxes to the IRS is also treated differently than taxes that are not withheld from an employee's wages.

When Social Security is withheld from an employee by an employer, the term generally applied to the tax withheld is "trust fund" tax. The logic is that this amount never becomes a resource owned or controlled by the employer. The tax is included in the amount paid to an employee and held back "in trust" to be paid to the government. It is as if the employee says to his employer, "Please take this money and pay it to the IRS for me."

The obligation to pay this amount over to the government existed from the date the wages accrued. Thus, if an employer fails to pay them over, not even bankruptcy guarantees protection against the ultimate responsibility to pay the tax to the IRS. Referring to these as trust fund taxes makes sense.

What happens once those funds are paid over to the IRS? Earlier, I said they were placed in the Social Security Trust Fund, creating the belief held by many Americans that withheld and employer-contributed Social Security taxes are deposited into some fund to be held in trust for their benefit. But they are not. Using the word *trust* to describe these taxes once they are paid to the IRS is a true misnomer.

Nonetheless, trust fund nomenclature notwithstanding and Roosevelt's political acumen aside, withheld Social Security taxes do not belong to the wage earner. Workers have no right, legal, contractual, or otherwise, to any benefit as a result of their actual Social Security contributions.

The Supreme Court has held that workers are not unconditionally entitled to benefits, even benefits based on payments they made. So much for the idea of a trust fund into which workers pay taxes. So much for President Roosevelt's assurance that these payments provide workers with a guaranteed legal, moral, and ethical right to benefits.

I don't have a problem with the court's determination, at least conceptually. I do, however, have a serious problem with the imposition of a regressive tax for which the determination of future benefits has no basis in any actuarial calculation, and from which the benefits are largely perceptual for many wage earners.

Sauce For The Goose

In the prior chapter, I demonstrated the tax inequity due to the different treatment afforded capital gains. Inequity under our federal tax system also results from the fact that FICA and SECA (self-employment) taxes are only assessed against earned income. Capital gains, passive income, and other types of income are not subject to payroll tax. This fact magnifies the regressive impact of these taxes.

However, implementation of the Affordable Care Act now subjects some passive income, limited to very-high-income earners, to the net investment income tax (NIIT). This tax, assessed at 3.8%, is equal to the combined employee and employer Medicare rate plus the new additional Medicare tax.

Section II – Every Means Necessary, Fair And Unfair

Assume a family includes two working spouses with no dependents. If they both earn $45,000, they would report total income of $90,000 and incur a federal tax burden of $16,496 (income tax of $9,611 and payroll tax of $6,885). This equates to an effective federal tax rate of 18.3%.

If a second couple likewise reported $90,000 in total income, this taxpayer would also realize an income tax liability of $9,611. But if all income came from rental activity, or from distributions from an S corporation, or any of a number of other income sources other than earned income, this taxpayer would not incur a payroll tax liability. Thus, the effective federal tax rate paid by this second taxpayer is 10.7%.

Despite the apparent inequity, you may conclude that the first couple would be eligible to draw Social Security on retirement while the second would not. Although the subject of Social (in) Security is addressed in a later chapter, allow me to briefly address this seemingly mitigating fact here.

First, as structured, Social Security tax imposes double, perhaps even triple, tax on low-income wage earners. Social Security is assessed on the full amount of wages below the wage base, withheld through payroll deduction. For an employee earning $100,000, payroll tax totaling $7,650 is withheld from those wages. He only receives $92,350 *but must report* $100,000 as income and then pay income tax on that full amount.

Bottom line, the employee pays payroll tax and income tax on the full wage of $100,000. If that is not double taxation, the tool in the shed is much duller than I originally thought. Finally, if and when benefits were actually paid to this taxpayer, those benefits may also be subject to income tax.

The F-Word

As described in the chapter on capital gains tax, Congress has tried, perhaps appropriately and fairly, to develop policies to avoid taxing the same income twice. Yet the combined effect of payroll taxes and income tax does exactly that. When assessing payroll taxes, Congress has adopted a different demeanor and says, "Let's play double jeopardy!"

In this last comparison, our wage earning couple is compelled to set aside $6,885 in Social Security contributions for retirement. If no other relevant facts exist and the current tax code remains in effect, this couple would be entitled to receive Social Security benefits at retirement while the second couple would not. This statement is generally true but has exceptions.

However, for this assertion to be true and to be financially relevant, we must also suppose that couple number one lives long enough to be paid benefits at least equal to the net future value of their contributions. Otherwise, their contributions were just another income tax. Nothing more! Nothing less!

Consider, however, just what the second couple is able to do with an extra $6,885 each year. At a minimum, that money could be deposited into a qualified retirement account, which would further reduce their income tax liability.

Section II – Every Means Necessary, Fair And Unfair

[1] Scenario One	First Couple	Second Couple
Wage Income	$90,000	$0
Passive Income	$0	$90,000
Total Income	$90,000	$90,000
Standard Deduction	$12,200	$12,200
Exemption	$7,800	$7,800
Taxable Income	$70,000	$70,000
Income Tax	$9,611	$9,611
Social Security Tax	$6,885	$0
Total Federal Tax	$16,496	$9,611
Marginal Tax Rate	25%	25%
Effective Tax Rate	18%	11%
[2] Scenario Two		
IRA Contribution	$0	$6,885
Adjusted Gross Income	$90,000	$83,115
Disposable Income after Retirement Contribution [3]	$83,115	$83,115
Taxable Income	$70,000	$63,115
Income Tax	$9,611	$8,576
Social Security Tax	$6,885	$0
Total Federal Tax	$16,496	$8,576
Marginal Tax Rate	25%	25%
Effective Tax Rate	18%	10%

Table 11 - Impact of Social Security on 2013 federal tax liability for two different taxpayers.

[1] In the first scenario, our first couple pays a higher total tax because of social security.

[2] In the second scenario, the second couple contributes an amount equal to the Social Security tax paid by the first couple into an IRA.

[3] The first couple only contributes to Social Security. The second couple contributes a like amount to a qualified retirement plan.

Assuming they are not covered by an employer-sponsored retirement plan, our wage earning couple could also contribute to an IRA, but are limited to $5,500 each. Taxpayers with passive income

The F-Word

have myriad ways to structure ownership of property, or other entities allowing them to set aside up to three times the amount allowable for our hardworking couple.

The fact that Social Security tax, which is an income tax despite the nomenclature, is only assessed against earned income, capped by a wage base, makes this tax unfair *and* regressive.

Payroll taxes are not trivial. Under the original act passed in 1935, the maximum total payroll tax burden for an employee was only $30. Allowing for inflation, that same burden would approximate $521 in today's dollars. Yet the maximum payroll tax burden today approximates $8,698. That equates to a fifteen-fold increase in the payroll tax burden.

At the risk of starting a firestorm of demagoguery, it is time to have a real discussion on the issue of Social Security taxes. Leave aside the fact that America has accepted a societal commitment to assist working Americans with retirement income. We can honor that commitment whether we employ a separate, unfair tax structure or implement a tax code that makes sense. Let's stay focused on the question of whether payroll taxes make our tax structure more or less fair, whether or not they make any sense at all.

You have probably heard the duck analogy—if it looks like a duck, quacks like a duck, and walks like a duck, it's probably a duck. What about payroll taxes vis-à-vis income tax?

In order to have a meaningful debate on income tax reform, Congress, as we used to say in the army, must get all of its ducks in a row. If our elected leaders fail to include payroll tax in the conversation, they will be a few ducks shy of a brace. (Author's note:

Section II – Every Means Necessary, Fair And Unfair

What do you call a group of ducks? Answer—it depends. It can be called a flock when in flight, a paddling or team when on the water, or, in general, a brace.)

Where the hell is my bourbon decanter?

Chapter 9

What Choice Do I Have?

> [A]..."tax reform" consisting in closing revenue "leaks" and reversing the "erosion" of the tax base concomitant to the many preferences that had crept into the tax code...
> Professor Sheldon Pollack, Esq.

> The establishment of some sort of minimum tax on persons with large incomes...
> Hon. Wilbur D. Mills, Congressman

> Special preferences in the law permit far too many Americans to pay less than their fair share of taxes.
> President Richard Nixon

Merriam-Webster lists one definition of *alternative* as "offering or expressing a choice." The application of that definition to the word *alternative* when used as an adjective for *minimum* might imply that a taxpayer is offered a choice from among two tax liabilities and could choose the least of those. If you used that interpretation, you would be wrong. Really wrong!

The F-Word

Given Congress's propensity for misnomers, perhaps I can suggest a better name to give to this tax provision. Maybe it could be more appropriately titled "possible mandatory minimum tax rate—two actually—except if."

Just as with much of the language contained in the Internal Revenue Code, the description of the alternative minimum tax (AMT) can be confusing. Look again at the quotes listed at the beginning of this chapter. President Nixon clearly stated the underlying problem that led to the development of a minimum tax. And despite the fact that Congressman Mills graduated from Harvard law school, he also expressed in simple terms what he wanted to do. Professor Pollack, on the other hand, used the overly complex legalese that typically finds its way into the tax code to describe the AMT.

The FY2003 report submitted by the National Taxpayer Advocate stated

> The problem that I believe requires the most immediate and thorough response is the growing reach of the individual Alternative Minimum Tax. This problem is looming over all of us—taxpayers, Congress, the IRS. In the years to come…increasing numbers of taxpayers will discover they, too, "won" the AMT lottery. For that is how the AMT appears to function—randomly, no longer with any logical basis in sound tax administration or any connection with its original purpose.

So just what is this complex, controversial tax provision called the AMT? The predecessor of this tax first appeared in the Tax Reform Act of 1969. Initially designed as a parallel tax system aimed at negating tax loopholes available to high-income taxpayers, the

Section II – Every Means Necessary, Fair And Unfair

AMT is becoming familiar to an increasing number of Americans, even those firmly ensconced in the middle class.

The AMT was specifically created to ensure that wealthy people were unable to use loopholes in the tax code to evade paying taxes. However, it is commonly understood that most of the loopholes that enabled taxpayers to completely escape paying income tax have long since been closed. A rational tax system would render the rest of this chapter unnecessary as an obsolete and unneeded tax provision would have been appropriately repealed long ago. Not so with our Congress; not so under our tax code.

However, due partly to the absence of loopholes and partly because, until just recently, AMT rates were not adjusted for inflation, the AMT now targets the middle class almost as much as it does the very wealthy. Several years ago, the *New York Times* reported that "by 2010, nearly 30 million taxpayers will be hit—among them, a staggering 94% of married filers who have children and make $75,000 to $100,000."

The AMT includes a separate set of rules to determine income, separately defined deductions, and separate tax rates. Although these rules closely resemble the rules of the regular tax system, the AMT has a broader definition of income and a less generous set of deductions. The fact that few Americans understand this tax is, in itself, understandable. Here is how the IRS defines the AMT.

> Section 55 of the Internal Revenue Code provides that the alternative minimum tax is a tax equal to the excess (if any) of the tentative minimum tax for the taxable year over the regular tax (defined in § 55(c)) for the taxable year.

Tentative minimum tax is defined in § 55(b)(1)(A) for noncorporate taxpayers as the sum of 26 percent of so much of the taxable excess as does not exceed $175,000, plus 28 percent of so much of the taxable excess as exceeds $175,000.

The term "taxable excess" is defined in § 55(b)(1)(ii) as so much of the alternative minimum taxable income for the taxable year as exceeds the exemption amount provided for in § 55(d).

Alternative minimum taxable income is defined in § 55(b)(2) as the taxable income of the taxpayer for the taxable year determined with the adjustments provided in §§ 56 and 58, and increased by the amount of the items of tax preference described in § 57.

Section 56(b) contains the adjustments applicable to individuals.

That's enough of that nonsense. I can just imagine ice cubes clinking in highball glasses all across America. Regardless of good intentions leading to its creation, the AMT no longer serves its original purpose. According to the Office of the Taxpayer Advocate, "The AMT is left to punish taxpayers for engaging in such 'classic tax-avoidance behavior' as having children or living in a high-tax state." This statement alone should be sufficient to lead to its repeal.

Due to the ambiguity in calculating AMT and the unintended consequences (for example, penalties for underpayment of taxes) of its implementation and enforcement, any reasonable evaluation of this tax provision demands its elimination. The National Taxpayer

Section II – Every Means Necessary, Fair And Unfair

Advocate first recommended repeal of the AMT in the Annual Report to Congress for 2001 and has consistently advocated for its repeal ever since.

The demand to rescind the AMT is virtually unanimous. At one time or another, the American Bar Association Section of Taxation, the American Institute of Certified Public Accountants Tax Division, and the Tax Executives Institute have called for the repeal of the AMT. The National Association of Enrolled Agents also advocated repeal or substantial reform of the individual AMT. Both the 2005 Tax Reform Panel and the 2010 National Commission on Fiscal Responsibility and Reform (the Simpson-Bowles Commission) also recommended its repeal. Senate and House leaders of both parties consistently propose repealing the AMT.

When the alternative minimum tax was created in 1969, the first ever minimum tax rate was set at 10%, affecting those with incomes in excess of $200,000 (approximately $1,450,000 in 2013 inflation-adjusted dollars). Since that time, several tax reform measures have increased the minimum tax rate.

Currently, the AMT includes two separate rates for individuals—26% and 28%. Doesn't the existence of two rates conflict with the idea of a minimum tax? Does this mean we have two minimums? Perhaps that is the justification for the use of the word *alternative*. Not!

Regardless, the logic behind the initial rate of 10% is difficult to grasp. The lowest marginal tax rate in 1969 was 14%. It seems to me that if Congress intended to establish a minimum tax rate for wealthy taxpayers, that rate should be at least as high as the lowest rate ordinary taxpayers are assessed. But maybe my criticism of the 1969 law, based on hindsight, is not very fair. After all, Warren Buffett had not yet made his now-famous comment about paying as high a rate when comparing his tax rate to that paid by his secretary.

As stated earlier, the AMT today does not achieve its original goal of ensuring that all wealthy people pay income tax. According to IRS data for 2009, nearly 21,000 taxpayers with adjusted gross income of more than $200,000 paid no income tax at all. Considering total income rather than AGI, that number increases to nearly 35,000 taxpayers.

Perhaps more remarkably, the AMT potentially affects a higher percentage of middle-income and upper-middle-income taxpayers than wealthy taxpayers. For tax year 2013, not considering "patches" or tax law changes, the AMT was originally projected to affect an estimated 33% of taxpayers with incomes between $75,000 and $100,000 and 44% of taxpayers with incomes between $100,000 and $200,000—yet only 14% of taxpayers with incomes above $1 million. Doesn't that seem backward given the intent of this provision?

Just as with most significant tax changes, the AMT originated during a time of war. The Vietnam War peaked between 1968 and 1969, requiring that the federal government raise significant additional revenue to finance the war. Immediately prior to that time, the *Washington Post* reported that 155 individuals with incomes over $200,000, twenty of whom were millionaires, did not pay any federal income tax for 1966. These individuals legally used all available tax loopholes to successfully avoid paying any federal income tax. The report attracted widespread attention and led to public shock and political anger.

In April 1969, the Nixon administration presented a proposal for tax reform to Congress. The proposal was accompanied by this message (excerpted):

Section II – Every Means Necessary, Fair And Unfair

> We must reform our tax structure to make it more equitable and efficient...Much concern has been expressed because some citizens with incomes of more than $200,000 pay no federal income taxes. These people are neither tax dodgers nor tax cheats...But where we can prevent it by law, we must not permit our wealthiest citizens to be 100 percent successful at tax avoidance.

After considering Nixon's proposals and hearing testimony regarding wealthy taxpayers who did not pay any federal income tax due to tax preferences or loopholes, the House Ways and Means Committee, chaired by Democrat Wilbur Mills, considered legislation that would establish a minimum tax to rein in those "who escape all taxation at present because their income is entirely from sources that receive preferred tax treatment."

As a result, Congress enacted a minimum tax which was the forerunner of today's alternative minimum tax.

The AMT that Americans now struggle with was established by the Revenue Act of 1978, enacted as part of the tax reform effort undertaken that year. In that law, Congress included tax cuts totaling almost $19 billion, in particular cuts in capital gains taxes and corporate taxes, many of which only benefited upper-income groups. To offset these cuts, the final legislation included a provision that formally transformed the minimum tax devised in 1969 into the alternative minimum tax and increased the minimum tax percentage.

In 1986, Congress approved a major reform of the tax code as proposed by President Reagan. Once again, the alternative minimum tax was included in the final tax package. In addition, Congress approved an expanded Corporate Alternative Minimum Tax.

Despite continued congressional intent to ensure wealthy taxpayers paid their fair share, the *Philadelphia Inquirer* reported that the AMT of 1986 actually reduced taxes on the wealthy:

> When Congress enacted the Tax Reform Act of 1986, lawmakers hailed its alternative minimum tax provision as the most stringent ever, guaranteeing that nobody would ever escape paying at least some tax...[But] passage of "the toughest minimum tax ever" resulted in a 75 per cent drop in the number of people who paid the tax, and a 90 per cent drop in the amount they paid. On average, a millionaire in 1986 paid an alternative minimum tax of $116,395. Three years later, a millionaire paid $54,758. That amounted to a 53 per cent tax cut.

The AMT rate was again raised in 1991, this time increasing from 21% to 23%. The final major tax legislation of the twentieth century, approved in 1993, included another increase in the AMT rate. The rate was increased to 26% for those who earned between $100,000 and $175,000, and 28% for those who earned above $175,000. Those rates remain in effect today.

Even though the AMT was designed to ensure wealthy people paid at least some minimum amount of tax, because it was not indexed for inflation, limited to high-income thresholds, or focused on tax loopholes, it has increasingly impacted taxpayers other than those in the highest income brackets.

The AMT hits middle-income taxpayers for getting married, having children, and paying state and local taxes while allowing some who earn much more to pay a lower effective rate. This is largely because the AMT eliminates the tax benefit of children (dependency exemptions are lost under the AMT) and marriage (the

Section II – Every Means Necessary, Fair And Unfair

AMT contains marriage penalties) and disallows the deduction for state and local taxes.

While it is hard to imagine that the drafters of the original AMT provision would view incurring expenses to raise a family and living in a high-tax state as tax-avoidance loopholes, that is exactly how those expenses are treated under today's AMT.

The AMT replaces the personal exemption and standard deduction with an AMT exemption. For taxpayers who itemize, AMT rules exclude some itemized deductions, including the deduction for state and local taxes. After deducting the AMT exemption or itemized deductions allowable under AMT rules, the appropriate AMT tax rate is applied to the resulting taxable income to produce an AMT amount.

The AMT is complicated and burdensome, even for those who are not subject to it. Many taxpayers must fill out a lengthy form only to find they do not owe any AMT after all. Keep in mind that AMT effectively requires taxpayers to compute their tax liability twice—once under the regular tax rules and again under the AMT rules. If the tentative minimum tax liability exceeds the regular tax liability, the difference is reported separately on Form 1040 as AMT tax. The two amounts are then added to produce total tax liability. Normally, once a taxpayer has calculated total tax liability, available tax credits are subtracted. As a final insult, AMT may also limit the use of certain credits.

Frequent AMT patches combined with the inherent complexity of the AMT make it nearly impossible for taxpayers to estimate their tax liabilities in advance. The AMT is so complicated that the IRS's wage withholding calculator does not even include AMT in determining how much taxpayers should have withheld.

The F-Word

Many taxpayers first learn they are subject to the AMT only after preparing their returns. It is then too late to increase their withholding or make estimated tax payments. Taxpayers who did not withhold or pay sufficient estimated tax are then subject to penalties. While the number of taxpayers subject to estimated tax penalties because of the AMT is unknown, IRS data show that, for tax year 2011, about 17% of those subject to the AMT were liable for estimated tax penalties, as compared to 4% of individual taxpayers overall.

Just to make this even more confusing, AMT allows for a look back. A taxpayer who paid AMT in a prior year, and who does not owe AMT for the current year, may be eligible to receive a credit for some or all of the AMT paid previously. In order to claim credit for AMT paid in prior years, a separate form must be completed.

AMT is a two-edged sword within our tax policy. The AMT is almost always projected to raise a large amount of revenue, estimated to generate between $1.2 trillion to $2.3 trillion in revenue from 2011 to 2022. Despite these glowing estimates, reality has consistently demonstrated that AMT revenue falls drastically short of projections. In 2010 and 2011, AMT will have raised less than $40 billion per year, equaling the most it has ever raised.

Why is that? Because Congress repeatedly enacts short-term patches to protect middle-class taxpayers and maintain popular tax benefits that increase the AMT exemption amount. Congress has passed ten such patches since 2001, thereby preventing the AMT from raising expected revenue. Further, as if the AMT were not already complicated enough, Congress typically enacts these AMT patches at the last minute or makes them retroactive or, worse, does both.

Section II – Every Means Necessary, Fair And Unfair

In essence, we end up with a basic tax code (IRC) that grants generally accepted, popular tax benefits, but that also includes a provision (AMT) that eliminates many of those same benefits. This hodgepodge is modified by a series of laws or temporary amendments (AMT patches) that reverse the impact of the elimination of those benefits—a legislative Rube Goldberg contraption involving needless confusion and difficulty.

One glaring problem of the AMT that is often overlooked is the inherent inconsistency with another major provision of our tax code: treatment of capital gains. It is generally understood that the wealthiest among us derive significant income from investments, much of which is treated as capital gains and subject to a much lower fixed rate than that set by the AMT. Currently, the top rate for long-term capital gains is set at 15% (set at 20% for AMT), compared with the 26% and 28% AMT rates. Again, so much for a minimum tax rate!

It is this contradiction that led to the furor over Mitt Romney's tax return and the Buffett rule because of the relatively low effective tax rates these two paid. Because both men derived much of their income from capital gains, that income was largely shielded from the AMT. Until the discrepancy between tax treatment for ordinary income and capital gains is truly and fairly addressed, discussions around minimum effective tax rates for the wealthy are largely irrelevant.

Let's look at a real-life example, comparing two taxpayers with total reportable income of $275,000, one of whom reports significant wage income and the second who receives primarily investment income. This income difference produces nearly a 100% variance in tax liability.

Income Source	Mixed Source Income	Investment Income
Wage Income	$206,125	$0
Interest	$17,485	$40,173
Tax Exempt Interest	$0	$17,488
Capital Gains	$13,255	$127,675
Passive Income	$38,135	$107,152
Total Income [1]	$275,000	$292,488
Itemized Deductions	$34,250	$34,250
Exemption	$7,800	$7,800
Taxable Income	$232,950	$232,950
Income Tax	$50,968	$37,327
FICA Tax	$15,769	$0
NIIT*	$950	$950
Alternative Minimum Tax	$3,951	$1,309
Total Federal Tax	$71,638	$39,586
Marginal Tax Rate	33%	33%
Effective Tax Rate	26%	14%

Table 12 - 2013 federal tax liability for two different taxpayers with the same taxable income but from different sources.

*NIIT is an acronym for Net Investment Income Tax.

[1] For display only. Total Income reported on Line 22, Form 1040 does not include Tax Exempt Interest.

I have already pointed out the inconsistencies of the tax code due to capital gains treatment. That difference accounts for most of the discrepancy in the income tax paid. But why is there a difference in the AMT? The taxpayer with lower actual income pays almost $4,000 in additional taxes, ensuring he pays a "minimum' amount.

Section II – Every Means Necessary, Fair And Unfair

This example is deliberate. Itemized deductions for the taxpayer with wage income include state income tax while the other does not. Despite the fact that this taxpayer earned less income and paid almost $10,000 more in state taxes, he must also pay the AMT. The taxpayer who earned a larger percentage of his income from employment is not only subject to a higher income tax rate, but then must pay AMT. Who writes this stuff?

To put the entire federal tax picture into perspective, when you add payroll taxes to the income tax and AMT, our unlucky wage earner pays total federal taxes approximating 26% of income earned. That contrasts rather unfavorably with the total federal tax rate of 14% paid by our investor.

Now here comes a curve ball. If you consider *only* the AMT, not within the IRC, but as a stand-alone policy, it actually makes more sense than the rest of the tax code. You may ask, "Why do I say that?"

The answer is simple and straightforward. The AMT eliminates most tax preferences and deductions. It keeps rates low and tax policy simple. It expands the tax base and offers nearly flat tax rates. It does offer an alternative—replace the entire individual income tax system with the AMT and name it the minimum tax plan.

Despite the curve ball, among a number of other major changes to our tax code, Congress should eliminate the AMT. Failure is yet another swing and miss. And those changes should not include various opt-in or opt-out provisions, or other alternative tax methods. Remember Adam Smith's warning: the tax must be certain. Certainty in the tax code presupposes that an alternative tax is not included among its provisions.

During the drafting of this book, the American Taxpayer Relief Act (ATRA) solved one of the triggers requiring frequent patches.

The F-Word

This law finally indexed the AMT exemption amount to inflation. It did not index income, however. As a result, as incomes rise due to inflation, more taxpayers will find themselves subject to AMT.

Do you prefer bourbon? Or would you rather have scotch? As an experienced host, I keep a fully stocked bar, offering several alternatives.

Section III

Social Engineers or Social Dilettantes?

Overview

> Whatever affects one directly, affects all indirectly.
> Martin Luther King Jr., Statesman and
> Civil Rights Leader

> There's a lot of evidence you can sell people on tax increases
> if they think it's an investment.
> President Bill Clinton

> The taxing power of government...must not be used
> to regulate the economy or bring about social change.
> President Ronald Reagan

While politicians argue about the level of taxes, taxpayers debate who should pay and who actually does pay. Meanwhile, pundits discuss the social impact of our tax code. Collectively, we weigh the advisability of and effects from income redistribution while we disagree whether our code creates an upward or downward redistribution of income.

I started this section with a quote from Martin Luther King Jr., as I thought it was appropriate for this topic. Regardless of one's point of view, Americans typically discuss tax reform in a vacuum. Ignoring which view is correct, many believe the boon or burden of different tax preferences only accrues to a particular group of taxpayers. But to paraphrase Dr. King, if the effect of anything done or caused to be done under the Internal Revenue Code impacts any of us, it impacts all of us.

The power and influence of the IRC over our nation, on our individual freedom, and on our economic future concerns me—deeply. Innumerable comments have been made about the foundation of our country and the seeds of its genesis. Admiration has been expressed about the Great American Experiment.

For this American, that genesis sprang from the germination of the seeds of two basic freedoms: religious freedom and political freedom. One only has to look closely at the world we now live in to gain a deeper appreciation of the importance these two freedoms have held for America and Americans. Nonetheless, absent economic freedom, their significance is drastically diminished.

I do not want to make this book a discourse on political philosophy, but, given that the subject of this section is the social engineering that now forms the core of our tax code, I felt the concept of freedom merited some commentary.

In the movie *The Last of the Mohicans*, a conversation, argument really, occurs between Cora Munro, the heroine of the story, and Major Heyward, a senior British officer.

Section III – Social Engineers Or Social Dilettantes?

> Maj. Heyward—"And who empowered these colonials to pass judgment on England's policies, and to come and go without so much as a 'by your leave'?"
>
> Cora Munro—"They do not live their lives 'by your leave'! They hack it out of the wilderness with their own two hands, bearing their children along the way!"

In my view, that determination and that indomitable spirit gave colonial Americans the confidence and mettle to embark on this experiment. They came from many places and many different cultures. Most came because they could not exercise their beliefs or pursue their dreams of a better life for their families. Relying only on the strength of those beliefs and the courage of their convictions, they came in pursuit of their dreams. I can scarcely imagine the daring required to embark across the Atlantic Ocean to points unknown and uncharted, and to do so on what would now be viewed as a very small wooden boat.

Yet they came, from countries all across Europe and other continents, prepared to accept the consequences of the success or failure of their efforts. Often, they left behind a country governed by those from whom they were compelled to gain "by your leave" dispensation in order to proceed on their own path. Whether through direct edict or indirectly through taxes or social structure, those headed for the New World were often told what they could or could not do; they were told where they could or could not live; and they were told where and how they could or could not worship.

How the passage of time has changed our attitudes! A significant number of present-day Americans, many of whom are descended from those early pioneers, now think decisions about what society needs should be left to the federal government. They believe most problems should be, and in many instances can only be, solved by that same government.

In the minds of many in this camp, whatever the task, almost any job is too big or too important for any individual or any market entity. The responsibility cannot be entrusted to a private individual with all his human frailties. Whether true or false, ceding that responsibility necessarily permits a "by your leave" prerequisite to begin an insidious intrusion into many personal choices.

The implication of that last paragraph is worrisome. If we are rightly and fairly concerned about the potential harm an individual can wreak, what constraints on potential harm exist for a government with unlimited power? Are we so naïve that we believe those in government are bereft of human weaknesses? Or are we bereft of our senses?

Have we forgotten the lessons of our own disassociation from Great Britain? Are we now so far removed from that spirit of freedom, of individual choice and undaunted spirit, that we are willing to cede our economic freedom to the government? And with that, are we then willing to relinquish our social freedom?

In "Common Sense," Thomas Paine wrote

> Some writers have so confounded society with government, as to leave little or no distinction between them; whereas they are not only different, but have different origins. Society is produced by our wants, and government by our wickedness; the former promotes our happiness POSITIVELY by uniting our affections, the latter NEGATIVELY

Section III – Social Engineers Or Social Dilettantes?

> by restraining our vices. The one encourages intercourse, the other creates distinctions. The first a patron, the last a punisher.
>
> Society in every state is a blessing, but government even in its best state is but a necessary evil; in its worst state an intolerable one; for when we suffer, or are exposed to the same miseries BY A GOVERNMENT, which we might expect in a country WITHOUT GOVERNMENT, our calamity is heightened by reflecting that we furnish the means by which we suffer.

His last sentence suggests that if we believe we are mistreated and that mistreatment comes from a government to which we have relegated our freedom, the injury is that much more painful.

Just as Paine forewarned, our government, through implementation and manipulation of a complex, intrusive tax code, has woven a dependent social structure in which many individual decisions are controlled by that same government. Congress pulls an enormity of economic resources from the private sector and redistributes them as they deem most appropriate. Do we now believe government officials are better able than individual Americans to judge how money should be spent and what investments make economic sense?

Almost everyone, wealthy or poor, benefits from one or more provisions of our tax code—in one way or another—at one time or another. Despite the largesse offered under our tax code, those who benefit, even if only temporarily, should pause to assess the cost to society as a whole. If we are all waiting in line for our turn at the goose's neck, what then? If together we kill the goose that lays golden eggs, will we be better off or worse?

If you disagree with the notion that our tax code is now used largely to influence behavior, answer this: Why does it matter how many children a family has under the code? You may rightly answer because it costs money to raise children, and a family should get some tax relief for that cost. Fair enough, perhaps. But why then is it that the number of children is limited for various credits?

Why should it matter whether a taxpayer owns a home or rents? Even if we agree that home ownership is a desirable national goal, why should the government penalize those who cannot afford or choose not to buy a home? Even more to the point, how is it that owning a second or third home, owning an RV or a houseboat, is in any way a socially beneficial outcome? Why is the ownership of a vacation ski lodge in Aspen rewarded with a tax preference?

The Affordable Care Act includes a tanning booth tax of 10%. When hearing this, comedian Jay Leno suggested, "You know what this means? This whole thing could be funded by the cast of *Jersey Shore*." Comedy aside, it is true that the IRC now includes a federal excise tax on the use of tanning booths. Why is that? The answer is simple: social engineering.

Under social engineering, activities that the government believes should be discouraged are taxed. Conversely, activities that Congress wants to encourage are favored with tax credits. By including the language, "promote the general welfare," in the preamble to the Constitution, our founding fathers expressed their belief that the government should take steps to promote our well-being. Nevertheless, it is not clear to me that they ever imagined that this concept would be used as justification for all of the social efforts now undertaken by the federal government.

Section III – Social Engineers Or Social Dilettantes?

What about that tax on tanning behavior? According to the Centers for Disease Control and Prevention, a federal agency funded by tax dollars:

> Using a tanning bed, booth, or sunlamp to get a tan is called "indoor tanning." Indoor tanning exposes users to both UV-A and UV-B rays, which damage the skin and can lead to cancer. Indoor tanning has been linked with skin cancers including melanoma (the deadliest type of skin cancer), squamous cell carcinoma, and cancers of the eye (ocular melanoma).

I don't know about you, but that all sounds serious to me: squamous cell carcinoma, ocular melanoma, and melanoma! Instead of taxing this form of behavior, Congress could outlaw it. The government already imposes a fine on automobile drivers who fail to wear a seat belt. Why not punish the next *GQ* cover model for using a tanning bed? Sarcasm aside, I am not advocating that the federal government regulate personal grooming behavior, but I question why this tax has been included in our tax code.

Today, most social engineering is done through tax expenditures—specifically, tax credits. The number of credits available, affecting the scope and amounts paid, has risen dramatically over the past several decades. One key reason that these expenditures have become so popular with Congress is the way the federal budget is developed. Despite the fact that these constitute an actual expense, either through reduced revenue or an actual payment, they are not considered an expense under federal budget rules.

For an average taxpayer, it does not matter whether costs increase or revenue decreases. In either case, if a household experiences a shortfall, the deficit must be addressed. A family facing this reality must figure a way to reduce expenses or increase income. Not so for Congress. Credits that reduce total tax are considered a reduction in revenues rather than an increase in costs. As a result, tax expenditures are not subject to the same annual appropriations review as actual federal outlays (defense spending, as an example). Congress can legitimately deny that spending has increased, even as they write more and larger refundable credit checks to taxpayers.

Using the tax code to socially engineer our economy raises a second concern—unintended consequences. It is generally accepted that changes to the tax code often produce unforeseen, unintended, and, ultimately, undesirable results. Given this fact, I am left wondering whether Congress and the IRS are actually trying to act as social engineers or simply playing as social dilettantes.

Conventional wisdom suggests we cannot fundamentally change our code. In particular, many assert that we cannot eliminate tax preferences. Some suggest that an economic apocalypse would result if we even tried. I understand that doing so will not be easy; nothing worthwhile ever is. But considering the alternatives, the loss of freedom, the distortion of a free market, by maintaining the status quo, we have to try!

Under the circumstances, I feel obligated to once again contribute to the general fund by paying federal excise tax on some distilled spirits.

Chapter 10

The American Dream
(or Nightmare on Main Street)

> The sentiment for home ownership is embedded in the American heart [of] millions of people who dwell in tenements, apartments and rented rows of solid brick.
> President Herbert Hoover

> Those who should have known better persuaded themselves that they were not their brother's keeper.
> Vice President Hubert Humphrey

> You want to reinforce family values in America... Make it easy for people to own their own home.
> President Bill Clinton

The term "American Dream" was first coined by James Truslow Adams in *The Epic of America*, published in 1931. In his book, Adams said it is, "that dream of a land in which life should be better and richer and fuller for everyone...It is not a dream of motor cars and high wages merely, but a dream of social order in which each man and each woman shall be able to attain to the fullest stature of which they are innately capable."

Good words. The term "home ownership"—a status symbol during colonial times that separated the middle class from the poor—has since become synonymous with the American Dream.

From the early days of the Great Depression, the federal government has felt it necessary to get actively involved in helping Americans bring the dream of home ownership to reality. However, although President Hoover believed in the value and importance of home ownership, his approach was to make mortgages more affordable through his Home Loan Discount proposal. He believed that government's role was "to stimulate industrial action," not "to set up government in the building of homes."

That changed when President Roosevelt took office. With White House support, the National Housing Act of 1934 was enacted as part of the New Deal in order to make housing and home mortgages more affordable. This law created the Federal Housing Administration, the Federal Savings and Loan Insurance Corporation, and the United States Housing Authority. It seems the government had embarked on "the building of homes."

Those early efforts were directed primarily at the lending side of the home ownership equation. In 2008, the government dove into the deep end of the home ownership pool when, on July 24, 2008, the Housing and Economic Recovery Act of 2008, commonly referred to as HERA, was enacted. This law included a credit, up to a maximum of $7,500, designed to help low- and middle-income families purchase a home. The credit was named the first-time homebuyer credit.

The idea sounds good. It even looks good—on paper. The federal government gives money to people to help them buy their first

Section III – Social Engineers Or Social Dilettantes?

home. But this isn't what really happened, because, in practice, the government doesn't have anything to *give*. Either it must borrow the funds, transferring the cost of its beneficence to future generations, or it must tax some citizens, in order to give to others. All of this raises the question: Is our government treating all of its citizens equally?

That is a hard question to answer, particularly with respect to paying taxes. But equal treatment—a complex legal concept—is actually a simple idea to comprehend. And although many legal scholars agree that the intended scope of the Equal Protection Clause of the Fourteenth Amendment is much narrower than commonly believed, in modern practice, the legal mandate to treat persons equally extends to all actions taken by the government.

Nothing could be further from this concept than the results caused by the implementation of HERA. And this can be clearly demonstrated by the remarkably different financial results that HERA, as amended, provided to two brothers.

A Tale of Two Brothers

Jake and Mike grew up in a middle-class home, in a small city in America's heartland. Separated in age by two years, they were closer than most brothers and inseparable as young boys. When not in school, they could be found playing baseball or basketball together. As they grew older, they even agreed on the three subjects that family and friends are not supposed to discuss—politics, religion, and money. Eventually, they attended the same college.

After college graduation, Jake took a job as an engineer with a local manufacturer. Mike graduated two years later and joined that same company as a sales representative. During his senior year in college, Mike began dating the younger sister of Jake's fiancée. Six months later, the two brothers married sisters, both of whom taught elementary school in the local school district.

A quick review of the couples' 2007 Form 1040 showed that both households included two wage earners and that neither couple owned a home and neither itemized deductions and neither had any dependents. Jake and his wife reported adjusted gross income (AGI) totaling $97,632. The return filed by Mike and his wife reflected AGI of $98,887.

Both couples dreamed of buying a home in the neighborhood in which the boys grew up, now a trendy area for first-time home buyers. Fortunately, with the help of the new first-time homebuyer credit, their dreams could come true. The four began scanning the real estate listings, and by early November, each couple found a house they liked on the same street the brothers had lived as young boys.

Preapproved for mortgages, each couple made an offer for the house they had chosen. Jake's original offer of $79,900 was accepted. Mike's offer of $78,500 was countered with an offer of $80,000, to which he agreed. Both Jake and Mike were scheduled to close on December 22, 2008.

Everything went smoothly with Jake's purchase. All required paperwork was correctly prepared, organized, and submitted in a timely fashion. He and his wife closed on their new home on December 22, 2008, as scheduled.

Mike's approach was less organized. Paperwork was often misplaced or incomplete, and another two weeks passed before he had all of the necessary documents submitted. Mike's closing finally took place on January 5, 2009.

Section III – Social Engineers Or Social Dilettantes?

As usual, Jake had all tax documents quickly assembled and categorized. When he received his and his wife's W-2, he immediately scheduled an appointment for February 6, 2009, with his accountant. As expected, he was told that his refund would include the $7,500 homebuyer credit but he was disappointed to learn that it had to be repaid over the next fifteen years. He had interpreted the word *credit* differently than the meaning intended under the law. When he met Mike for a beer later that evening, he told him about the repayment requirement.

Unlike his older brother, Mike was not quite as prepared. But by early March, Mike had all of his paperwork ready and went to the local office of a national tax preparation service to have his 2008 tax return prepared. His preparer recommended that he choose to treat the home purchase as if it had closed in 2008, despite the closing date of January 5, 2009.

Mike was glad to learn that, rather than waiting a year, this choice allowed him to immediately claim the homebuyer credit. He was even more surprised to learn that the credit had been changed and, rather than $7,500, he would get $8,000. Remembering Jake's warning, he asked how long he had to repay the credit. If he was surprised at the amount of the credit, he was astonished when told he would not have to repay the credit unless he moved out of the house. The $8,000 was not a loan—it was a gift.

(Author's note: Pay particular attention to the IRS FAQs listed later. Note particularly the language "For homes purchased in 2009…with some exceptions, does not have to be repaid." It should include "including those elected to have been made in 2008.")

As a result of a diligent, focused effort, Jake received a fifteen-year, $7,500, interest-free, government loan. Mike, due to a more laid-back approach, unwittingly received an $8,000 gift from that same government. Jake was probably muttering that well-known advertising slogan, "I wanna be like Mike," interspersed among frequent, muffled *F* word expletives.

Like peas in a pod, these two families lived under indistinguishable social, financial, and geographic conditions. Although both returns had been correctly prepared, accurately reflecting a first-time home purchase, the tax benefit received by these two families was dramatically different. These incredibly dissimilar outcomes occurred as a result of identical actions taken only two weeks apart but which were completed *under the same tax law in effect at the time each purchase had closed.*

Forget trying to comprehend the tax code and thereby make rational decisions. Luck must also smile down on you. Not only is the Internal Revenue Code complex, it is changed so frequently, so randomly, that understanding it has become nearly impossible. The following excerpt regarding this credit was taken directly from the IRS FAQ web page:

> The first-time homebuyer credit is a tax credit for individuals and couples who purchase a new home after April 8, 2008, and before May 1, 2010. There are several versions of the credit depending upon when the home was purchased:
>
> - For homes purchased in 2008, the credit, with some exceptions, must be repaid and takes the form of a $7,500 interest-free loan.
> - For homes purchased in 2009 prior to November 7, the credit is for a maximum of $8,000 and, with some exceptions, does not have to be repaid, but it's only for new home owners who have not owned a home in the prior three years.

Section III – Social Engineers Or Social Dilettantes?

- Beginning November 7, 2009, an additional category of new homebuyers, long-time residents (who owned their own homes), was added. The credit for this group is a maximum of $6,500, which, with some exceptions, does not have to be repaid.

As with almost all provisions of the IRC, nothing about this credit was clear. Consider the name originally given to this credit. I suspect when taxpayers initially heard or read the expression—"first-time homebuyer credit"—many incorrectly assumed they were ineligible for the credit if they had ever purchased a home. The IRS definition of the term is excerpted here:

> (c) Definitions.—For purposes of this section—
> (1) First-time homebuyer.—The term "first-time homebuyer" means any individual if such individual (and if married, such individual's spouse) had no present ownership interest in a principal residence during the 3-year period ending on the date of the purchase of the principal residence to which this section applies.

This first-time homebuyer credit was not limited to a true first-time home buyer but was available to a taxpayer who had made any number of previous home purchases. The restriction is more accurately described as excluding anyone who had owned a home within the previous three years. The initial language also confused taxpayers by portraying the benefit as a "credit."

The truth, as belatedly stated in the IRS guidance reprinted before, is that the credit was actually a fifteen-year, interest-free loan. The taxpayer had to repay any credit received. In *Gone with the Wind*, Rhett Butler told Scarlett that they could, "Look things in their eyes and call them by their right names." Why can't Congress do the same? The original tax credit might have been more accurately named "Restricted, Limited, Fifteen-Year, No Interest, Home-Buyer Assistance Loan."

But even before eligible taxpayers could claim the credit, Congress changed several key provisions by enacting the American Recovery and Reinvestment Act of 2009. Section 1006 of this law was titled "Extension of and Increase in First-Time Homebuyer Credit; Waiver of Requirement to Repay."

Think about the meaning of the phrase "Waiver of Requirement to Repay." Taken at face value, the last phrase of the title negates repayment of the credit, changing it from a de facto loan to an actual credit. And in fact, with one caveat, that is what the amendment did. What was the caveat, you may wonder? It was the applicable dates.

The original act covered the time period April 9, 2008, until July 9, 2009. Under the initial version, any credit received had to be repaid. The amended version extended the end date until December 31, 2009, and exempted credits received for purchases made in 2009 from repayment. This exemption applied to 2009 purchases "elected" to have been made in 2008, hence Mike's good fortune.

It is as if Congress opted to take literally a line from the book of Matthew, "So the last shall be first, and the first last." Had the bill's sponsors used sarcasm, they might have titled this section "Extension of and Increase in First-Time Homebuyer Credit; *Limited* Waiver of Requirement to Repay—*Hope You Waited to Close.*"

Section III – Social Engineers Or Social Dilettantes?

Although the original measure was signed into law July 30, 2008, the credit was retroactively effective for any purchase made after April 9, 2008. The first amendment to the law was signed on February 19, 2009. The effective date for the waiver provision was made retroactive, as was the beginning date under the original law. Why not make the repayment exemption provision of the amendment retroactive to the original effective date, April 9, 2008, rather than January 1, 2009? While I may not be the sharpest tool in the shed, it is unclear to me how or why these dates were selected.

I can just picture it. A number of legislative aides are congregated in a large conference room, jackets draped over chairs, sleeves rolled up, and ties askew. Stacks of paper are piled around the table strewn with several weeks' worth of paper cups and plates and Chinese takeout cartons. Sighs of relief are heard from around the room. The law has been crafted and drafted. Softly, from one corner of the room, in a tired voice, hoarse from hours of debate, one of the cohort says, "We haven't inserted the effective dates."

Two of the younger participants quickly spring from their chairs. Opening a wood cabinet at the end of the room, they reveal a dart board. Those who had any energy left half-heartedly join the first two and pick up darts from a box.

It may be hard to imagine, but the expiration date, having been extended once already, was delayed once again. On November 6, 2009, Congress passed the Worker, Homeownership, and Business Assistance Act that made several changes to this credit, one of which was notable. In a consistent effort to maintain inconsistency, these changes *were not* retroactive.

In what can be reasonably interpreted as a deliberate attempt to randomly bestow fortune on a select few taxpayers, Congress changed the income eligibility limits—significantly. For purchases made before November 7, 2009, married taxpayers with modified adjusted gross incomes over $170,000 were ineligible. For purchases made after November 6, 2009, married taxpayers with modified adjusted gross incomes up to $225,000 were eligible for the full credit.

In plain English, a husband and wife who made $170,100 and purchased their home on November 6, 2009, received no credit, while a couple who earned $224,900 and who closed their home purchase one day later received an $8,000 credit. Like the earlier amendment, perhaps the relevant section of this law might have been similarly titled "The Worker, Homeownership, and Business Assistance Act—*Hope You Waited to Close—Again.*"

To quote Nina Olsen, the National Taxpayer Advocate, our tax code has become a lottery. Amendments to the IRC often pick winners and losers from among American taxpayers. Forget insider stock trading. I want to get early intelligence on changes to our tax code.

In 1832, South Carolina took exception to tariff laws passed by Congress and attempted to nullify those laws. It has been argued that South Carolina's attempt contributed to the friction that led to the Civil War, frequently described as "brother against brother."

Equal treatment? Not hardly. Fair treatment? You decide. Was this tax preference a dream come true or a nightmare on Main Street? Either way, as this story demonstrates, inequities in our tax code are once again pitting brother against brother.

I need a nightcap to help me sleep.

Chapter 11

Congress's Pet Is Our Peeve

> *Preference* (n)—(1) a feeling of liking or wanting one thing more than another thing;
> (2) an advantage that is given to some people and not to others.
> *Merriam-Webster Dictionary*

> I cannot undertake to lay my finger on that article of the Constitution
> which granted a right to Congress of expending, on objects of benevolence,
> the money of their constituents.
> President James Madison

> For every benefit you receive, a tax is levied.
> Ralph Waldo Emerson, Author

The practical application of that first definition of *preference* is seen throughout our tax code. Elected officials frequently reveal their favorites by adding or removing credits or changing the benefit derived from a particular tax provision. This is all done in an attempt to increase societal involvement in activities more preferable to members of Congress.

The F-Word

Even if that makes sense, even if we can trust those we elect to Congress to make the right decisions, isn't there something disturbing about the second definition of *preference*? How can it be that, in America, significant stipulations in our laws provide an advantage to some over others?

Ben Baack and Edward J. Ray claimed that passage of the income tax in 1913 "signaled voters that the federal government had the wherewithal to provide something for everybody." But is that even possible? Can the government actually *provide* something for everyone? Doesn't the government have to first *take* something away from someone else?

We have all heard the term "teacher's pet." In school, we disliked or were jealous of any student known as the teacher's favorite. But we didn't really care whether the teacher had favorites; we just wanted the same consideration, whatever it was. That same state of affairs exists under our tax code. Congress has a multitude of pets—a limitless number of favorite people and programs. The challenge to the average taxpayer has now become how to get on that list of favorites.

In no particular order, Congress's pets include energy research, students, teachers, Native Americans, New Yorkers, the disabled, and Americans living overseas. Congress rewards these pets with favorable tax treatment. But just as when we were in school, unless we are also a recipient of that most favored treatment, we are jealous. We want ours too.

Under the IRC, it matters whether a taxpayer is engaged in the production of alternative fuels, or whether a taxpayer buys an alternative fuel car. Investors are given special consideration. Saving, whether for education, retirement, or health care, is rewarded through tax preferences. Alternatively, spending is favorably

Section III – Social Engineers Or Social Dilettantes?

supported, as long as a taxpayer is buying a new car or the right appliance or the home improvement du jour. Those less well-off are given tax breaks for working, up to a point, more so if they have children—even more so if they elect to stay unmarried.

Is it the right time to buy a home? How about buying a second or maybe even a third? Is buying a home now better than saving for retirement or setting aside money for the children's college tuition? And if a taxpayer chooses to set aside money for college, what plan gives the greatest return? Should the furnace be replaced? If so, which one should be purchased? Is it time to replace the clunker in the driveway? These and other similar questions commonly arise within every American household. They encompass everyday life.

Prior to the increase in the pervasive reach and influence of the tax code, answers to these and similar questions were generally based on available finances, on priorities centered on the family's values, and on need—in short, on customary social and economic factors. Before the growth of the social mandates within the IRC, answers to all of these questions involved private considerations.

Now, though, these decisions are influenced as much by our tax code, perhaps even more so, than by traditional concerns. The question is no longer simply "What is the cost?" or "What is the return?" but "What is the after-tax…?" If a taxpayer fails to compare the financial results of a decision based solely on traditional considerations with the after-tax results of alternative choices based on tax preferences, such failure may result in economic loss. Let me remind you of our two homebuyers, Jake and Mike.

Businesses use this present-day reality in much of their marketing. Financial institutions attempt to sway customers to invest in order to reap the tax benefits. Real estate agents typically advise clients of the after-tax cost of buying a home. Big box stores, plumbers, electricians, and contractors often lead their sales pitches with the tax savings of buying this or that appliance, of replacing windows, of taking some specific action favored by the tax code.

Form 1040 contains seventy-seven separate lines for specific information. Of these, almost one in three deals with some type of preference, some different treatment or recognition of income or expenses. Our ever-changing tax code has influenced, intentionally or by accident, whether or not we marry, have children, live in one or another state, buy a home or rent, borrow or save, or go to college. The code influences where we work and whether and what kinds of insurance we buy.

In this chapter, I examine three common tax preferences, beginning with one of the largest and best known. Unlike some other tax preferences, this one has assumed something of the status of a birthright. Which preference is it? Why it is none other than the home mortgage interest deduction (MID).

This deduction has a number of vocal supporters including real estate brokers, home builders, and mortgage lenders. These supporters suggest that this tax preference must not be changed; indeed, it cannot be changed. They propose that restricting or eliminating this benefit would wreak havoc on the US economy. Their view notwithstanding, it is hard to understand how any precise conclusion can be drawn without comparing the elimination of the mortgage interest deduction with a specific alternative tax structure. Arguments to the contrary are based on abstract assumptions.

Advocates for this tax benefit suggest it should be retained because it makes the cost of home ownership more affordable and leads to increased home ownership. The evidence, however, is not so clear. Comparisons with developed countries that do not offer a similar

Section III – Social Engineers Or Social Dilettantes?

tax deduction do not support that the United States has a statistically significant higher percentage of home ownership.

Even absent increased home ownership, proponents argue that eliminating this deduction would result in a higher cost of home ownership to middle-income families. That contention also is not so obvious. The argument is somewhat diminished by those same advocates who decry the drop in real estate prices—estimated to be as high as 15%-20%—that would inevitably result from the elimination of the deduction.

As an aside, this last assertion necessarily supports the criticism levied against tax preferences by many economists—our tax code serves to unnaturally inflate different sectors of our economy. They almost universally agree that artificial inflation of home prices is not a good thing. Once again, our tax code works at cross-purposes. Congress intends to make home ownership more affordable, yet economists agree that this effort actually increases home prices.

Caveat Emptor

Say a young couple currently rents a home in a modest bedroom community outside a medium-sized city. Intending to buy their first home, they find a starter home that meets their budget with a purchase price of $119,000. Absent closing costs, a 20% down payment would leave a mortgage of $95,200. Because interest rates fluctuate, let's use 5% on a twenty-year, fixed-rate mortgage. The ballpark monthly principal and interest payment would be $628.

Annual interest for the first year would approximate $4,462, which could be claimed as an itemized deduction on their tax return, assuming the couple itemizes. A typical argument asserts that, at a marginal tax rate of 15%, our couple would realize an effective monthly principal and interest payment of $573. If this assumption holds true, the after-tax payment results in a $55 reduction of the monthly payment, producing an annual savings of $660.

Real estate agents typically use this argument in their zeal to persuade a potential buyer to take the plunge. But remember the discussion about precise language. To actually realize the projected savings, the total of itemized deductions must exceed the standard deduction by at least the amount of interest—else no real savings. Using this example, itemized deductions, including interest, must total $16,662 to produce the promised tax savings.

To demonstrate, say property taxes approximate $2,800. Assume the couple lives in a state with an income tax, and they paid $2,300 in state income tax. Assume further that they tithe 10% to their church for an additional $6,100. Eligible itemized deductions, with interest of $4,462, total $15,662. In this case, they would reduce their tax burden by only $549, not the $660 promised. This difference is due to the fact that total itemized deductions only exceeded the standard deduction by $3,662. Applying the 15% marginal tax rate on that amount produces the $549 tax savings. Less generous tithing would reduce MID savings even more.

However, who knows for how long they would continue to own the home, or what their income would be over the life of the mortgage. Still, those are questions for which we can make an educated guess. How about this question? How will the tax code read in five years or in ten? Anyone want to hazard a prediction on that?

Regardless, let us assume this couple generally falls within the 15% tax bracket throughout their working lives. Under the current mortgage interest deduction, the total cost of their home approximates $168,249 ($23,800 down plus loan principal of $95,200 plus interest of $55,587 less tax savings of $8,338).

SECTION III – SOCIAL ENGINEERS OR SOCIAL DILETTANTES?

Now let's assume, as some worry, that political insanity infects Congress and the mortgage deduction is eliminated. In the movie *Ghostbusters*, Dr. Venkman appropriately describes this eventuality as envisioned by those who worry over the elimination of MID. He said we would be "headed for a disaster of biblical proportions… dogs and cats living together…mass hysteria!"

Seriously, suppose the mortgage interest deduction were eliminated and the bottom fell out of the real estate market, causing a 15% decline in home values. Assuming the tax code remained the same in all other respects, what would be the impact on that young couple described earlier?

In this case, our couple might pay $640/month, reflecting a 2% higher monthly mortgage payment compared with the pretax cost cited earlier. The total cost would be roughly $135,190 ($20,230 down plus principal of $80,920 plus interest of $34,264).

Wait, what? Is that right? A higher monthly cost should produce a higher total cost, not a lower one. Why the difference? Using the logic of those who suggest that real estate values would plummet, I inferred that home prices would decrease by 15%. In this case, the purchase price for this same home would be $101,150.

Given that the earlier payment of $628 was within the couple's budget, the lower purchase price likely makes a fifteen-year mortgage payment of $640 affordable. The total number of monthly payments is sixty less than the number of payments made in the first example. The reduced purchase price and shorter mortgage term produce a much lower total cost.

It is not clear to me how lowering the total cost of ownership almost 20% can be determined, in any shape or fashion, to put the cost of owning a home out of reach for middle-class Americans.

Many economists agree that providing a tax preference for home mortgage interest has served to artificially increase real estate values. They suggest that it has unnaturally encouraged home investment—buying a home—as opposed to other forms of consumption or investment. Generally, economists have held that investing for a profit, for economic gain or necessity, typically results in an economic benefit. Conversely, if an investment is made to take advantage of a tax preference, they generally hold that economic harm may result.

In my view, proponents of the home mortgage interest deduction cannot have it both ways. They cannot express concern that home prices will drop if the deduction is either limited or eliminated, and simultaneously claim that elimination of the deduction will make home ownership unaffordable for many families. I do not believe the one necessarily follows the other.

Let's examine a different tax preference. This one takes a number of forms and may be limited based on income. This congressional pet is fed by nonrefundable credits, refundable tax credits, or both. Alternatively, the benefit may be realized by claiming an adjustment to income, producing a lower AGI.

How well do you know the tax code? With the information just provided, can you state with certainty to which of the myriad of tax preferences I refer? Are you sure? Are there any others that meet these criteria?

Take Care

Let me come back to this credit later. Instead, let's examine a third preference: tax treatment of health care costs. The expenses of health care and health care insurance are addressed in a number of separate sections of the IRC. Like much of our tax code and the resulting implications of that code, these adjustments, deductions,

Section III – Social Engineers Or Social Dilettantes?

credits, and penalties are confusing and, in many instances, applied in a way that leads to inequitable treatment. Although the ACA changed the impact of various health care preferences, it did not change the overriding issue of equitable treatment.

True or false? Can premium costs for health care coverage be taken as a deduction against total income, resulting in a lower adjusted gross income? Answer: It depends!

In limited instances, health care premiums may be taken as an adjustment to total income. A self-employed taxpayer, defined either as a sole proprietor, a partner, or a 2% owner of an S corporation, *may* deduct the cost of health insurance premiums as an adjustment to income. Why *may*? Because the deduction is limited to the net income derived from self-employment. As an example, if a partnership loses money, a partner cannot take the cost of health insurance as an adjustment to income.

Conversely, a taxpayer whose income is only wage income or unearned income, including passive activities and capital gains, cannot take this expense as an adjustment to income. (Author's note: I can just imagine Twitter crashing now. "Yes Dorothy, everyone can take health care premiums as an itemized deduction—read further.") How or why this differentiation exists is beyond me.

To consider the incongruity of the tax treatment of health care costs, let's compare three different types of taxpayers. First, consider a taxpayer who works for an employer that offers health care coverage as a condition of employment. Although our tax code does not consider this employee benefit as income, it clearly is an economic benefit. If this employee did not receive this benefit and wanted health care insurance, he would be forced to purchase health coverage individually. The cost of that coverage would have to be paid with after-tax dollars.

Nonetheless, the taxpayer who is provided such coverage receives that benefit tax free. Additionally, the company can deduct the cost of those premiums. It may even qualify for a tax credit by virtue of providing health care coverage.

As a subset of this preferential treatment, if an employer offers health care coverage under Section 125 of the IRC (more commonly referred to as a cafeteria plan), premiums paid by the taxpayer through payroll deduction are excluded from taxable income.

Compare the after-tax results of a single taxpayer who does not receive employer-sponsored health care with one who does. Both are single with no dependents and claim the standard deduction. The impact of this disparate treatment is shown in table 13.

	Covered Employee	Noncovered Employee	Noncovered Employee [2]
Gross Wages	50,000	50,000	52,100
Annual Health Care Cost	4,200	4,200	4,200
Employer Contribution	2,100	-	-
Employee Contribution [1]	2,100	-	-
W-2 Wages	47,900	50,000	52,100
Standard Deduction	6,100	6,100	6,100
Personal Exemption	3,900	3,900	3,900
Taxable Income	37,900	40,000	42,100
Income Tax	5,410	5,935	6,460
Payroll Tax	3,664	3,825	3,986
Disposable Income After Health Care	38,826	36,040	37,454

Table 13 - After tax impact of health care coverage for a covered and non-covered employee.

[1] The company has established a Section 125 (Cafeteria Plan) Plan. Deductions for health care reduce taxable wages for Social Security and federal income tax.

[2] Stepped up wages allowing for market pressure on the value of labor.

Section III – Social Engineers Or Social Dilettantes?

Summarizing this first example, an employee who receives health care benefits does so tax free because the monetary value of the premiums is not included in taxable income. Conversely, an uncovered worker must seek coverage and pay for that coverage with after-tax dollars. Said differently, an uncovered worker pays premiums with money included in his taxable income.

Two wage earners, each making the same wage, each of whom elect to carry health care insurance, end up with different disposable income. But you might argue that if the market determines this labor is worth $52,100 (the wage paid plus the employer's premium contribution for health care), an employee not eligible for health benefits would be paid a wage of $52,100. Fair enough. The result: the noncovered employee still ends up with $1,370 less in disposable income. He would incur income and payroll taxes totaling $10,446 compared with $9,074 for the covered employee.

Using an example similar to the previous one, let's compare the tax liability for a self-employed person with a noncovered employee, both of whom elect health care coverage. In this example, they work at the same company, doing the same job. As is common for self-employed individuals, the negotiated contract rate was slightly higher than the employee rate to offset higher SECA taxes. Again, note the disparity in total tax liability and disposable income.

	Noncovered Employee	Self-employed
Gross Wages/Gross Self-employment Income	50,000	53,825
Annual Health Care Cost	4,200	4,200
Adjustment to Income	-	8,003
Adjusted Gross Income	50,000	45,822
Standard Deduction	6,100	6,100
Personal Exemption	3,900	3,900
Taxable Income	40,000	35,822
Income Tax	5,935	4,928
Payroll Tax	3,825	-
Self-Employment Tax	-	7,605
Net disposable Income After Health Care	36,040	37,092

Table 14 - After tax impact of health care coverage for a self-employed taxpayer and a non-covered employee.

Considering these last two examples, the least desirable condition of employment for a taxpayer who secures health care coverage is working as a W-2 employee for an employer who does not provide health care coverage. Why is it that our tax code creates an environment in which one type of employment or one employer is preferable to another?

Continuing this analysis of preferential tax treatment for health care costs, consider actual treatment costs. These costs receive favorable tax treatment and may be deducted on Schedule A. Earlier, I asked if health care premiums could be claimed to lower AGI. I answered that this expense could only be claimed by self-employed taxpayers. Although that answer is correct, all taxpayers can include health care premiums on Schedule A as an itemized medical deduction to possibly reduce taxable income. To do that, however, and to actually benefit from the preferential

Section III – Social Engineers Or Social Dilettantes?

treatment of health care costs, several factors, must exist, as detailed here.

First, total medical costs, including health care premiums, must exceed 10% of AGI to be included in the total of itemized deductions. Second, the taxpayer must have incurred allowable itemized costs, including health care costs in excess of the 10% threshold, for which the total excess is more than the standard deduction. Said differently, total itemized deductions must exceed the standard deduction by the amount of medical expenses, or else no medical deduction is realized.

As an aside, prior to the Affordable Care Act, the threshold for the medical deduction was 7.5%. Doesn't it seem contradictory to include raising the deduction threshold for health care costs in a bill titled Affordable Care Act? The practical effect of increasing the deduction threshold for itemized health care costs is the reduction of the tax benefit for medical expenses, which, for many middle-income households, made health care less affordable. The quantifiable impact on a family with AGI of $70,000 is that this family just got an additional bill for medical expenses approximating $225.

Like the humorous name I suggested "hope you waited to close" in the story of Jake and Mike, with the increased medical deduction threshold, I hope no taxpayer delayed surgery from one year to the next. The result could be hundreds of dollars in higher tax liability. As I said before, this change is inconsistent with a law named the Affordable Care Act.

Discussion of tax preference for health care costs could take several chapters with all of the various exceptions, allowances, definitions, and exclusions, but the point has been made. Do you think a homeowner can deduct the cost of installation of a swimming pool as an allowable medical expense? The answer comes later in the book.

Get Smart

Have you figured out what that second preference was that I mentioned earlier in the chapter? The preference I had in mind is that which is provided to offset tuition expenses for higher education. While direct support of higher education has been debated since the 1960s, specific tax credits came to be in the Clinton administration with passage of the Tax Relief Act of 1997. These credits were first announced by President Clinton in a commencement speech delivered to graduating students at Princeton University in June 1996. His goal was to provide assistance to middle-income families.

Education has long been supported by the federal government. Prior to World War II, most Americans thought college was available only for the wealthy few. The Servicemen's Readjustment Act of 1944, better known as the G.I. Bill of Rights, changed that perception. That law made college affordable for many veterans who might never have attended college. The G.I. Bill was an unexpected success, leading to almost eight million service veterans enrolling in higher education—ten times the number originally predicted.

More recently, Pell grants provided direct relief to low-income families for higher education costs. Subsidized and unsubsidized Stafford loans have helped many middle-income families. These two programs pale in comparison to the support of higher education provided to taxpayers through the tax code. In fact, the total amount provided for higher education through the tax code now dwarfs the amount spent on primary and secondary programs such as Head Start and Title I.

Section III – Social Engineers Or Social Dilettantes?

Although I do not intend to get into a discussion of the rising costs of higher education, as with many things, government efforts to help families with the cost of higher education may have backfired. Many economists hold that, when the government made it exceptionally easy to borrow for college by opening the floodgates to government-backed student loans without income restrictions, it spurred tuition increases. This rapid increase in tuition costs was further fueled by the proliferation of education tax credits.

Under President Clinton, the government introduced a new form of aid to college students: federal tax credits for higher education. Unlike the EITC, which was targeted to low-income households, or the benefit that capital gains treatment affords wealthier households, education credits were specifically designed to provide tax relief to middle-income families.

Higher education is supported by four potential tax preferences. Education tax credits are provided under (1) the American Opportunity Credit, successor to the earlier Hope Credit, or (2) the Lifetime Learning Credit, either of which can be claimed by a taxpayer as a nonrefundable tax credit. The American Opportunity Credit can also be taken as a partially refundable tax credit. Alternatively, (3) education expenses can be taken as a deduction against total income, lowering adjusted gross income. Finally, (4) student loan interest can be taken as a deduction against total income, lowering AGI.

Each of these possible tax benefits must be calculated separately, but a taxpayer can use the method that results in the lowest tax liability. The ability to benefit from any education tax preference is also limited by specified AGI thresholds above which eligibility ceases. One thing is certain: Congress did not want to make education preferences easy to understand or calculate. But then what else is new?

The F-Word

Just as with many of our preferences, the changing nature of the credits and eligibility requirements make timing just as important as any other factor. It seems clear that this aspect of our tax code conflicts with basic fairness.

Consider two couples, both of whom raised two children. The two husbands work for the same employer as do both wives. The adjusted gross income reported by each couple is nearly identical from 1995 until 2005. The one difference is age. In 1995, Martha and George turned forty-five and forty-three, respectively, while Napoleon and Josephine turned thirty-nine and thirty-eight.

Our first couple has two daughters who both attended the nearby state university. The son and daughter of our second couple attended that same university although exactly four years later. Both couples had set aside money to pay for a college education for their children.

Despite the similarity between these two families, when the IRC is introduced into the financial equation, especially the timing of various provisions, significant differences ensue. Table 15 highlights this disparity.

	George and Martha						Napoleon and Josephine					
Year	Total Wages	AGI	Taxable Income	Gross Income Tax	Education Credits	Net Federal Taxes	Total Wages	AGI	Taxable Income	Gross Income Tax	Education Credits	Net Federal Taxes
1994	$50,913	$48,367	$32,217	$4,834	$0	$4,834	$50,409	$47,888	$31,738	$4,759	$0	$4,759
1995	$51,901	$49,306	$32,756	$4,916	$0	$4,916	$51,134	$48,578	$32,028	$4,804	$0	$4,804
1996	$51,903	$49,308	$32,408	$4,864	$0	$4,864	$50,885	$48,341	$31,441	$4,714	$0	$4,714
1997	$53,311	$50,646	$33,146	$4,969	$0	$4,969	$52,011	$49,410	$31,910	$4,789	$0	$4,789
1998	$54,318	$51,602	$36,402	$5,464	$715	$4,749	$52,865	$50,221	$32,321	$4,849	$1,500	$3,349
1999	$56,958	$54,110	$41,410	$6,214	$0	$6,214	$55,569	$52,791	$34,591	$5,186	$3,000	$2,186
2000	$59,141	$56,184	$43,234	$6,484	$0	$6,484	$57,981	$55,082	$36,532	$5,479	$2,276	$3,203
2001	$60,853	$57,810	$44,410	$6,664	$0	$6,664	$59,953	$56,956	$37,756	$5,666	$1,000	$4,666
2002	$60,413	$57,392	$43,542	$5,929	$0	$5,929	$59,815	$56,824	$39,974	$5,396	$888	$4,508
2003	$59,302	$56,337	$40,737	$5,409	$0	$5,409	$59,007	$56,057	$40,457	$5,371	$0	$5,371
2004	$58,485	$55,561	$39,661	$5,236	$0	$5,236	$58,741	$55,804	$39,904	$5,274	$0	$5,274

Total Wages	$617,499		Total Wages	$608,370
Total Federal Taxes	$60,268		Total Federal Taxes	$47,623
Total Education Credits	$715		Total Education Credits	$8,664
Percent Education Costs Subsidized	3%		Percent Education Costs Subsidized	28%
Effective Total Income Tax Rate	9.8%		Effective Total Income Tax Rate	7.8%

Table 15 - The effect of the timing of changes to the tax code on the after tax educational costs borne by two families.

SECTION III – SOCIAL ENGINEERS OR SOCIAL DILETTANTES?

As demonstrated, despite similar income and education costs, one couple realized noticeably higher disposable income. Why? Timing differences under the tax code create winners and losers. Everyone wants to "be like Mike."

Speaking of time, perhaps it's time to join Jake and Mike at their favorite watering hole.

Chapter 12

Fair or Foul?

> [EITC] The best anti-poverty, the best pro-family,
> the best job creation measure
> to come out of Congress...
> President Ronald Reagan

> Much-needed tax credit for working Americans...
> Hon. John McCain, Senator

> If you raise the earned income tax credit
> significantly,
> that would definitely help people who've gotten the
> short stick in life.
> Warren Buffett, Businessman and Philanthropist

The debate over tax equity has created a deep and wide gulf between Republicans and Democrats. The real issues often get clouded in vitriolic political rhetoric. During the 2012 presidential campaign, Mitt Romney was excoriated for off-the-record remarks regarding the working poor. His comments included the assertion that "forty-seven percent of Americans pay no income tax." Notwithstanding the criticism leveled against Romney for his proclamation and disregarding the lack of political sensitivity demonstrated by his remarks, his assertion is reasonably accurate.

Taken a step further, a significant plurality of American households effectively pays neither federal income tax nor payroll tax. The primary reason behind this is the earned income tax credit (EITC).

Republicans have praised and criticized the EITC. Most Democrats have expressed unabashed adulation for the program. Supporters laud the benefits and obscure the problems. But whether one is for or against the EITC, this tax policy clearly has significant glitches, not the least of which is the fraud and abuse sustained by the program.

The IRS has long recognized the EITC to be a tax preference subject to the highest incidence of abuse. The Final Audit Report, prepared by the Deputy Inspector General for Audit on December 31, 2008, stated, "Alternatives to traditional compliance methods are needed to stop billions of dollars in erroneous payments." The report pointed out further, "Potentially erroneous EITC claims identified continue to be paid in error. The IRS reports $10 billion to $12 billion annually in erroneous EITC payments."

The EITC, a federal tax spending program, provides more than twenty million low-income adults, most with minor children, with total payments exceeding $30 billion through refundable tax credits. Proponents assert that this program successfully meets its explicit goal of encouraging low-income parents to work by effectively lowering their income tax rate and providing a financial bonus to offset payroll taxes. Advocates argue that the alternative, traditional welfare programs, leads to the opposite conclusion—discouraging recipients from entering the workforce.

Section III – Social Engineers Or Social Dilettantes?

Government statistics reflect that the EITC lifts more children out of poverty than any other government program. Advocates see it as promoting family and work values and contend the cost of the EITC is partially compensated by a reduction in the number of welfare recipients.

However, due to design weaknesses, the EITC attaches a significant marriage penalty to intended beneficiaries and creates an extraordinarily regressive marginal-rate structure, particularly at the income level at which the credit begins to phase out. Taken together, these two factors mitigate arguments in support of the program's effectiveness. In particular, opponents contend that the EITC has increased single-parent households in low-income families.

The EITC began in 1975 as a modest program aimed at offsetting the Social Security tax paid by low-income working families with children. The actual design was the result of a heated public debate over implementation of a negative income tax (NIT) proposed by the Nixon administration.

Opponents claimed NIT would be a disincentive to work. To offset that possible effect, the EITC was made available only to those with income earned from employment. Further, the maximum amount of the credit increased as income rose, up to a defined income level. It was argued that this method would not only encourage individuals to work, but encourage recipients to work harder or longer, thereby increasing income.

To be eligible, a taxpayer must have earned income—defined as wage income or net income from self-employment. Eligibility has other restrictions as well. The taxpayer's adjusted gross income and total income must not exceed specified limits. Additionally, unearned income, such as income from investments, must also fall below allowable limits.

The amount of the EITC is based on the amount of earned income and the number of qualifying children. In 2013, for example, the maximum allowable income for a married taxpayer filing jointly with three or more children was $51,567. The credit ceased for income above that level.

The tax credit is refundable. Eligible taxpayers with no federal tax liability receive a tax refund from the government for the full amount of the credit if they file a tax return together with required forms.

Prior to 2011, low-income wage earners could file Form W-5 and receive an advance EITC (AEIC) payment with each paycheck. However, in 2010, President Obama signed the Education, Jobs and Medicare Assistance Act, which repealed the AEIC, effective with tax year 2011. As a result, eligible employees could no longer elect to receive AEIC through their payroll. That method was abandoned, replaced by large refunds issued when eligible taxpayers file their federal tax returns.

However, many economists suggest that a large lump-sum payment does not have the same positive economic multiplier as does a series of equal payments. More to the point, in a materialistic society, deluged with "buy now and save" messages, receipt of these large, lump-sum refunds does not provide the same benefit to a family as would an extra $25 to $75 dollars each week.

Over time, the reach and scope of the EITC has expanded with the most significant changes arising from the Tax Reform Act of 1986 and the Omnibus Reconciliation Act of 1993. Between 1990 and 1996, the cost of the program more than doubled in real dollars.

Section III – Social Engineers Or Social Dilettantes?

The popularity of the program is shown by the fact that, as of 2014, twenty-six states have instituted similar EITC programs to supplement the federal credit. The largest group of EITC recipients is composed of single mothers, typically in their late twenties or early thirties with a high school diploma.

Expansion of the credit has led to a dramatic decline in average effective tax rates for eligible taxpayers. From 1985 until 2000, effective rates have dropped from 14.5% to (4.1%) in 2000. In plain English, a negative tax rate means the federal government subsidized affected households—increasing disposable income by slightly more than 4%.

Some studies suggest that the EITC has possibly contributed to a slight reduction in the number of working spouses in a two-parent household. This occurs because the credit is based on family income. If, for example, the husband is the primary earner, and any additional income earned by the wife puts the family in the phase-out range of the EITC, the family receives the maximum credit if the wife remains out of the labor force. But if she seeks employment, additional earnings will likely decrease the credit received.

Thus the real boost in family income may be much smaller than the nominal extra earnings. One unintended result may be an incentive for the second earner to stay out of the labor force. At $10 an hour, for example, the tax rate for a spouse could exceed 35% of her earnings. That is a punitive marginal tax rate for low- to moderate-income families.

It has also been argued that the design of the program leads to fewer hours worked by those already employed. Eligible taxpayers may decline to work additional hours if doing so increases income to a level that the EITC begins to decrease or stop altogether.

However, the most potentially serious, unintended consequence of this credit might be the impact on the family unit. The benefit to children living in two-parent households is commonly accepted. Yes, many children do well in families of all types, including extended families, with stepparents, grandparents, and foster and adoptive parents. As a society, we have moved past the idea that children cannot be raised by two parents of the same sex. Okay, maybe we have not moved past that notion, but we do recognize that what is most critical is that all children have loving, caring, and involved parents in all aspects of their lives.

Assuming this concern is valid, how is it possible that a section of our tax code discourages parents staying together? To answer that question, consider the following example.

Horns of a Dilemma

A teenage girl gets pregnant and delivers a healthy baby. With only a high school education, she works at a local franchise of a fast-food chain. She works hard, but, with limited income, she continues to live with her parents. With their help, she takes good care of her child. She finally gets a promotion, and, with annual income approximating $24,000, she moves into her own apartment. She meets someone she cares about, and nine months later, she delivers a second baby.

She and her partner talk of marriage, but they realize that doing so could be costly. He is employed as a night watchman earning $10 an hour and works a lot of overtime. His annual wages approximate $29,000. At the time they met, he lived with his four-year-old son. Our young mother continued to live in her apartment with her two children.

Let's compare the tax implications of marriage. For this comparison, leave aside personal beliefs and opinions of what these two

Section III – Social Engineers Or Social Dilettantes?

taxpayers should or should not do. Forget your emotional response to the story. Just as they must do, consider the financial implications of the tax code on their decision to marry. The impact of getting married and filing a joint return compared with two separate returns filed as head of household is shown in table 16.

	Married Filing Jointly	Filing Individually		
	Combined	Father	Mother	Total
Adjusted Gross Income	53,000	29,000	24,000	53,000
Standard Deduction	12,200	8,950	8,950	17,900
Total Exemptions	19,500	7,800	11,700	19,500
Taxable Income	21,300	12,250	3,350	15,600
Income Tax	2,306	1,228	338	1,566
Child Tax Credit	2,306	1,000	338	1,338
Additional Child Tax Credit	694	-	1,662	1,662
EITC	-	1,413	4,004	5,417
Net Income Tax Liability	(694)	(1,185)	(5,666)	(6,851)
Payroll Taxes	4,055	2,219	1,836	4,055
Net Federal Tax Liability	3,361	1,034	(3,830)	(2,797)
Effective Federal Tax Rate	6.3%	3.6%	-16.0%	-5.3%
Disposable Income	49,640	27,966	27,830	55,797

Table 16 - Comparison of the impact of the tax code on low-income taxpayers, eligible for the EITC, if they marry and file jointly or stay unmarried.

If they marry, perhaps even if they move in together, they incur a total federal tax liability of $3,361. If they remain apart, they incur no tax liability and actually receive a net payment from the government. Bottom line, these two parents have a significant financial decision to make. They can marry and give up $6,158, or they can stay separate. They may even decide to continue to live apart but have another child. That child could live with the father providing an additional $3,600 in refundable tax credits.

Does it make sense that our tax code should have this degree of influence on parents' family choices? If the tax code is designed in a way that compels these parents to surrender an amount of income sufficient to have a serious lifestyle impact, the design is ludicrous.

Fair or foul? The answer is hard to determine. Whether fair or foul, the earned income tax credit provision is just like all other sections of our tax code. Complex and confusing, the EITC frequently works at cross-purposes with itself and often leads to results that penalize those it was designed to benefit. This is typically the result of unintended consequences.

This is so depressing that I don't know whether to pour a shot of bourbon or swear off drinking. In the movie *The Angel and the Bad Man*, a doctor opines, "It's amazing the varied uses to which men put alcohol…a stimulant, a depressant or an anodyne." That country sawbones went on to say, "Just now I'm using it as an anodyne."

Makes sense to me. Just now I am pouring a shot of bourbon as an anodyne.

Chapter 13

No Such Thing as a Free Lunch

> The American Republic will endure until the day
> Congress discovers
> that it can bribe the public with the public's money.
> Unknown

> The Government that robs Peter to pay Paul
> can always count on the support of Paul.
> George Bernard Shaw, Playwright

> In general, the art of government consists in taking
> as much money as possible
> from one party of the citizens to give to the other.
> Voltaire, Philosopher

These opening quotes are particularly relevant in light of our present-day tax code. Congressional candidates have embraced that first quote, often attributed to de Tocqueville, for a long time and now espouse support for this or that tax credit as patronage for their specific electorate. As a result, we all now dine at the trough of congressional largesse.

Whether such bounty is legitimate under our Constitution is another question entirely. Even if justifiable, it begs the question of reasonableness. The founding fathers understood the monster that could arise from the words "power to lay and collect taxes." But it is likely they did not foresee the tax credit cornucopia that Congress has since created.

One only has to read the various letters, articles, and speeches written by many of those men to recognize a common thread—they did not consider the federal government to be the final arbiter of all behavior. They did not envision that the government would mete out punishment or grant rewards for different actions through the tax code.

Yet this is the circumstance in which we now find ourselves. Preferences, exclusions, deductions, and allowances abound. Carry-back provisions and look-ahead methods create or address timing inconsistencies. However, these myriad preferences typically apply unequally even to similar circumstances.

Lunch is on Me

Consider the deduction for meals and entertainment. This deduction is restricted by a number of rules and tests and is limited to 50% of the amount spent.

Imagine three senior executives of a small manufacturing company eating lunch together at a nice midtown restaurant. Don't confuse this purposeful meeting with the much maligned three-martini lunch. It's just three executives at lunch discussing important issues of the day. One of the three picks up the $135 tab and turns it in with his weekly expense report.

As required, the executive properly recorded all attendees on the back of the receipt. He further indicated that, during lunch, they

Section III – Social Engineers Or Social Dilettantes?

discussed improving next quarter's sales projections, price modeling, blah, blah, blah. The company reimbursed the executive for the expense. Thus the executives had a free lunch. Or did they?

Because this expense properly met all IRS requirements under the "directly related" test, and the receipt properly substantiated the expense, the company is able to deduct 50% of the amount reimbursed from its income for tax purposes.

Now imagine three tool men—journeyman tool and die makers—employed by that same manufacturer, eating lunch together in the factory cafeteria. Feeling generous, having just won a $50 Lotto scratch-off, one of our trio trails the others through the serving line and tells the cashier to put all three charges on one check. (Author's note: Under the IRC, our benefactor should properly enter $50 as gambling winnings on line 2 of the Other Income Statement, reported on Line 21—Other Income, on Form 1040.)

The cashier totals the three checks, and he pays the freight, totaling a whopping $27.85. Having heard that the company frequently reimburses meal expenses, he turns in his receipt to human resources. He provides the names of his two co-workers and notes that they had discussed recommendations for changes to the latest die blueprint. The receipt comes back with a note thanking him for his submittal but explaining that the meal is not eligible for reimbursement.

Not one to give up so easily, he holds onto his receipt and attempts to deduct it when he prepares his tax return for the year. He learns that the deduction is limited to 50% of the expense and is further limited by a threshold equal to 2% of his adjusted gross income. This confused him because he had also read that a corporation could deduct meal expenses, also limited to half of the actual cost, but with no such income threshold.

Pressing ahead, he calculates that, because he does not currently itemize, he must buy enough lunches so that half of the total amount spent, in excess of 2% of his adjusted gross income, creates an amount larger than his standard deduction.

As a highly skilled worker, our generous benefactor earns $45,000 a year. Ignoring any other possible deductions, he concludes he has to buy $7,056 worth of deductible business lunches in order to claim the $28 he spent for his friends.

Finally, he concedes that he simply cannot deduct the expense. That evening, he retires to the bar with his two comrades. Over a shot of bourbon chased down with an icy mug of draft beer, he describes the tax code for his buddies, using a number of *F* word variants.

The IRC contains a multitude of preferential tax treatments. Besides an allowance for meals and other entertainment, these include distinct treatment for different types of income, including capital gains, tax-exempt interest, passive income, and various retirement and disability payments. The code further contains many provisions that lower taxable income, including deductions, exclusions, and exemptions, or that lower or eliminate the amount of taxes owed, including tax credits.

Americans must understand that any preference that lowers one taxpayer's liability simply transfers the monetary benefit of the payment associated with that activity onto the backs of all taxpayers.

The lion's share of these preferences is now implemented through various tax credits. Since 1975, tax credits may be either refundable or nonrefundable. Refundable tax credits differ from all other tax preferences in a significant way. Whereas other preferences reduce the amount of taxes owed, either by reducing the amount

Section III – Social Engineers Or Social Dilettantes?

of income subject to tax, or by offering a credit to offset such tax, refundable credits can result in a net payment to the taxpayer.

Specifically, if a refundable tax credit exceeds a taxpayer's tax liability before the credit is applied, the government pays the excess to the taxpayer. Within the federal budget, the portion of refundable credits that reduces taxes owed is counted as a reduction in revenues, and the amount that exceeds the tax liability is treated as a tax expenditure. The total cost of refundable credits is the total of these two components.

Since the introduction of the earned income tax credit (EITC), the first of the refundable tax credits, the number and cost of refundable credits have grown substantially. Advocates and opponents argue over their real effects on the economy. They debate the administrative challenges associated with providing such subsidies and the inherent inefficiencies. By adding more complicated rules, more tax forms, and more computations, refundable credits increase the costs incurred by taxpayers in complying with the tax code and by the government in administering those laws. Additionally, rivals maintain they diminish the transparency of our tax system.

Not only have the number and cost of refundable tax credits grown over the years, the nature of those credits has evolved. While eligibility for the EITC was premised on earned income, many of the newer refundable tax credits are not limited to those with earned income. Instead, these credits are used to compensate taxpayers for expenses incurred for items such as health insurance and higher education.

This explosion of refundable tax credits has contributed to a decline in average tax rates among households that fall below the median income. That decline is most notable for households in the bottom two-fifths of income distribution. By 2009, individual income tax rates became increasingly negative for many of these households. On average, households in the bottom fifth of income now receive a tax payment—refundable credits—from the IRS instead of paying income taxes to the IRS. Many of those households, however, do pay federal payroll taxes.

Most refundable tax credits were created to meet social policy goals, such as providing income support for low-income households, expanding health insurance coverage, or increasing college enrollment. Alternatively, those same goals could be supported through spending programs (such as the Supplemental Nutrition Assistance Program, the Temporary Assistance for Needy Families program, Medicaid, the Children's Health Insurance Program, and the Pell Grant program).

Playing With Monopoly Money

The choice between using the tax system and relying on spending programs hinges largely on administrative considerations. These include the effectiveness in reaching the target population, timeliness, and the ability to ensure compliance with rules. Each of those factors affects the administrative cost incurred by the federal government and the compliance burden imposed on those eligible for the benefit and on the third parties required to support an applicant's eligibility.

The decision whether to use tax expenditures or actual budget outlays is also influenced by federal budget rules. Tax credits are considered a reduction in revenue. Because they are not viewed as an expense, they are not subject to the same scrutiny as, for example, defense spending.

Stated simply, the government cannot spend money it does not collect; therefore, it neither has to appropriate that money nor

Section III – Social Engineers Or Social Dilettantes?

monitor its expense. I know eyebrows went up all across America and shot glasses taken out of cabinets after reading this statement. I am not talking about deficit spending. Rather, I am describing budget methodology. In fact, it could be argued that this methodology facilitates deficit spending.

There are some serious flaws with this budget methodology. Not the least of these is that unless such a program has a spending cap, and most do not, expenditures could outstrip estimates. Rather than an estimated thirteen to fifteen million students claiming an education benefit, suppose thirty million did so? Remember the earlier comment regarding participation under the G.I. Bill? How many government programs can withstand an outlay twice the original estimate—no less ten times the expected cost?

Some analysts have suggested that the magnitude of federal commitments is hidden because as much as half of the cost of all refundable tax credits is recorded as a reduction in revenues, thereby making the budget appear smaller and the readily identifiable budgetary costs of refundable tax credits appear less than their actual cost. As a result, ensuring congressional review and oversight for tax expenditures is more difficult than for traditional spending programs.

One major problem is that overpayments occur more frequently with tax expenditures than with ordinary spending subsidies. This is generally caused by the fact that the Internal Revenue Service cannot verify that applicants meet all eligibility requirements before refundable tax credits are paid. Additionally, tax expenditure payments are commonly larger than payments made under spending programs.

Despite political rhetoric, the EITC is not, nor has it been, the sole method of social welfare administered through the tax code. In

The F-Word

2009 and 2010, American taxpayers were given yet another form to include with their tax return. That form is Schedule M, which had to be completed in order to calculate the Making Work Pay credit.

This credit only lasted two years and was replaced by the Payroll Tax Holiday or Payroll Tax Cut. In 2011 and 2012, working Americans—those with earned income and my apologies to those earning money from their investments—received a lower federal tax bill through a reduction of the employee Social Security tax rate from 6.2% to 4.2%.

It might be said that these two tax expenditures comprised EITC for middle-class families. Schedule M was a refundable credit while the reduction in Social Security tax was simply a lower tax rate. In order to receive either of these credits, the taxpayer had to be employed.

As I frequently asserted in the chapter on marginal tax rates, determining the net tax liability paid is crucial in assessing the actual tax burden carried by individual taxpayers. However, while the distribution of the tax burden is commonly debated, the allocation of government spending through tax expenditures is often ignored in the debate. Just as taxes fall more heavily on some households than others, so too do tax expenditures flow unequally to different households.

The complexity and scope of today's tax expenditure programs make this issue much more intricate and critical than in prior years. The Tax Foundation models the total impact of a tax system with the following equation:

Household Income plus Government Spending less
Tax Burden equal
Household Resources

Section III – Social Engineers Or Social Dilettantes?

Simply, the economic impact of a tax system to a household must consider both the tax burden on that household, in resources taken, as well as tax expenditures for that household, in resources provided. Sadly, it is difficult if not impossible to truly assess the tax burden on a particular household or the benefit of government spending on that same household.

Earlier, I discussed one of the largest tax expenditure programs, Social Security and Medicare. As we all know from media coverage, political commentary, and legislative debate, we now spend far more in Social Security benefits than we currently receive in Social Security taxes.

Each year, the Social Security Trust Fund board of trustees issues a report. In the 2014 Annual Report, it reported, "In 2013, OASDI expenditures were paid to almost 58 million recipients. Total payments approximated $823 billion while tax collections approximated $752 billion."

Whether paid with taxes deposited into the general fund or into the Social Security Trust Fund, these tax expenditures sound nice. The government gives money to students, to the elderly, and to those who work and those who don't. It subsidizes those who buy newer cars and newer energy-efficient furnaces. It even buys an occasional lunch. Has anyone stopped to ask where all of that money is coming from? Does this strategy make any sense?

Looking a Gift Horse in the Mouth

Remember our three executives. Having eaten on the company's nickel, they enjoyed a free lunch, getting away scot-free. Although the company paid the bill, in turn, it claimed a meal deduction on its tax return. The amount deducted was limited to 50% of the expense. Assuming a 35% tax bracket, the lunch actually cost the company $91.00, not the $135.00 reimbursement made to the executive. As it turns out, the company didn't get away scot-free.

Speaking of getting off scot-free, one urban myth suggests that the etymology of that term stems from an old English expression that applied to Scottish subjects who were able to avoid paying the royal tax. Hence, they were Scot-free. Whether true or not, it's an interesting notion.

If you are wondering who paid the difference between the cost paid by the company and the actual cost of the lunch, look in the mirror. But you are not alone. Consider this: the annual interest payment on the US debt approximates $400 billion. With the US population estimated at just over 300 million, the per capita share of that interest payment equals $1,333. Maybe even our three executives didn't get away completely scot-free.

Perhaps it is time that we all looked in the mirror. Better still, every American taxpayer should look this gift horse in the mouth. Imagine if we all stopped trying to get someone else to pay for lunch. Perhaps we could begin to trim the deficit and, just maybe, our national debt would not be so high. After all, there is no such thing as a free lunch. We can't all get off scot-free—someone always has to pay.

But under our tax code, unknown and unknowing taxpayers often pick up the tab for a couple of bourbon cocktails during lunch. Waiter, another round!

Section IV

Fool's Gold in Our Golden Years

Overview

> You should never depend on the government for
> your retirement,
> your financial security, for anything. If you do,
> you're screwed.
> Drew Carey, Actor and Comedian

> I advise you to go on living solely to enrage those
> who are paying your annuities.
> Voltaire, French Philosopher

> You can be young without money but you can't be
> old without it.
> Tennessee Williams, Author and Playwright

A retirement plan is a financial strategy designed to replace employment income when a person stops working. Plans may be set up by employers, insurance companies, trade unions, the government, or other institutions, or they may be established by individuals for themselves. The US government encourages saving for retirement by granting favorable tax treatment to such efforts within the Internal Revenue Code (IRC). Retirement plans in the United States are generally defined by the IRS and regulated by the Department of Labor under the Employee Retirement Income Security Act (ERISA).

Sounds simple enough, doesn't it? The IRC even includes one qualified retirement plan that uses the word *simple* in its name: SIMPLE IRA. Be warned, however, any resemblance to simplicity stops there. The subsections of the IRC that govern retirement accounts include rules, restrictions, limits, definitions, and reporting requirements as complex and confusing as any other sections of the code. The pragmatic application of these various plans is to treat individual taxpayers differently, often drastically so, even if they have the same level of income.

How you earn your money, where you work, for whom you or your spouse work—all can have a significant impact on how much you can contribute toward your retirement with favorable tax treatment. Additionally, major differences exist regarding how and when you can use the money you have set aside for retirement, depending on the type of retirement plan you have used.

If the assertions made in this last paragraph are true, it may trigger an idea in your mind that the code is not fair. It isn't.

Retirement planning is important, make no mistake. Whether one agrees that saving for retirement should or should not receive favorable tax treatment, it seems to me that, under the concept of "equal treatment under the law," every American should be given the same options and same tax treatment for retirement investments. I am not implying that the federal government should mandate what an employer provides for its employees, although that seems to be the current political trend.

Section IV – Fool's Gold In Our Golden Years

What I am suggesting is this: if an employee can contribute X (insert your own desired number) to a 401(k) plan, then another taxpayer should be able to contribute that same amount to an IRA, or to any other qualified retirement plan—or vice-versa—at least as far as any special tax treatment is concerned. Although allowable contributions to any qualified plan are treated the same, the difference in what is allowable, based on employment, is bothersome.

One argument frequently raised is that Social Security somehow mitigates any disparity in the financial impact on American families under qualified plan provisions of the IRC. But if ever a time existed that Americans could realistically rely on Social Security for a financially viable retirement, that time has come and gone.

Today, other savings plans must be put in place. The idea of retiring with some measure of economic security is a good one. Taking steps to achieve this goal might even be something that the government should encourage. But to the extent it encourages such behavior with a tax incentive, that incentive should be equally available to all taxpayers.

Finally, there needs to be some assurance that retirement plans that are in force today, under tax laws as they now exist, will not be adversely affected by future changes to the tax law, such as taxing future distributions that are currently not subject to tax (taxing Roth IRA distributions is one example) or modifying other plan provisions. Retirement for many Americans comes with enough uncertainty without Congress playing with its tinkertoys.

The following chapters detail the different plans mandated by the IRC and the tax treatment of various retirement benefits. I also offer a dramatic comparison of taxpayers earning the same

The F-Word

income, and the drastically different impact on those taxpayers as a result of the preferential tax treatment of retirement planning.

Shall we retire to the neighborhood bar and grill?

Chapter 14

Social (In)Security

> We have tried to frame a law which will give some
> measure of protection
> to the average citizen and to his family against…
> poverty-ridden old age.
> President Franklin D. Roosevelt
>
> I have today signed [legislation which]…constitutes
> a major breakthrough for older Americans, for it
> says at last that inflation-proof Social
> Security benefits
> are theirs as a matter of right.
> President Richard Nixon
>
> Social Security…represents our commitment as a
> society to the belief that workers should not live in
> dread that…old age could leave them
> or their families destitute.
> President Jimmy Carter

Republican and Democrat alike, presidents from both ends of the political spectrum stand second to none in their endorsement of the sacred trust we know as Social Security.

The F-Word

The three quotes attributed to different presidents concerning the protection afforded by Social Security express fine sentiments—each of them. The belief that our government is committed to the financial security of our elderly population is clearly affirmed by each of these presidents. However, I take exception to all three.

I have so many concerns about the three comments that it is hard to know where to begin to address them. Possibly the first is the whole idea of security. In the words of President Roosevelt, Social Security would provide protection against poverty-ridden old age. His hope notwithstanding, most experts—economists, social scientists, and political scientists—contend that Social Security alone is insufficient to meet the needs of our senior citizens. Simply, Social Security falls short of meeting the financial demands of the elderly. The "security" offered is an illusion.

To depend on Social Security alone is to live in poverty.

If that last statement is true, then one has to ask the question whether the benefits of providing merely a stopgap benefit, a subsidized lifeline to economic well-being, is worth the costs of the program as currently structured. Even more to the point, what is the actual benefit?

Initially, Social Security benefits were not subject to income tax. Taxing these payments began following passage of tax code amendments in 1983. One amendment mandated that up to half of a recipient's Social Security benefits could be added to taxable income if the taxpayer's modified adjusted gross income (MAGI) exceeded a specified threshold.

In 1993, that provision was changed yet again by legislation that raised the percentage of Social Security benefits subject to taxation from 50% to 85%. Again, the amount subject to tax was based on MAGI. As of this writing, the income threshold above which Social Security benefits are subject to tax is not indexed for inflation. If unchanged, it is only a matter of time before virtually everyone will be paying federal income tax on their benefits.

Taxing Social Security benefits raises another important consideration: fairness. Assume that a middle-class wage earner elects to begin saving for retirement by opening a Roth IRA. When this worker retires and begins taking distributions from that Roth IRA, those distributions are not subject to tax, regardless of income level. The reason is that the money invested in the Roth IRA was contributed with after-tax dollars. Said differently, that worker initially paid income tax on his full income and then set aside after-tax dollars for retirement. Logically, therefore, when he begins to draw on those funds, they should not be taxed again.

But isn't that same set of circumstances true for an elderly taxpayer who relies on Social Security in addition to any other income? The last time I checked, withheld Social Security tax is not deducted from gross income to determine taxable income. In effect, those who have only climbed up a few rungs of the socioeconomic ladder and who do not have sufficient discretionary income to set aside additional funds for retirement are potentially subject to income tax on their Social Security benefits—retirement income derived from income on which they have already paid income tax.

Purists may argue that this scenario is no different than that of the middle-class wage earner referenced earlier. While he will not pay tax on his Roth IRA distributions, should MAGI exceed the threshold, he will pay tax on any Social Security benefits he receives. I think the argument is disingenuous.

As noted, Social Security is insufficient to the task. As a result, retirees are faced with a Morton's Fork choice. They must earn additional income or choose to live a substandard lifestyle. Should older taxpayers elect to continue to work, however, it is possible they will have to pay income tax on their Social Security benefits. Yet our middle-class retiree can receive Social Security benefits and distributions from the Roth IRA and possibly pay tax on neither. One other recent change makes this difference even more insidious.

Keep in mind that the Supreme Court has ruled that there is no limit to the changes Congress can enact regarding Social Security. Remember that Congress has increased the full retirement age and may do so again and again. The ruling of the court demands that one other recent modification—the repayment provision of Social Security benefits—should be examined.

If an individual needs Social Security in addition to any earned income and applies for benefits before reaching full retirement age, part of the benefit received may be required to be returned—given back to the government. The rules governing that repayment, like everything else about our tax code, are complex and confusing.

If a senior citizen makes this election, four things happen. The first is that the amount of the monthly benefit is reduced. Second, despite the consensus that Social Security is often not enough on which to live comfortably, should this individual elect to keep working and should earned income exceed the earnings threshold, half of the excess benefit must be returned. Third, he must pay Social Security taxes on earned income. Fourth, to add insult to injury, if his MAGI exceeds a defined threshold, up to eighty-five percent of his remaining Social Security benefit may also be subject to income tax.

Section IV – Fool's Gold In Our Golden Years

The earned income threshold is birth-year dependent. Assume a $15,480 threshold is applicable. If an unmarried beneficiary receives $1,000 a month in Social Security and earns an additional $20,000 in wage income, he would be required to repay $2,260 (half of the amount that earned income exceeds the threshold) of the Social Security benefit he received. This is the equivalent of two and a quarter months of the Social Security benefit received.

This just does not make any sense. A senior citizen begins taking Social Security while continuing to work because that income—$32,000—was necessary. But, after income tax and Social Security tax on wages, and income tax on part of the Social Security benefits and the payback of part of the Social Security received, net income approximates $27,097. For those keeping score, if you consider the wages earned as marginal income, this taxpayer incurs an effective marginal rate of 25%. That rate typically does not apply until income reaches $72,500.

To put this in a nutshell, if you work—in other words if you have earned income—the IRC imposes a ceiling on your earnings, above which you are required to give back half of your excess Social Security benefit. But no such limit exists for unearned income. If a person decides to retire at age sixty-two, he or she can begin drawing Social Security and take distributions from available retirement accounts, and earn tens of thousands in passive income, all without the need to give back anything.

On a related note, clients often ask which plan is better, a Roth IRA or a traditional IRA? Assuming all else is equal, without blinking I always answer "traditional." Asked why, I respond that I can calculate the tax benefit of the contribution to a traditional IRA under the tax code today. I further comment that I have no way of knowing the future benefit, real or perceived, of establishing a Roth IRA. Generally my clients look at me askance, assuring me that the benefit is that distributions taken when they retire would not be taxable. Shrewdly I inquire, "How do you know?"

They typically answer, "That's what the tax code says." With an amazed look, I continue to press the point. On nicer days, I try not to laugh. On other days, with my belly hurting from the guffaws, I ask how they know what the tax law will read in five or ten years, no less in thirty. When I am told that Congress couldn't change the taxability of those distributions, I point out the changes to the tax assessed against Social Security benefits.

America Embarks on a Social Welfare Journey

Social Security retirement benefits, as we currently know them, were ushered in by the Social Security Act, signed by President Roosevelt on August 14, 1935.

Returning to the quotes printed at the start of this chapter, President Roosevelt said the law would give some measure of financial protection. If we are to assume that workers earn this benefit by virtue of a separate, special tax, then the law is not *giving* them anything. More to the point, the law makes them do something. Specifically, workers are required to contribute to a general government retirement fund.

President Nixon affirmed that he had taken measures to ensure Americans retain inflation-proof Social Security benefits. To that I say, "So what?" Yes, absent such protection, the real value of such benefits may be effectively reduced by inflation. Again I ask, "So what?" The more important question, once again assuming workers have paid for this benefit—as opposed to receiving some form

Section IV – Fool's Gold In Our Golden Years

of welfare—is whether they received a reasonable return on this government mandated retirement savings.

Finally, President Carter assured us that our Social Security program somehow demonstrates a societal commitment to our aged citizens, that they need not fear poverty. His comment, indeed the entire argument about Social Security, revolves around the question of whether benefits are somehow "earned." Is it true, as Roosevelt stated that workers have a "legal, moral and political" right to receive such benefits? Or are such benefits actually welfare payments?

Whether one agrees that Social Security is a valuable program, with demonstrated benefits to all Americans, asserting that the program demonstrates society's commitment seems to argue that it is a welfare program.

This question is further clouded by the Supreme Court ruling in *Flemming v. Nestor* (1960), cited later. That ruling states with certainty that Social Security benefits are not earned and workers do not have an absolute right to future payments.

I do not have the space to put forth a complete argument to make the point, but I will make a general observation. Social Security is about more than simply forcing workers to save for retirement or demonstrating our commitment to our elderly. Truth is, the government is taking tax funds and using them for a designated purpose. Have we ever taken time to think about the real implications of Social Security taxes? Who really benefits and who really pays?

It seems to me that any money paid by a worker, ostensibly set aside in trust, in an account for that specific worker, should in fact carry with it a right of receipt for that worker. If you deposit money in a bank, it is yours to withdraw. Once you have withdrawn all of it, the bank has no further responsibility to give you any additional funds. If you die, any remaining funds are given to your heirs. Not so with Social Security.

Leaving aside the insignificant death benefit paid to the family of a deceased worker, if a worker dies before receiving the future value of the full amount contributed, that money is just lost. The impact to the taxpayer is no different than that of any other tax paid. Conversely, if benefits continue to be paid, even if a person outlives the actuarial basis of his contributions, then the benefit is not earned, it is provided by others. It seems difficult to equate that dichotomy with other savings or investments made by that same worker with personal funds.

This apparent conflict once again begs the question: Are Social Security benefits actually earned by a worker for retirement, or are they just an extension of social welfare?

The fact that workers contribute to funding for Social Security through a dedicated payroll tax theoretically establishes a unique connection between those tax payments and future benefits. More so than federal income tax, payroll taxes can be said to establish rights to certain government services. This right is often expressed by the idea that Social Security benefits are an entitlement.

True enough, perhaps, in a moral and political sense, as Roosevelt originally intended, but like all federal programs, Congress can change eligibility rules. It has done so many times over the years. The rules can be more generous, or they can be more restrictive. Benefits granted at one time can be withdrawn. Wages taxed at one point can be exempted in the future or vice versa.

Throughout the program's history, workers have assumed that payment of FICA taxes entitles them to a benefit in a legal,

Section IV – Fool's Gold In Our Golden Years

contractual sense. In other words, if a person makes FICA contributions, Congress cannot change the rules in such a way that deprives a future benefit. Under this reasoning, if benefits could be changed at all, such benefits could only be increased, never decreased.

Congress clearly had no such limitation in mind when crafting the law. Section 1104 of the 1935 act, entitled Reservation of Power, specifically reads: "The right to alter, amend, or repeal any provision of this Act is hereby reserved to the Congress." Congress's unlimited authority to amend this law, even if such amendment serves to take away benefits, has been upheld by the Supreme Court.

Under a 1954 law, Social Security benefits were denied to persons who were deported for, among other things, being a member of the Communist party. Accordingly, having been a member of the Communist party, Nestor's benefits were terminated. He appealed the termination, arguing that promised Social Security benefits were a contract and that Congress could not renege on that contract. In its ruling, the court rejected this argument and established the principle that entitlement to Social Security is not a contractual right.

Few Americans are aware that the Supreme Court has held that benefits are not guaranteed. Congress has the ability to amend those benefits any way it chooses. In *Flemming*, the Supreme Court held that workers were not entitled to benefits, even though the appellant had contributed to the program for nineteen years and was already receiving benefits.

The court went on to state that depriving a worker of any benefits would not violate due process and that Social Security benefits were not analogous to a contractual annuity. But, most importantly, the

The F-Word

court reaffirmed the ability of Congress to essentially do whatever it wanted with respect to Social Security. The court's statement is excerpted here.

> To engraft upon the Social Security system a concept of "accrued property right" would deprive it of the flexibility and boldness in adjustment to ever-changing conditions which it demands and which Congress probably had in mind when it expressly reserved the right to alter, amend or repeal any provision of the act.

While the denial or termination of benefits is rare, a number of changes to the Social Security law make the actual value of such benefits less beneficial. Although the amount of the benefit has increased over the years due to changes to the formula as well as automatic cost-of-living increases, increased benefit payments come with hidden costs: taxation of benefits, give-back requirements, and higher payroll tax rates.

Make no mistake. Although there are valid arguments specifically for and against the current Social Security methodology, I am not denouncing a commitment by our country to set aside tax dollars to make some minimum level of income available to retired elderly citizens. I just do not understand the love affair, the fatal attraction that we have with a separate Social Security tax.

Here is why.

> First, few people make the case that a retiree can have any meaningful standard of living if Social Security is the sole source of income.

Section IV – Fool's Gold In Our Golden Years

> Second, most agree that a tax assessed on the first dollar earned and limited by a wage ceiling constitutes a regressive tax.
>
> Third, the Social Security Trust Fund, because of legal restrictions, has historically produced a significantly lower rate of return than almost any other reasonable investment.
>
> Fourth, benefits are almost meaningless to the wealthiest citizens of our country.
>
> Fifth, the earned income tax credit relieves many families on the lowest end of the socioeconomic ladder from paying either income or payroll taxes.

In reality, the cost and benefits of Social Security are largely immaterial to the very wealthy. They are simply unaffected by Social Security taxes or benefits. Conversely, the poorest among us effectively pay neither income nor Social Security taxes. However, given the absence of any vesting, coupled with the fact that the majority of Americans receive benefits only after retirement, unless actuarial tables reflect that low-income taxpayers outlive the rest of us, they also do not receive a significant benefit (considering only the old age and survivor benefits—not disability or Medicare).

Where does that leave us? The middle class—the silent majority, albeit a shrinking majority given our tax code—pays the highest percentage of income in payroll taxes but also receives the greatest benefit. On its face, this seems appropriate.

However, to be thorough, another question must be asked. What is the real return on the investment made by these middle-income families? How does the benefit they receive, for which it is argued they have paid, compare with any other benefit they might receive for the same investment? As stated before, Social Security is insufficient to meet their financial needs; hence, they must invest elsewhere. Why not allow them to invest the entire amount in investments of their own choosing?

We cannot, critics reply, because if workers do not save for retirement or earn sufficient income in their sunset years, they would become elderly wards of the state. Assuming the societal commitment expressed by President Carter, that is quite likely true. At least, if that is the argument, make it. Do not hide behind an earned right that in reality does not exist.

But let's take a hard look at this social benefit, which, according to most proponents, is paid for by the recipients. Let's compare this benefit with the after-tax value of benefits received under a private retirement plan, for example, a 401(k).

Consider a husband and wife, both college educated, and both employed for most of their adult lives as midlevel executives. They diligently saved and invested during their working years. They both paid Social Security and both contributed to 401(k) plans while they worked. When they reached the age of sixty-five, they converted their 401(k) accounts to annuities.

They each retired in 2013, and having attained the full retirement age of sixty-six, both applied for Social Security. The husband receives a monthly Social Security benefit of $1,911 while the wife receives $1,455. His annuity began paying a monthly benefit of $2,042 at age sixty-five. Her annuity will begin paying a monthly payment of $1,171 when she attains the age of seventy. Total income for 2013 approximated $64,896. They no longer have a mortgage, so this modest retirement income allows them to live

Section IV – Fool's Gold In Our Golden Years

comfortably. Total federal income tax assessed on this income is $868—a rate of 1.3%.

A second couple, neither of whom attended college, comprised a two-worker household for most of their married life. Like the first couple, they are both sixty-six years old. The husband lost his job with a local manufacturer several years earlier and has worked various jobs ever since. The wife is employed at a local lodging establishment where she has worked for many years. They were unable to save much for retirement on their modest incomes but were always able to pay their bills.

Both the husband and wife of our second couple applied for Social Security in 2013. The husband receives a monthly Social Security benefit of $1,024, and the wife receives a benefit of $972. This second couple, having worked just as hard as the first couple, yet at a lower wage, find themselves in a situation where they must continue to work in order to earn sufficient income over and above their Social Security benefit. It is difficult for an elderly couple to live on an annual fixed income approximating $24,000.

Thus, because Social Security benefits are not sufficient to provide them with a comfortable living, both continued working. The husband worked as a night watchman, earning wages of $16,882. Her wage income was reported as $17,744. Total annual income for 2013 approximated $58,578.

What does the Internal Revenue Code make of their situation? The result is that this couple pays income tax of $2,171, and Social Security taxes on their wages of $2,649. Total federal tax equals $4,820—an effective rate of 8.2%. The second couple pays six times the total federal tax on 10% less income. This stark difference is highlighted in table 17.

	First Couple	Second Couple
Gross Wages		34,626
Social Security Benefits [1]	40,392	23,952
Distributions From Retirement Accounts	24,504	0
Actual Income	64,896	58,578
Adjusted Gross Income (Form 1040) [2]	31,099	42,838
Standard Deduction	14,600	14,600
Personal Exemption	7,800	7,800
Taxable Income	8,699	20,438
Income Tax [3]	868	2,171
Payroll Tax	0	2,649
Total Federal Tax	868	4,820
Marginal Tax Rate	15%	15%
Effective Tax Rate	1%	8%

Table 17 - Comparison of the impact of the tax code on Social Security recipients, those who are fully retired and those who continue to work.

[1] Social Security benefits are based on a formula tied to income earned during a worker's life. FICA taxes paid on earned income produce the benefit.

[2] Adjusted Gross Income includes a percentage of Social Security benefits based on a formula. The first couple includes $6,595 while the second couple includes $8,212.

[3] The second couple reports $6,318 less income, receives $16,400 less Social Security, pays income tax on 34% of its benefits while the first couple only pays tax on 16% of its benefits. As a final insult, our working couple, with less income, pays two and one-half times the amount of income tax.

These issues are complex, mostly because our tax laws make them so. How much money a family needs to live is not complex. The need for the second couple to earn additional income is also not complex. Arguing that Social Security makes sense of this nonsense is, on its face, nonsensical.

Again, I want to be perfectly clear. I am not arguing against America's commitment to the elderly. Nor am I arguing that those who earned higher wages should not receive a higher benefit.

Section IV – Fool's Gold In Our Golden Years

What I am arguing is that the notion this program is sacred, that any change would bring about doomsday for America, is bunk. When I hear statements that such benefits are earned, that paying benefits constitutes some sacred trust, I want to hit something.

Just as with capital gains and with many other aspects of our tax code, the fact that we treat income differently, coupled with the regressive nature of payroll taxes, places our two couples in decidedly unequal positions.

The following statements attempt to explain Social Security in plain English.

- The federal government requires all working taxpayers to set aside money for retirement. Such savings are mandatory and are enforced through a payroll tax.
- The requirement to save applies to everyone with earned income, even those for whom such savings will be irrelevant and those who cannot really afford it.
- The requirement to contribute excludes those with only investment income.
- Social Security provides a modest level of income for retirees. Modest will become insufficient as the years pass.
- These taxes are set aside in a trust fund—a fund from which the government borrows.
- At present, the trust fund pays out more in benefits than it receives in contributions income. That shortfall will increase over time.
- Our highest court has ruled that a worker is not guaranteed any benefit for taxes withheld under the plan.

- The tax places the highest burden on the poorest; it provides a lower rate of return to the middle class than other savings programs; and it is irrelevant to the wealthiest.
- Benefits may be added, changed, modified, increased, or decreased as Congress deems appropriate.

If I understand Social Security correctly, workers must contribute into the system, by virtue of a mandatory tax, even if the amount paid might make a difference in their standard of living when paid. If a worker dies before retirement, that investment is lost. Said differently, workers contribute whether or not they ever receive any benefits. And should a worker actually receive any future benefits, that income may also be taxed. Is it any wonder that I keep looking over at the liquor cabinet?

And the Two Will Become One (Taxpayer)

One unintended consequence of the income tax treatment of Social Security benefits makes it difficult for older Americans to marry someone they meet and with whom they fall in love. If that is not completely true, at a minimum, the tax code exerts a financial penalty on such behavior. Maybe the two should not become one. Consider the following example.

A widow, sixty-six years old, receives Social Security benefits and a small pension. Total reported income is $35,500 (Social Security of $24,225 and pension of $11,275). On this income, she suffers no federal tax liability.

A sixty-eight year old gentleman, divorced, also receives Social Security benefits and takes a distribution from his IRA account. Total reported income is $38,311 (Social Security of $27,205 and distribution of $11,106). On this income, he also incurs no federal tax liability.

The two meet at the local senior citizens center. They discover they enjoy the same things, particularly each other's company. After a few months, they talk of the loneliness inherent in living alone. He asks if she would marry him. They wed on December 20, 2013.

In January, after they pay off the expense of their honeymoon cruise, they contact the agency that prepares tax returns at their senior center. When they meet with the representative, they learn that, unlike prior years, the tax man cometh. The IRS presents a bill for slightly less than $1,000. Same income—different tax bill!

Might want to rethink those wedding vows.

Not only are questions surrounding Social Security confoundingly complex, we cannot even have a rational discussion on the subject. If a politician dares to raise the issue, as President Reagan observed, a witch-hunt ensues with demagoguery the only rule of engagement. President Eisenhower opined, "Should any political party attempt to abolish Social Security…you would not hear of that party again in our political history."

The word *security* is defined in the *Oxford English Dictionary* as a state of "feeling safe, stable, and free from fear or anxiety." Every few years the subject of insolvency of the Social Security Trust Fund arises. Using any reasonable actuarial assumptions, few economists believe that the fund can meet its future needs under current law. The system requires significant reform.

I don't believe I have ever talked with any American who has not expressed concern about Social Security. Does that sound like freedom from fear or anxiety? What, if anything, about the discussion

The F-Word

of Social Security in this chapter does not lend itself to meaningful debate?

But rather than debating the issue, I could just be sociable and offer you a drink.

Chapter 15

Plethora of Plans

> *plethora* (n)—a very large amount or number; an amount that is much greater than what is necessary.
> Merriam-Webster Dictionary

> Take, for example, my Keogh Plan. If you're wondering what a Keogh Plan is, the technical answer is: Beats me.
> Dave Barry, Comedian

"Greater than what is necessary." Perhaps Webster should have added "see the Internal Revenue Code" to the definition of *plethora*.

The federal government believes retirement planning is so important that it partially underwrites taxpayers' efforts by providing a tax break to those who actually set aside some gold for their golden years. Most Americans are familiar with the terms *IRA* and *401(k)*, whether or not they have ever invested in such accounts, and *401(k)* is quite possibly the most recognized term within the Internal Revenue Code.

But how many of us are really familiar with the overabundance, this plethora, of qualified retirement plans? Under Congress's watchful eye and the protective auspices of our tax code, these plans have been fruitful and have multiplied past all understanding. Who among us truly comprehends the significant differences among them? More importantly, how many of us realize the favorable treatment afforded to one or another group of taxpayers, not only as a result of how much they earn and how much they elect to set aside, but by virtue of where they work?

Before one can understand the differences, it is important to understand some terms. Referring to retirement plans defined by the IRC, a "qualified" plan is an employer-sponsored plan established for the exclusive benefit of employees and their designated beneficiaries. The provisions necessary for a retirement plan to be qualified are enumerated within the IRC.

There are two basic types of qualified plans. Defined benefit plans are employer-sponsored retirement plans that provide designated future benefits based on several factors, including salary history and length of employment. Investment options and risk are entirely managed by the employer. Unlike earlier pension funds, under which benefits were tied to fund performance, defined benefit plans require an employer to fund any shortfall out of earnings. Simply, the amount of the future monthly benefit paid to eligible retirees is specified in the plan and may not be reduced.

Defined contribution plans are employer-sponsored retirement plans under which an employer sets aside a certain amount of money each year for the benefit of its employees. Unlike a defined benefit plan, the amount ultimately received by a retiree is dependent upon the return on the money invested in the plan. Typically, with certain restrictions, investment options are managed by the employee, and the risk of loss is borne by that same employee.

Section IV – Fool's Gold In Our Golden Years

The plethora of qualified employer-sponsored retirement plans provided for under the IRC is listed here.

401(k) is a defined contribution plan generally available to any private employer, defined in subsection 401(k) of the Internal Revenue Code, in which an employee can make pretax or after-tax contributions, depending on the options offered in the plan. Contributions are deposited into a 401(k) account managed by the employee. The employer may also contribute to the employee's account either through matching contributions or elective contributions such as profit sharing. SIMPLE and safe harbor 401(k) plans include mandatory employer contributions.

403(b) is a tax-sheltered annuity retirement plan offered by public education organizations, some nonprofit employers (limited to 501(c)(3) organizations), and cooperative hospital service organizations. An individual's 403(b) annuity can be obtained only under an employer's Tax-Sheltered Annuity (TSA) plan. Generally, these annuities are funded by elective deferrals made under salary reduction agreements and nonelective employer contributions.

457 deferred compensation plans are described in IRC section 457 and are available to certain state and local governments and nongovernmental tax-exempt entities. They can be established as eligible plans under IRC 457(b) or ineligible plans under IRC 457(f). One notable difference from other plans is that 457 plans allow participation by nonemployees—independent contractors.

The F-Word

Profit-sharing plans are yet one more employer-sponsored plan under the Internal Revenue Code that also permit contributions for retirement to be made with pretax dollars. Any contributions into the plan must come from the employer. Such contributions are completely discretionary, but an employer who makes such contributions must have a set formula for determining how the contributions are divided. Contributions are deposited into a separate account for each employee. One advantage of this plan is that it can be used in conjunction with other qualified plans.

Money purchase plans are employer-sponsored plans that, unlike profit-sharing plans, must include a defined contribution based on a specified percentage of income. Employer contributions are not discretionary. Like profit-sharing plans, a money purchase plan can be used in conjunction with other qualified plans.

It is easy to understand why Dave Barry was confused about a Keogh plan. This plan was named after the law that initially permitted an unincorporated business owner—sole proprietor—to establish a retirement plan. Because the IRC no longer distinguishes between incorporated and unincorporated employers for the purpose of establishing retirement plans, the term is seldom used anymore.

Even if all of this makes sense, be warned that the hits just keep on coming. Not only does the Internal Revenue Code regulate employer-sponsored plans, it also controls the ways that individuals can save for retirement, at least if taxpayers use savings methods that include a tax break. The **IRS** refers to these types of individual plans as "no muss–no fuss."

SECTION IV – FOOL'S GOLD IN OUR GOLDEN YEARS

The code provides for the creation and operation of two different types of individual retirement arrangements. Under the IRC, amounts in these plans are immediately vested and always controlled by the individual investor. The two plans listed here add to the plethora.

> **Traditional IRA** is a way to save for retirement that offers immediate tax advantages. Contributions made to a traditional IRA may be fully or partially deductible from your income, and earnings from a traditional IRA are not taxed. Distributions taken from the account at retirement are taxed as ordinary income.

> **Roth IRA** is a mirror image of a traditional IRA. Although subject to many of the same rules (such as allowable investments, contribution limits, and so forth) as a traditional IRA, a Roth IRA has two significant differences. As now provided in the IRC, contributions made to a Roth IRA are not tax deductible, but distributions taken at retirement are not subject to tax.

With respect to retirement options, we have to applaud Congress once more. It has left no stone unturned in its effort to make planning for retirement under our tax code as complex and confusing as possible. In addition to the employer-sponsored plans and individual retirement arrangements, the code allows employers to create and participate in a number of individual retirement options.

> **Payroll deduction IRA** is established by an employee with a financial institution. The employee authorizes the employer to make a payroll deduction for the IRA.

SARSEP is a Salary Deferral Simplified Employee Pension plan that existed prior to 1997. This plan permits employee contributions through salary reduction and has several restrictions. At least 50% of eligible employees must choose to make employee salary reduction contributions for the year. Also, the employer must not have more than twenty-five eligible employees at any time during the year.

SEP is a Simplified Employee Pension plan. This plan replaced the SARSEP, although certain SARSEPs are grandfathered, allowing them to continue. A SEP provides employers with a simplified method to make contributions toward their employees' retirement by allowing employers to contribute to a traditional IRA (SEP-IRA) established for employees.

SIMPLE IRA is a Savings Incentive Match Plan for Employees. Under a SIMPLE IRA, employees may choose to make salary reduction contributions. Whether or not an employee chooses to do so, an employer must make either a matching or nonelective contribution for all employees. All contributions are made directly to an IRA set up for each employee.

Forget for the moment whether the numbers, types, qualifications, and restrictions of retirement plans are needed. Let's assume that they are absolutely necessary and that we would be unable to save for our later years without this plethora of possibilities. But why can one taxpayer, one citizen of this country, save more than another and receive favorable tax benefits?

I believe how much a taxpayer can save for retirement and receive advantageous tax treatment should be the same across all plans.

Section IV – Fool's Gold In Our Golden Years

Can we say "equal treatment under the law"? Some would say that eliminating the differences resulting from this plethora is not necessary. My answer to that was expressed by Captain Algren in *The Last Samurai*, "What could be more necessary?"

Not only do permissible contribution amounts vary across separate plans, but the ability to play catch-up also fluctuates from plan to plan. In the tax reform bill passed in 2001, Congress added new catch-up contribution options to retirement plans. This provision was included out of concern that baby boomers hadn't been saving enough for retirement. As a result, taxpayers age fifty and over could make additional contributions to their retirement plan. These catch-up contributions are allowed in 401(k), 403(b), and 457 plans, as well as IRAs, but the rules differ among plans. Again, why is that?

Assume that a majority of Americans are in harmony about government involvement in individual retirement savings. Add to that a consensus of opinion that baby boomers have not saved enough. Finally, add universal agreement that those who have reached age fifty should be given a tax incentive to save more. Given these conditions, why restrict the amount that can be saved across different plans? Why allow one taxpayer to save an additional $5,500 while permitting another to save only an additional $1,000?

This catch-up provision is even more curious if you carefully examine the underlying premise—baby boomers have not saved enough for retirement. Employer plans that allow a higher catch-up contribution are those that already permit a higher normal contribution. Participants in a 401(k) plan can contribute up to 25% of their income, to a maximum of $17,500. The catch-up limit for taxpayers fortunate enough to participate in a 401(k) plan is $5,500. Those not covered by an employer plan, but who choose to contribute to an IRA, are limited to a standard contribution of $5,500. The catch-up limit for these taxpayers is $1,000.

Consider two different scenarios, disregarding changes made to contribution limits. Assume an employee who participates in a 401(k) plan had contributed $10,000 each year. Now assume that a second taxpayer had contributed the maximum allowable to his IRA, say $5,000 per year over the same years as the first taxpayer. The 401(k) plan participant has contributed twice as much, *yet* is allowed to contribute *five times* the amount allowed for the IRA participant in order to catch up. Am I missing something here? As I have asked before, "Who writes this stuff?"

The difference among various plans does not stop with contributions. Whether a distribution must be taken—and when and how much—also varies by plan. Whether a contributor to a retirement plan can borrow from that plan differs from one plan to the next. Whether early distributions are penalized also fluctuates among different plans. Again, why is that?

Table 18 shows a comparison of the major elements of each plan type applicable for the 2014 tax year. To make this even more confounding, the limits shown can be increased or reduced based on a number of other factors including term of service, income limits, and discriminatory testing within employer-sponsored plans. Employer contribution limits can vary based on whether the contribution is an elective matching contribution or nonelective contribution.

Any individual contribution, regardless of plan type, is limited to earned income. (Author's note: A working spouse can make a contribution to a nonworking spouse's IRA.) Limits for most plans must be aggregated, that is, contributions to multiple plans are subject to the annual single limit. Wait for it. You guessed it. There is an exception to this rule for contributions made to a 457 plan.

Section IV – Fool's Gold In Our Golden Years

Type of Plan	401(k)	403(b)	457	SARSEP	SEP	Simple IRA	Traditional IRA	ROTH IRA
Plan Sponsor	Employer	Employer	Employer	Employer	Employer	Employer	Individual	Individual
Contributions Deductible	Yes	Yes	Yes	Yes	Yes	Yes	Yes	No
Contribution Limit	17,500	17,500	17,500	17,500	-	12,000	5,500	5,500
Catch up Contribution Limit	5,500	5,500	35,000	5,500	-	2,500	1,000	1,000
Total EE/ER Contribution	57,500	57,500	35,000	65,000	52,000	62,500	N/A	N/A
Loans Permitted	Yes	Yes	Yes	No	No	No	No	No
Distributions Taxable	Yes	Yes	Yes	Yes	Yes	Yes	Yes	No
Hardship Distributions	Yes	Yes	Yes	No	No	No	No	No

Table 18 - Comparison of major plan features of different qualified retirement plans

Despite the different treatment among these plans, each plan includes a number of exceptions. Note the following language issued by the IRS regarding exceptions to 403(b) contribution limits.

> While the age 50 catch-up is subject to an annual limit, the 15-year catch-up is subject to a use test, lifetime limit and an annual limit. When both catch-up opportunities are available, the law requires deferrals exceeding the standard limit ($17,500 in 2014) to be first applied to the 15-year catch-up (to the extent permitted), and then to the age 50 catch-up.

If this is not confusing enough, yet one more curve ball must be thrown into this already convoluted mix. Contributions to an IRA may be lowered or eliminated if either spouse is covered by a retirement plan at work, based on the couple's adjusted gross income.

In an effort to thoroughly befuddle American taxpayers, rather than reducing the number of qualified plans, President Obama recently offered a proposal that would add yet one more qualified retirement plan, myRA. The president has stated that low-income taxpayers do not have sufficient reward for saving for retirement. Whether true or not, just make the existing code work for all taxpayers. Don't make a bad situation worse!

The F-Word

Since 2002, taxpayers who contribute to a retirement plan may also qualify for a federal tax credit. The Retirement Savings Contribution Credit—Saver's Credit, for short—is a tax credit intended to encourage low-income individuals to save for retirement. The credit can be taken for contributions to almost all qualified retirement plans, including 401(k), traditional IRA, Roth IRA, SEP-IRA, SIMPLE IRA, or 403(b) plans.

Prior to this, the federal government partially subsidized retirement savings by allowing the amount saved to be, in most cases, deducted from income, thereby lowering taxable income and, as a result, lowering the tax liability. The subsidy equaled the difference in the tax liability pre- and post contribution. Now, in addition to reducing taxable income and income tax, the actual tax liability can be offset by a credit.

Just as with most tax credits, eligibility for this credit depends on AGI and filing status. The credit is based on a percentage of the amount contributed, from 10% to 50%. The maximum credit amount is $2,000 for single filers and $4,000 for married filing jointly.

In chapter 5, Complexity or Insanity? I referred to the idea of gaming, defined as any action undertaken by a taxpayer to leverage the complexity, inconsistency, and contradictory nature of the tax code to lower tax liability or, in a perfect sense, actually produce a windfall. When the Saver's Credit was introduced in 2001, Congress's intent was to encourage saving for later years. However, some resourceful taxpayers found a use that was quite different.

Let the Games Begin

Almost immediately, with the assistance of creative tax preparers, taxpayers began gaming this provision. Some tax professionals advised taxpayers to contribute the maximum allowable amount

Section IV – Fool's Gold In Our Golden Years

to an individual retirement plan, file a return claiming the credit, then withdraw the amount originally contributed. What follows is an example of how this game might have been played.

A married taxpayer with no dependents filed a joint return for 2002. She and her husband each earned approximately $16,000. This couple elected to take their information to a tax preparation office to have their tax return prepared. Adjusted gross income reflected on the return totaled $31,750. After claiming the standard deduction and two personal exemptions, taxable income equaled $17,900 producing a tax liability of $2,089.

Assuming that a knowledgeable tax preparer would ask if they had made a contribution to an IRA, imagine a dialogue something like this:

> Tax Preparer: "Tell me, how much did either of you contribute to a retirement account?"
>
> Couple: "Oh, we couldn't afford that. We need everything we make just to get by."
>
> Tax Preparer: "Well, I have good news for you. The government will pay part of your contribution."
>
> Couple: "Thank you, but we can't possibly save anything. We are behind in our bills even with what we make."
>
> Tax Preparer: "Yes, but it won't cost you very much. As it stands, you have a total tax liability of $2,089. You had $2,375 withheld from your paychecks so you are getting a refund of $286. But if you each make a $1,500 contribution to an IRA, the government

The F-Word

will give half of that back to you. Your refund would increase from $286 to $2,138."

Couple: "Wow. We wish we could do that but we don't have the money. We might be able to come up with $400 or $500, but not $3,000."

Tax Preparer: "Look, I have an idea. I just need each of you to open an IRA account and make a deposit of $1,500 before April 15. As long as you promise to do that, I can prepare your return as if you made the deposit. I can file for a rapid refund so you would actually get the money before you made the deposit. Then, you could go back in a month or so and withdraw all of the money. You just have to wait until after April 15. You would end up with almost $2,000 more than you had to start with."

Couple: "No way! That's really awesome! Could you tell us exactly what we need to do? That extra money would really come in handy."

Tax Preparer: "Certainly. In fact, I have a good friend at a bank that manages IRA accounts. Let me give him a call."

Tax Preparer: (while dialing the phone) "But I need to tell you that your tax liability will be higher than it otherwise would be next year. The IRS will penalize you for withdrawing that contribution. But you are still better off. You are getting an extra $2,000 this year."

(Looking at each other, the couple smile and nod their heads.)

Section IV – Fool's Gold In Our Golden Years

> Tax Preparer: (talking into the handset) "Hello, Bill. Tom here. I have some clients with me right now…"

Seems crazy doesn't it? Remember the admonishment of the Taxpayer Advocate in her FY2005 report to Congress, "Our tax code creates opportunities for taxpayers to game the system or deliberately push the envelope. The IRS responds with increased enforcement actions which begin an endless cycle—complexity drives inadvertent error and fraud, which drive increased enforcement or new legislation, which drives additional complexity."

As an aside, you may recall my typical response when asked whether a traditional IRA or Roth IRA was better. I always responded "traditional." With the advent of the Saver's Credit in 2002, taxpayers who contribute to a Roth IRA also receive an immediate, identifiable benefit. In truth, for some low-income taxpayers, a Roth IRA actually became more beneficial.

In summary, taxpayers who are covered by an employer-sponsored plan can earn more and be taxed less than those not covered. They can set aside a greater sum for retirement, largely subsidized by a preferential tax treatment. Despite the fact that these taxpayers have been allowed to set aside more, in the event they determine that they have not saved enough, they are permitted a larger "catch-up" contribution. In the event of an emergency, these same taxpayers are often allowed to borrow against their account or, in a severe crisis, might even be able to take a hardship distribution. After all, as J. G. Wentworth is known to say, "It's your money; use it when you want to."

Conversely, taxpayers who are relegated to simple IRA plans (not to be confused with a SIMPLE IRA) are limited to a smaller contribution amount. In the event of an emergency, they cannot borrow against their account but must withdraw needed funds, incurring both income tax and a 10% penalty on the amount withdrawn. So much for it being their money.

Speaking of plethora, did you know that there are well over a hundred different brands of distilled corn whiskey recognized as bourbon? Right now, all I need is one.

Chapter 16

Same Peanut Butter on Different Bread

> Take free money…if your employer offers a
> matching contribution on a 401(k)…
> you must sign up and contribute enough to get the
> maximum company match each year.
> Think of it as a bonus.
> Suze Orman, Author and Entertainer

> Retirement-income inequality has grown in part
> because most 401(k) participants
> are required to contribute…in order to participate,
> whereas workers are automatically enrolled in
> defined-benefit pensions.
> Monique Morrissey, Economist

The term "retirement planning" seems clear enough. Whether a family believes it has sufficient resources to actually save for retirement, the idea is straightforward.

Let's assume that this effort is imperative and that all of us should set aside funds for retirement. One idea—same peanut butter for all of us. Advertisements aside, most individuals cannot tell one peanut spread from another.

The F-Word

But, as demonstrated in the previous chapter, the Internal Revenue Code provides a variety of plans and incentives for retirement saving. Within the IRC, there is no such thing as spreading the same peanut butter on the same bread. The code allows for everything from pumpernickel to whole wheat. We may not be able to tell Jif from Skippy, but most of us can tell the difference between rye and cornbread.

This chapter clearly exhibits that taxpayers who save for retirement are treated differently. This difference exists even if two taxpayers earn approximately the same income and take almost identical steps to save for retirement. To demonstrate, consider two workers who make about the same income. One is self-employed, and the other a W-2 employee.

Let's compare how each is treated if they save for retirement. Assume the employee does not work for a company that offers retirement plans. Any contribution made to a retirement must reduce disposable income. Because the other taxpayer is self-employed, by definition, any money contributed must also reduce net income. Given that our tax code promotes the idea of saving for retirement, America's commitment to "equal treatment under the law" must result in the same treatment. These two taxpayers can save the same amount and receive the same benefit, correct?

Not so fast. Hold your horses. Back the truck up, Chuck. How do you spell *assume?*

To keep it simple, let's call our sole proprietor Joe Plumber. After expenses, Joe reflects self-employment income for the year approximating $65,500. After self-employment taxes, Joe nets $55,225. Our wage earner, also a plumber, is Jack Plumber (no relation). Jack works for Beanstalk Enterprises and earns $60,000 a year including overtime pay. After payroll taxes, Jack nets $55,410. So far it seems that they earn about the same amount.

Section IV – Fool's Gold In Our Golden Years

Neither is married and both have paid off the mortgages on their homes; thus, neither itemizes expenses. Having had a good year, both are considering setting aside some money for retirement. Jack, fifty-two years old, learns that he can set aside $6,500 on a pretax basis. A rough calculation reflects that his income tax liability before making a contribution to an IRA would approximate $8,435. If he made the maximum contribution, his tax would be reduced to $6,810.

What does this really mean to Jack? He worked all year and earned a respectable income of $60,000. The tax code allows him to set aside $6,500 for retirement resulting in total payroll and income tax approximating $11,400. This leaves discretionary income of $42,100, after taxes and retirement savings, and a retirement account balance of $6,500. Looked at a different way, Jack received a federal subsidy of his retirement account in the amount of $1,625—the difference between his tax liability pre- and post contribution.

Let's look at Joe's situation. As a sole proprietor, he learned that he had a variety of retirement options available. Wanting to maximize his savings, he established a Savings Incentive Match Plan for Employees (SIMPLE IRA). Because he is fifty-one years old, Joe discovers that he can set aside his entire net earnings up to a maximum of $14,500. He also learned that his business can make a matching contribution up to 3%, for a total contribution of $16,337. Before establishing a retirement account, his total tax liability approached $17,903. What does this all mean for Joe?

He worked all year, earning $65,500. The tax code allows him to set aside over 20% of his income for retirement, resulting in total self-employment and income tax approximating $13,988. This leaves him discretionary income, after-tax and retirement savings, of $37,012 and a retirement account balance of $16,337. Is he less or more well-off than his colleague?

The F-Word

Joe made more money, but has $6,687 less discretionary income. Have you decided yet? Is his financial condition better or worse? Although he has less discretionary income, he has $16,337 in his retirement account, almost $10,000 more than Jack. Where did this difference come from? Solely by virtue of different treatment under the tax code, Joe, who effectively earned the same as Jack, receives a $3,915 retirement subsidy, $2,280 more than that received by Jack.

	Jack Plumber	Joe Plumber
Wage Income	$60,000	$0
Net Profit From Self-employment [1]	$0	$63,663
Net Income After FICA/SECA Taxes	$55,410	$54,408
Retirement Contribution	$6,500	$14,500
Matching Contribution	$0	$1,837
Adjusted Gross Income	$53,500	$46,372
Standard Deduction	$6,100	$6,100
Exemption	$3,900	$3,900
Taxable Income	$43,500	$36,372
Income Tax	$6,810	$4,733
Self-employment Tax	$0	$9,255
Payroll Taxes	$4,590	$0
Total Federal Tax	$11,400	$13,988
Net Disposable Income	$42,100	$35,175
Retirement Account Balance	$6,500	$16,337
Federal Subsidy	$1,625	$3,915

Table 19 - Impact of retirement preferences in the tax code on the 2013 federal tax liability for an employed taxpayer and a self-employed taxpayer.

[1] Net Income of $65.500 less matching retirement contribution of $1,837.

Section IV – Fool's Gold In Our Golden Years

Two men, approximately the same age, working in the same profession, earning approximately the same income, receive decidedly different benefits. One is enjoying a peanut spread on marbled rye. The other is trying to swallow his peanut butter on sourdough. Is this refrain beginning to sound familiar?

To continue the demonstrated differences among plans and the significant impact of these, compare the effect of our tax code on two other taxpayers, one of whom utilizes a traditional IRA and the other who participates in a 401(k) plan.

The traditional IRA was introduced with the Employee Retirement Income Security Act of 1974 (ERISA) and made popular with the Economic Recovery Tax Act of 1981. Contributions are generally, although not always, tax deductible. Additionally, all transactions and earnings within an IRA, other than early distributions, have no tax impact. Finally, with some exceptions, distributions taken at retirement are taxed as ordinary income.

A taxpayer cannot withdraw funds from an IRA, or use the funds in any way prior to the age of fifty-nine-and-a-half. On a separate note, can anyone tell me why the "half"? Regardless, if an early—premature—distribution is taken, the amount withdrawn is subject to a 10% penalty and must be included in taxable income. There are some limited exceptions to this rule, but by now you probably assumed that to be true.

Defined in subsection 401(k) of the Internal Revenue Code, a 401(k) plan is a tax-qualified, defined contribution account into which savings contributions are provided by, and sometimes matched by, an employer. The employee does not pay federal income tax on the amount of current income deferred into a 401(k) account on a pretax basis. Any employer contributions are also excluded from taxable income. The employee ultimately pays income tax on money withdrawn after retirement.

So far, an IRA and 401(k) plan sound alike, but they are not. They are definitely made by different bakers using different flour. The bread produced is decidedly different. Contribution limits, the ability to receive additional tax free compensation through employer matching, and restrictions on when and how contributions can be used prior to retirement vary greatly between these two plans. Let's examine these differences by taking a close look at two different families over an extended period of time.

To simplify the comparison, each taxpayer is married and files a joint return claiming the standard deduction. Both have two children whom they claimed as dependents until each moved away from home, the first in 1989 and the last in 1992.

The only significant difference between these two households is the employer for whom each spouse worked. One couple is composed of two wage earners, both of whom work for an employer who sponsors a 401(k) retirement plan. The second household also includes two working spouses, neither of whom works for a company with an established retirement plan. Both couples strive to save for retirement by saving as much as their family budget allows while getting favorable tax treatment under the IRC.

Table 20 illustrates the income, tax, and retirement savings for these two families from 1982 through 2012, a period of thirty years. Each household earns the same income, using the Internal Revenue Code definition as stated in Section 26, "except as otherwise provided in this subtitle gross income means all income from whatever source derived."

However, note that the same compensation results in different amounts reported on Form W-2 and on Form 1040: different

Section IV – Fool's Gold In Our Golden Years

total income, different adjusted gross income, and different taxable income. For consistency, each couple contributes an amount that produces approximately the same disposable income over the three decades.

	Mary and Joe [1]					Adam and Eve [2]				
Year	Total Wages	AGI	Taxable Income	Total Federal Taxes	Disposable Income	Total Wages	Adj. to Income [3]	AGI	Taxable Income	Total Federal Taxes	Disposable Income
1982	$20,193	$20,193	$12,793	$2,903	$17,290	$23,783	$3,500	$20,283	$12,883	$3,012	$17,270
1985	$23,840	$23,840	$16,130	$3,594	$20,245	$28,078	$4,000	$24,078	$16,368	$3,746	$20,331
1990	$29,931	$29,931	$18,331	$5,293	$24,638	$35,252	$4,000	$31,252	$19,652	$5,648	$25,604
1995	$34,458	$34,458	$22,908	$6,368	$28,090	$40,584	$4,000	$36,584	$25,034	$6,859	$29,725
2000	$42,587	$42,587	$29,637	$8,064	$34,523	$50,158	$4,000	$46,158	$33,208	$8,821	$37,337
2005	$46,830	$46,830	$30,430	$7,815	$39,015	$55,155	$9,000	$46,155	$29,755	$7,955	$38,200
2010	$49,750	$49,750	$31,050	$8,045	$41,705	$58,594	$11,000	$47,594	$28,894	$7,976	$39,618
2012	$52,173	$52,173	$32,673	$7,306	$44,867	$61,448	$12,000	$49,448	$29,948	$7,091	$42,357

Total Actual Compensation [4]	$1,363,727		Total Actual Compensation [4]	$1,363,727
Total Reported Wages	$1,157,881		Total Reported Wages	$1,363,727
Total Federal Taxes	$195,183		Total Federal Taxes	$204,477
Total Retirement Contributions	$205,845		Total Retirement Contributions	$182,000
Disposable Income	$962,698		Disposable Income	$977,250

Table 20 - Impact of retirement preferences in the tax code on two families over a thirty-year period. (Showing only beginning and ending years and every fifth year.)

[1] Mary and Joe participate in a 401(k) plan at work. The plan includes an employer match.
[2] Adam and Eve have set up an Individual Retirement Account.
[3] Contributions to an IRA are taken as a deduction to produce a lower adjusted gross income.
[4] Mary and Joe received beneficial value of $1,323,581, including deferred compensation and employer matching contributions. Adam and Eve received total wages of $1,363,727.

To summarize, both families actually received compensation of $1,363,000 over that thirty-year period. Mary and Joe end up with a balance in their 401(k) accounts totaling $551,000, while Adam and Eve were only able to accumulate $476,000. (Author's note: The balance assumes a return on investment tied to the increase in the Standard & Poor's index over that period.)

With a difference of $75,000 in their retirement accounts, it is fair to conclude that Adam and Eve must have realized a much higher disposable income. But that is not exactly true, although they did end up with $14,000 more than Mary and Joe. Taking these two numbers together creates a discrepancy. Part of that difference can be attributed to a difference in total tax liability. Adam and Eve incurred a total income and payroll tax liability over that period approximating $204,500. By comparison, Mary and Joe only paid a total of $195,000 in federal taxes.

The balance of the difference is due to another significant distinction between a 401(k) plan and an IRA—employer contributions. Mary and Joe enjoyed a total contribution over the period of $205,845. But they only contributed $129,000 of that amount out of their compensation. The balance—approximately $77,000—came from their employer. They did not report this amount as income and, as a result, paid neither income nor payroll taxes on this sum.

The same virtual income produced a higher tax burden on one couple of $10,000 and allowed the other couple to save $75,000 more toward retirement. They both saved for retirement—same peanut butter—but realized remarkably different results—different bread.

This last example compared two taxpayers with identical reported incomes. I assumed that each spouse had the same basic job and the market would determine the value of that labor. To compensate for the 401(k) benefit Mary and Joe received, allowing them to defer compensation and receive an employer-matching contribution, I grossed up the wages for Adam and Eve to end with that popular adage, equal pay for equal work. In this example, while the market offered comparable pay, our tax code shaped a quite different set of outcomes. (Author's note: I grossed up wages paid to Adam and Eve to equal the wages paid to Mary and Joe plus the matching contribution they received.)

Let's magnify the impact of this disparate treatment. Assume that both couples incur a health problem such that, even with excellent health insurance, both find that they need additional cash. For one reason or another, neither couple wants to take out a traditional bank loan. Mary and Joe discover that they can borrow

Section IV – Fool's Gold In Our Golden Years

from their 401(k) account. They are told that they can borrow half of the vested balance up to a maximum of $50,000.

Adam and Eve are told that they cannot borrow from their IRA. With no alternative, they are forced to withdraw funds. Both couples withdraw $40,000 from their retirement funds. Mary and Joe pay this amount back over six years through payroll deduction. The result of these actions is that Mary and Joe are now able to save $125,000 more toward retirement, while the tax burden carried by Adam and Eve has grown to be greater than their neighbors' by almost $22,000.

Table 21 summarizes the impact of the Internal Revenue Code on the tax impact of their use of their own savings, but taken from two types of retirement accounts. Both couples had to repay the funds. Mary and Joe paid themselves interest while Adam and Eve pay a penalty to the IRS and interest to a bank. Quite a disparity considering both taxpayers were using their own funds.

	Mary & Joe					Adam and Eve					
Year	Total Wages	AGI	Taxable Income	Total Federal Taxes	Disposable Income	Total Wages	Adj. to Income	AGI	Taxable Income [1]	Total Federal Taxes	Disposable Income
1982	$20,193	$20,193	$12,793	$2,903	$17,290	$23,783	$3,500	$20,283	$12,883	$3,012	$17,270
1985	$23,840	$23,840	$16,130	$3,594	$20,245	$28,078	$4,000	$24,078	$16,368	$3,746	$20,331
1990	$29,931	$29,931	$18,331	$5,293	$24,638	$35,252	$4,000	$31,252	$19,652	$5,648	$25,604
1995	$34,458	$34,458	$22,908	$6,368	$28,090	$40,584	$4,000	$36,584	$25,034	$6,859	$29,725
2000	$42,587	$42,587	$29,637	$8,064	$34,523	$50,158	$4,000	$86,158	$73,208	$8,821	$37,337
2005	$46,830	$46,830	$30,430	$7,815	$39,015	$55,155	$9,000	$46,155	$29,755	$7,955	$38,200
2010	$49,750	$49,750	$31,050	$8,045	$41,705	$58,594	$11,000	$47,594	$28,894	$7,976	$39,618
2012	$52,173	$52,173	$32,673	$7,306	$44,867	$61,448	$12,000	$49,448	$29,948	$7,091	$42,357

Total Actual Compensation		$1,363,727		Total Actual Compensation		$1,363,727
Total Reported Wages		$1,157,881		Total Reported Wages		$1,363,727
Total Federal Taxes		$195,183		Total Federal Taxes		$217,720
401(k) Account Balance at Dec. 2012 [2]		$567,141		IRA Balance at Dec. 2012 [2]		$441,707
Disposable Income		$962,698		Disposable Income		$977,250

Table 21 - The effect of retirement preferences in the tax code on two families over a thirty-year period. (Showing only beginning and ending years and every fifth year.) The impact of borrowing from a 401(k) is compared to withdrawing from an IRA.

[1] Taxable income for Adam and Eve includes the $40,000 withdrawn from their IRA in the year 2000.

[2] The 401(k) account balance for Mary and Joe benefited from interest they paid to themselves.

Let's take a look at one more stark contrast. For this illustration, Table 22 clearly demonstrates the uneven treatment of our tax code on two taxpayers with the same reported wages as reflected on Form W-2. However, one of these two taxpayers earned significantly more than the other under the same circumstances as before. Both are married and take the standard deduction. Both have two children that they claim until they move out of the house.

In this case, I compare the financial results realized by Adam and Eve with those of Isaac and Ruth. Isaac and Ruth work for an employer who provides a 401(k) plan with matching contributions. They both earn a significant salary so have always made a substantial contribution to their 401(k) accounts, ensuring they always get the largest employer-matching contribution possible.

Their W-2 forms reflect wages identical to that earned by Adam and Eve. After reviewing their family budget, they determine that they can also afford to contribute to an IRA and elect to do so. As a result of the contributions to individual retirement accounts, Isaac and Ruth report the same taxable income as Adam and Eve. A comparison of their financial results demonstrates a shocking dissimilarity. Adam and Eve are able to save the same $476,000 as before and paid total taxes of $204,500 also as shown earlier.

	Isaac and Ruth [1]					Adam and Eve [2]				
Year	Total Wages	Adj. to Income [3]	AGI	Taxable Income	Total Federal Taxes	Total Wages	Adj. to Income [3]	AGI	Taxable Income	Total Federal Taxes
1982	$23,783	$3,500	$20,283	$12,883	$3,012	$23,783	$3,500	$20,283	$12,883	$3,012
1985	$28,078	$4,000	$24,078	$16,368	$3,746	$28,078	$4,000	$24,078	$16,368	$3,746
1990	$35,252	$4,000	$31,252	$19,652	$5,648	$35,252	$4,000	$31,252	$19,652	$5,648
1995	$40,584	$4,000	$36,584	$25,034	$6,859	$40,584	$4,000	$36,584	$25,034	$6,859
2000	$50,158	$4,000	$46,158	$33,208	$8,821	$50,158	$4,000	$46,158	$33,208	$8,821
2005	$55,155	$9,000	$46,155	$29,755	$7,955	$55,155	$9,000	$46,155	$29,755	$7,955
2010	$58,594	$11,000	$47,594	$28,894	$7,976	$58,594	$11,000	$47,594	$28,894	$7,976
2011	$59,451	$11,500	$47,951	$28,951	$6,855	$59,451	$11,500	$47,951	$28,951	$6,855
2012	$61,448	$12,000	$49,448	$29,948	$7,091	$61,448	$12,000	$49,448	$29,948	$7,091
Total Actual Compensation 4			$1,842,318			Total Actual Compensation 4			$1,363,727	
Total Reported Wages			$1,363,727			Total Reported Wages			$1,363,727	
Total Federal Taxes			$204,477			Total Federal Taxes			$204,477	
Total Retirement Contributions			$660,591			Total Retirement Contributions			$182,000	
Retirement Account Balances at Dec. 2012			$1,283,736			IRA Balance at Dec. 2012 2			$476,326	

Table 22 - Impact of retirement preferences in the tax code on two families over a thirty-year period. (Showing only beginning and ending years and every fifth year.)

[1] Isaac and Ruth participate in a 401(k) plan at work that includes an employer match. They also contribute to an IRA.
[2] Adam and Eve contribute to an Individual Retirement Account.
[3] Contributions to an IRA are taken as a deduction to produce a lower adjusted gross income.
[4] Mary and Joe received beneficial value of $1,842,318, including deferred compensation and employer matching contributions. Adam and Eve received total wages of $1,363,727.

Section IV – Fool's Gold In Our Golden Years

But Isaac and Ruth have realized results that are far and away better. With the same W-2 income and the same contributions to their respective IRAs, they were able to set aside over $1.25 million dollars for retirement and pay the same tax as Adam and Eve. Although the two couples have the same disposable income, any similarity between the two stops there.

It is nearly impossible to present the discrepancies, disparities, complexity, and inequity of the Internal Revenue Code treatment of retirement planning. The bottom line: if we believe taxpayers should be subsidized in their effort to save for retirement, let's make the subsidy the same.

Our tax code offers shots, jiggers, and doubles on a wide choice of bourbon cocktails. Specials vary depending on which bar stool you choose and what bartender serves you.

Section V

The Whole Nine Yards

Overview

> The regulation of eating and drinking...is provided for in the power of taxation.
> Hon. Oliver Ellsworth, Chief Justice of the Supreme Court

> Excise: a hateful tax levied upon commodities and adjudged not by the common judges of property but wretches hired by those to whom excise is paid.
> Samuel Johnson, Writer and Scholar

> The necessity of preventing the danger of perpetual revenue which must of necessity subvert the liberty of any Country.
> George Mason, Founding Father

Besides federal income taxes, Americans pay many other assorted taxes. Some of these are obvious, and we understand their application. Many others are hidden. We may pay them directly, yet unknowingly, or we may pay them indirectly. These include federal, state, and local taxes.

The F-Word

I have discussed the largest federal tax other than income tax—payroll tax. The US government also assesses many other taxes. The most significant of these are estate taxes and corporate income taxes. But the list of federal taxes does not end with these. US taxes include a variety of excise and special use taxes, such as the Heavy Highway Vehicle Use Tax and the federal gas tax.

As of 2010, the federal government assessed forty-eight separate taxes on trade and commerce. While many of these could more properly be called ad valorem taxes or property taxes, they are generally referred to as excise taxes. Many of these taxes are assessed on transactions such as the manufacture and sale of alcohol and tobacco products, and receipts are included in the general fund. Others, including a tax on sales of automotive fuels, or on heavy vehicles, are deposited into designated trust funds (as an example, the Highway Trust Fund).

The total amount collected from these other taxes is not trivial. Estimates of federal tax receipts generated by excise and use taxes approximate $70 billion annually. Given the fact that so much of our tax code is centered on individual income taxes, it is unclear why we must also levy so many other different taxes.

However, levying use taxes on specific activities makes some sense. For example, taxes imposed on airline tickets and on aviation fuels are used for the Airport Trust Fund. In this and similar limited instances, such a tax appears to be fairly implemented because the tax is ultimately borne by the end user, in this case, an airline traveler.

The same is not true for all excise or use taxes. Consider taxes assessed on diesel fuels or taxes levied on heavy trucks. In theory, these taxes are paid by various freight companies. But these companies consider those taxes as a cost and set prices necessary to

Section V – The Whole Nine Yards

recover these costs. Their customers, wholesalers and retailers, then pay higher freight costs and pass that higher cost on to their customers. In the end, individuals buying shirts, washing machines, cans of tuna, or anything delivered by a freight carrier actually pay the full amount of the original taxes by paying a higher price. Again, the end user becomes the taxpayer.

This array of different taxes presents a number of challenges. First, it becomes difficult to assess the total tax burden faced by any individual taxpayer. Consider the earlier discussion on fairness. If total tax burden includes direct, indirect, and hidden taxes, the challenge of accurately assessing whether one component of that burden is fair or not becomes more complex.

Hidden taxes are the worst culprit in this mélange. Most business taxes are hidden because any tax levied on a business is actually and ultimately paid by someone other than the company. If the company passes on the cost, the consumer pays through higher prices. If the company cannot charge higher prices and tries to reduce other costs, employees frequently pay through lower wages. Finally, if the company is unable to recover the cost, either it closes its doors and we all pay, or shareholders pay with a lower return on their investment. Hidden business taxes include income tax, property tax, payroll tax, and various excise and use taxes.

There is no getting around the fact that everyone pays a multitude of hidden taxes. Renters pay property tax on the building they occupy. Even if every purchase made is exempt from sales tax, everyone who buys an item pays a hidden tax in the higher price necessarily paid to cover the corporate taxes incurred by the company that produced the product purchased. In fact, retail prices include all taxes paid by every company involved in the production, shipping, and sale of an item.

The F-Word

In addition to the array of taxes levied by the federal government, each state and local government also levies a multitude of taxes. The largest of these in terms of revenue and most prevalent in terms of use are income tax, property tax, and sales tax. Although individual income tax is a direct tax, most others, such as property taxes, result in an indirect tax—assessed on a landlord but passed on in the rent paid by the tenant.

Previously, I noted that many American families have been accused of not paying taxes due primarily to the impact of the earned income tax credit. But in America today, with a tax system so layered and intertwined, the only people who truly pay no tax are those who have absolutely no income. If someone has no income, by definition that person cannot pay any tax. In this case, I exclude government assistance payments from income. If a recipient pays tax with money received from government assistance, because the income derives from a source other than the taxpayer, that taxpayer does not actually "pay" the tax.

However, if an individual earns income, under our tax system, that person will pay tax, of one kind or another, either directly or indirectly. If he or she has wage income, at least payroll taxes would be paid. Although it is possible that a taxpayer pays neither income or payroll taxes because of an EITC refund, if this taxpayer buys anything, sales tax will be paid. While some goods and services are excluded from sales tax, all purchases are not exempt.

There can be no question that our society, our economy, and our culture are all more complex than when our founding fathers penned the Constitution. However, those learned men might look askance, if not aghast, at the current convoluted and layered mix of taxes.

Section V – The Whole Nine Yards

Most people, when faced with a complex situation, try to simplify their circumstances to reach an acceptable solution. Not so with Congress and our tax code.

Make mine simple—a glass, some ice and two fingers of bourbon.

Chapter 17

Playing Hide-and-Seek

> Despite all the attention given to income taxes...
> they are just a fraction
> of the total taxes Americans bear.
> In fact, personal income taxes
> represent much less than half
> (42%) of Americans' tax burden.
> Bryan Riley, Economist

> The government maintains the myth that
> employers pay half of
> Social Security and Medicare taxes because
> Americans would "go ape"
> if they knew the true tax burden these
> programs impose.
> Professor Walter Williams

> What the statute declares to be a requirement with
> a penalty [individual mandate],
> is instead an option subject to tax.
> Justices Scalia, Kennedy,
> Thomas, and Alito, dissenting

THE F-WORD

As of the editing of this book, public furor has arisen over the description used by the current administration when selling the Patient Protection and Affordable Care Act to Americans. In short, the administration originally denied that the individual mandate was a tax. According to one of the architects of the plan, Jonathan Gruber, "This bill was written in a tortured way to make sure CBO [Congressional Budget Office] did not score the mandate as taxes."

Yet the Supreme Court ruled that the penalty for failing to adhere to the mandate to buy insurance was constitutional precisely because it *was* a tax. This fact exposes what political scientists and economists have long known and taxpayers often fail to recognize. Taxes are frequently hidden by our government. Deliberately so!

Although this book is primarily focused on individual federal income tax, because of the overlapping, confusing nature of our tax code, this discussion must include some commentary on business taxes, including corporate income taxes. These taxes are hidden from prying eyes of individual Americans—those who actually pay the tax.

In order to play a game, one must have at least a basic understanding of the rules. Terms used by the coaches and referees must be defined. In the game of tax hide-and-seek, there are some words that must be understood.

First, *direct* and *indirect* are often used to describe the general nature of a tax. These two words were discussed in Chapter 3. While some disagreement exists over a precise meaning, in general, a direct tax is one assessed on something tangible, a person or property. Examples include a capitation tax (head tax or poll tax) assessed on a person, and property tax, assessed on real or

Section V – The Whole Nine Yards

personal property. The effect of a direct tax is that the entity on which the tax is assessed actually pays the tax.

Conversely, an indirect tax is typically assessed on an economic construct, a fabrication of economic activity. An example would be a tax levied on a sales transaction such as an excise tax or value added tax (VAT). The practical implication of an indirect tax is that it is assessed on one entity, collected and remitted to the government by that entity, but actually paid by a different entity.

An argument exists regarding whether an income tax is a direct or indirect tax. For the federal government, this distinction was important because of the constitutional requirement to "apportion" direct taxes. In *Springer*, the court rejected the plaintiff's argument that income tax was a direct tax because it was a tax on wages. In *Pollock*, the Supreme Court held that tax on income derived from real estate or personal property is a direct tax. But passage of the Sixteenth Amendment made moot the argument whether income taxes were a direct or indirect tax.

One other word is also used to describe various taxes and tax systems: *hidden*. It is used to describe a tax that is obscured from view, whether intentionally or simply as a result of its design and implementation. Sometimes just the amount is unknown, while in other instances both the existence and the amount are hidden from view.

Many of the taxes levied under the Internal Revenue Code are hidden or indirect or both. The hidden nature is often mandated by our government. Although little known, a federal excise tax was levied on all telecommunications service providers, designed to support universal access for high-cost service areas, including many rural areas. Carriers may pass this cost to consumers, which most do, and may refer to it is a Universal Service Fee or charge. But, by law, they may not call it a tax. Yet that is precisely what it is.

If the provisions of the code covering individual income taxes seemed unnecessarily complex, you should consider the complexity of the corporate income tax provisions. At least the IRS has made a formal acknowledgment of such complexity as it affects corporate taxpayers. Beginning with tax year 2010, Form 1120, used to report corporate income, has included the question, "Is the Corporation required to file Schedule UTP (Form 1120) Uncertain Tax Position Statement?" How have we allowed a major part of our tax code to become so complex that it contains language calling for an "uncertain position"?

Regardless, as our tax system is currently structured, corporations in the United States can incur any of the following federal taxes. This list is not intended to be all inclusive.

> **Corporate Income Tax**—Other than not-for-profit corporations, businesses are required to pay federal income tax on net income.
>
> **Payroll Tax**—A corporation must pay federal payroll taxes (Social Security and Medicare) on all wages paid up to the wage threshold.
>
> **Unemployment Tax**—All employers are required to pay federal unemployment tax on all wages paid up to the wage threshold.
>
> **Excise Tax**—A corporation may be required to pay federal excise taxes on the purchase or sale of specific items, or on the use of certain items such as heavy trucks.

Section V – The Whole Nine Yards

Corporations may also be subject to the following state taxes.

Corporate Income Tax—Depending on the state, a corporation may be required to pay state income taxes on its net income.

Franchise Tax—Depending on the state, a corporation may be required to pay state franchise taxes on its gross receipts or net assets.

Sales Tax—Depending on the state, a corporation may be required to pay state sales and use taxes on purchases not specifically exempted from such tax.

Unemployment Tax—Depending on the state, a corporation may be required to pay state unemployment taxes on all wages paid up to a wage threshold.

Excise Tax—A corporation may be required to pay state excise taxes on specified transactions.

To begin, I will defer discussion on corporate income taxes or franchise taxes. To a greater or lesser degree, all of the other taxes listed are either an indirect or hidden tax. If not completely hidden, each includes an element of hidden taxes. The reality is that each of those taxes is paid by the end users of the products or services supplied by the particular corporation. Those taxes are included in the costs incurred by the company and must be recovered through the price for which such goods and services are sold.

This statement must be accepted as axiomatic. A company cannot stay in business if the price for which it sells its products is insufficient to cover all of its costs, including taxes. I agree with the adage that businesses do not pay taxes, they collect them. However, I acknowledge that whether a business really pays any taxes is the subject of considerable disagreement.

Turning again to corporate income taxes, levying taxes on corporations rather than on individuals may seem appealing at first blush. But it's not that simple. When a government imposes income taxes on a corporation, the corporation will react. It will do so rationally to drive down its tax burden. Can we say "inversion"? And the truth is that none of the potential responses is favorable to the economy, to employees, or to customers.

While the maximum corporate tax rate is set at 35%, few corporations pay that rate. Just as with individual income tax, the numerous deductions, credits, exemptions, and other tax preferences result in a small percentage of companies paying the highest rate, with many companies paying no tax at all.

If corporate income tax is part of the economic environment, owners have to consider ways to increase pretax returns—lowering wages or raising prices, for example. Alternatively, they must compare the after-tax return with other forms of investment and choose the investment that offers the greatest total return—after tax.

Leaving aside whether corporate taxes are a hidden, indirect tax on consumers, it is generally accepted that corporations consider tax expense when making investment decisions. They stay or move, hire or fire, with an eye to the tax code. I think it is intuitive that this process cannot be good business and cannot be good for the overall economy.

This issue highlights inconsistent logic within our tax code. On one hand, those who have authored and approved our tax code over the past many decades have legislated preferential treatment of capital gains. The argument in support of such treatment is

Section V – The Whole Nine Yards

that it encourages investment. It seems self-evident that the bulk of intended investment is made in businesses, leading to an increase in jobs and growth of the economy. Fair enough.

But it also seems logical that corporations and corporate owners must consider a tax on profit as a cost, perhaps not a cost of doing business but as a cost of ownership. By inference, then, business income tax reduces the actual return, forcing the question whether our tax code encourages or discourages investment. Or does it just work at cross-purposes?

Owners charge their board and their executives with maximizing *return*—that is, return after taxes, not profit before taxes. Under a high, burdensome corporate tax code, those responsible for managing the company are obliged to ask what can be done to increase that return.

Answers are few.

A company can raise its prices if the market permits. If this approach is used, does it not follow that the consumer is actually paying the tax?

Alternatively, a company can cut other costs. Typically, the first cost that is examined is payroll. Costs are lowered either by cutting staff, lowering wages, converting full-time employment to part-time, or eliminating or reducing benefits. Who actually bears the tax burden in this scenario?

Finally, a company can close its doors entirely or move elsewhere. In this case, we all pay with lost jobs and a shrinking economy.

Answer this question! Who really pays taxes defined as employer Social Security taxes? Just like all business taxes, employer

The F-Word

FICA taxes are a hidden, indirect tax and are really paid by the owners through reduced profits, by employees through reduced wages, or by customers through higher prices. Yes, the employer calculates the tax and pays it over to the IRS, but the company does not truly pay the tax. Criticism that elimination of payroll taxes relieves employers from their responsibility is just not realistic.

Assume that a company realizes $10 million in gross receipts with ordinary and reasonable deductible expenses totaling $6,750,000 before any payroll costs. Imagine that same company pays $2,750,000 for wages. That would produce net income approximating $500,000 equal to 5% of sales. Not great but net income nonetheless.

Hold the phone. That payroll comes with a FICA price tag approaching $210,000, reducing net income to $290,000, less than 3%. Despite this result, the owners could elect to continue at a reduced profit. The effect of that decision is that the tax is paid by the owners. Realistically, however, the owners are not likely to make that decision. A company cannot survive at that profit level, at least not for long. Elimination of that option leaves the owners with three choices.

Just as before, owners could assume they would not be profitable and close the doors. The economic impact of that decision is not particularly desirable. Alternatively, they could investigate the market for their product(s) or service(s). If the market could support a higher price, the company could raise its prices. Assuming owners wanted to realize the same profit originally attained, prices must increase 2% to 3%. Perhaps not enough to be noticed by consumers, but if this choice were implemented, the tax would be paid by the consumer. Finally, the company could reduce wage costs. In order to realize the same profit, it would need to lower wages by 7.65%—the level of FICA tax. In this instance, the tax is paid by the employees.

Section V – The Whole Nine Yards

The rule book for this game of tax hide-and-seek is titled the Internal Revenue Code. Congress has decided to also include rules that allow corporate taxpayers to simultaneously play a game of tag—you're it. Companies can effectively pass along taxes paid to others.

Corporate taxpayers are besieged and beleaguered by taxes on every front, assessed by every level of government. But reality tells us that all of those taxes are ultimately paid by individual Americans—you and me—adding to the long list of taxes we already bear.

The number of taxes assessed on Americans, including fees, whether described as income, sales or property taxes, excise taxes, user fees, license fees, or other names, runs well over a hundred individual items.

Virtually every tax expert, every economist specializing in government finances, argues that hidden taxes are easier to assess and to increase than visible taxes. They also maintain that tax expenditures are an easier sell than direct subsidies because tax expenditures are sold as a tax reduction. When the government wants to subsidize an individual or activity, a direct subsidy is "spending" money. But, in reality, they are one and the same.

It has been said that the best place to hide is often in the open. Withholding, for example, has long been recognized as a way to hide a tax. How many of us examine our pay stub each payroll and make a mental calculation of the amount of tax taken out? Withheld taxes just become part of the background noise. Yes, they are visible under a strict interpretation of that word, but they are also well and deliberately hidden.

Although we all know about payroll taxes and withheld income taxes, openly displayed for all to see, they remain hidden in the confused and confusing structure of our tax system. Do we, as taxpayers, want to continue playing hide-and-seek?

How about a nice game of chess—perhaps while enjoying a bourbon on the rocks?

Chapter 18

Peeling Back the Onion

> She's like an onion, you have to peel her back one layer at a time.
> Sean Touhy, *The Blind Side*

> Use of the same kind of tax by two or more levels of government...becomes poor policy only when one level of government uses...in such a way that (a) the cumulative tax...does gross violence to an acceptable pattern of tax burden distribution.
> The Advisory Commission on Intergovernmental Relations

Peeling an onion is a common metaphor to describe digging through many layers to reach the core of something. You cannot just examine surface issues; you must look behind the façade to recognize a subject's true character. So it is with our tax structure.

The IRS, empowered by the Internal Revenue Code, is the white elephant at the federal level. But state and local governments also need revenue to run their affairs and they have myriad taxing options at their disposal. The two largest and most commonly used are income tax and a retail sales tax.

While most states assess an income tax, seven do not. Instead, these seven states get needed revenue from sales, property, and excise taxes. Two other states employ a limited income tax, assessing tax only on dividend and interest income. However, two states, Alaska and New Hampshire, have neither a state income tax nor statewide sales taxes. New Hampshire relies on relatively high property taxes, while Alaska depends on revenue from gas and oil. Finally, many states utilize a variety of corporate taxes, including corporate income taxes.

Aside from these commonly used taxes, states raise funds through a variety of excise taxes, including sin taxes such as a tax on alcohol and tobacco products. Every time you light up that smoke or enjoy an adult beverage, you are paying both a state and federal excise tax. User fees, including charges for vehicle registration and drivers' licenses, are common. Generally, residents must pay a license fee to hunt or to fish and to own a gun or a boat.

When you top off your gas tank, the state tops off its tax coffers. A smiling state tax collector is typically standing in the shadows because, with few exceptions, you pay a state gasoline tax at the fuel pump in addition to the federal gasoline tax.

Doubling Down

Although the United States, unlike many developed countries, does not have a national lottery—excluding multistate lotteries which resemble one, such as Powerball or Mega Millions—gambling has become a significant source of revenue for state governments. Yep, states have decided to compete with Caesars Palace and the Bellagio. In addition to the two multistate lottery behemoths, most states run lottery games restricted to their borders. But a government-run lottery is nothing if not an extraordinarily regressive, hidden tax.

Section V – The Whole Nine Yards

Lotto, Powerball, Mega Millions—all promise to make some lucky recipient the newest multimillionaire. The New York legislature authorizes the New York State Lottery to spend tens of thousands of dollars shouting across multiple media, "Hey, you never know." State governments now suggest, particularly to the least among us economically, "All it takes is a dollar and a dream." Advertisements plague the airways, barking out "Strike it super rich."

Once upon a time, the New York State Assembly asserted that "the lowest, meanest, worst form…[that] gambling takes in the city of New York, is what is known as policy playing." For the uninitiated, policy playing is a form of lottery. We should ask ourselves why we arrest gangsters for running a numbers game when we authorize our government to engage in identical activity.

These comments are not made by a modern Carrie Nation. I neither want nor intend to take an ax handle to all gaming tables. If you ask my closest friends, they would say that I have been known to make a wager. However, to the extent government holds sway in the private affairs of its citizens, it should encourage hard work, saving, and investment rather than gambling. Something is deeply troubling about government hinting, often with the loudest voice to those least able to afford gambling, "Somebody's gotta win, might as well be you."

As an aside, guess who is present at the award ceremony when that $100 million winning lottery ticket is redeemed? If you said the IRS and the State Department of Revenue, go to the head of the class. The government encourages gambling, keeps half of the take, distributes the remaining half, and then takes a large bite out of the amount paid to the winners.

Withheld taxes and hidden taxes are often described as out of sight, out of mind, making the tasks of levying, increasing, and collecting them much easier. A lottery is not just a hidden tax; it is better described as covert—kept out of our collective sight and hidden from our social consciousness.

Have you ever wondered who really pays this tax, and whether those paying can truly afford it? Do you care? If you read any reasonable study of lottery gambling, it may become embarrassingly and painfully obvious. Don't have time to read those academic tomes? No matter, just stand outside the nearest convenience store and observe for a few minutes.

Just as with many government endeavors, a lottery often works at cross-purposes with itself. As an example, state lotteries strive to make players habitual users. To be blunt, they try to get users addicted. Don't think so? Have you ever wondered why the various games change so frequently? It is likely that they are trying to avoid player boredom leading to disuse. But so what if a few hundred or even hundreds of thousands become addicted? Not to worry, the state spends some lottery dollars to support various gambling addiction treatment programs, even paying for billboards that provide a Gamblers Anonymous hotline.

I have an idea. Why not levy a tax on indoor tanning? If necessary, the government could spend some of that tax revenue to educate Americans about melanoma? Wait, isn't that already included in Obamacare? Have you ever observed a dog chasing its own tail?

The multitude of overlapping layers does not stop at the state level. Counties, cities, and towns also need money to constantly fill depleted government coffers. Currently, the number of different taxing authorities—school districts, utility districts, flood control districts—within the United States approximates ninety thousand agencies. Government agencies sprout as if fertilized and cultivated.

Section V – The Whole Nine Yards

Each has its own insatiable need for revenue. Most rely on sales and property taxes to meet their demands. Use fees of one sort or another are also employed. All of these taxes are simply layered on top of those already in place.

An average taxpayer does not know, cannot know, how much tax he is paying and to whom. The federal government begins with a payroll tax deducted from all wages, followed by income tax assessed on the full amount of the wages earned, plus an income tax levied on all other income. Individual states tax any transactions undertaken with that income, at two or more levels of government. Federal and state governments tax business entities with the understanding that they can pass that tax on to others. Local governments tax the property on which we live and work. States frequently tax the personal property we own.

Advocates have suggested a single tax at the federal level, or a flat tax rate. We should consider streamlining federal, state, and local taxes. We have to pay taxes. That much is certain. But we have to begin to make sense of our tax system. It starts with the Internal Revenue Code, but we must peel back the layers to get the full picture.

I don't know if the tears in my eyes are from peeling onions or from the realization of what our tax system is actually doing to me. I do know I can use a stiff drink.

Chapter 19

Just Say When

> Working Americans who believe in our country and
> who believe in our Constitution
> are saying, "Enough is enough!"
> Hon. John Boehner, Speaker, House of
> Representatives

> The only question as to whether it is worth living is
> whether you have had enough of it.
> Hon. Oliver Wendell Holmes, Associate Justice of
> the Supreme Court

> The art of taxation consists in so plucking the
> goose as to get the most feathers
> with the least hissing.
> Jean Baptiste Colbert, Controller General of
> Finances for Louis XIV

We all know the commonly used and generally understood gesture. A waitperson approaches with a pot of coffee, intending to refill your cup. As you make eye contact, you move your hand to cover your cup indicating you are done. You have had enough.

Often when a server or vendor is filling a container, a cup, a bag, a box, or a small child's hand, the action is accompanied by the directive, "Just say when!"

For Americans, it might be time to tell Congress "when."

What follows is an example of the tax burden borne by a typical, hardworking family. This family includes a two-worker household with two young children. Additionally, the couple owns rental property and a small business.

With a strong work ethic and a commitment to family, this couple does relatively well financially. Household income places them in the top quintile for 2013, though well below the median for that group.

The income reported on Form 1040 for 2013 is summarized in table 23. Just as with all households, the income earned by this couple and the economic actions taken with that income produce a tax liability. You may notice that they have not done so well with their investment portfolio. The capital loss reflected is a carry-over from the harsh economic downturn experienced in 2008 and 2009.

	Type of Income	**Amount**
Line 7	Wages, Salaries, Tips, etc.	$79,429
Line 8a	Taxable Interest	$3,885
Line 9a	Ordinary Dividends	$528
Line 13	Capital Gain or (Loss)	($3,000)
Line 17	Rental Real Estate, S Corporations, etc	$72,806
Line 22	Total Income	$153,648

Table 23 - Schedule of 2013 income reported on Form 1040.

Section V – The Whole Nine Yards

Table 24 illustrates the total tax liability incurred by this couple.

Tax Type	Amount
Federal Income Tax	$17,156
State Income Tax	$8,506
FICA Taxes	$7,568
Property Tax	$12,888
State Sales Tax	$8,177
Employer Payroll Tax	$6,853
Fuel Taxes	$1,373
Total Taxes	$62,521

Table 24 - Schedule of identifiable federal, state and local taxes paid by this family.

To better understand these numbers, let me point out the following.

Sales tax is relatively high as the couple purchased a vehicle in 2013. FICA taxes include tax paid on deferred income, not reported in wage income. Property taxes include amounts paid on their residence as well as their rental property. The taxpayer pays ordinary income tax on the profit generated by the business, due to its election as an S corporation. The employer payroll tax reflects Social Security and Medicare taxes paid by the business.

Just as with examples provided earlier in the book, it may be easy to conclude, "So what?" Clearly this family is doing well. They are making almost three times the median US household income.

But they are paying forty cents of every dollar earned in one or another form of tax. And the stark reality is that even this is not a complete picture.

When Mom or Dad goes to the store to buy groceries, including produce, it is possible, even likely, that the produce came from somewhere other than local farmers. If so, it would have been delivered by a freight carrier. That carrier paid federal and state fuel taxes. It also paid toll charges and license fees and federal tax for large vehicles. But all of that tax is ultimately paid by the end consumer, in this case, our family. All of those taxes are added to the other costs incurred to grow, prepare, and deliver that produce.

Although food products, other than prepared foods, are exempt from sales tax in most states, there are other taxes added by the grocer to the price paid for the produce. The grocer pays wages, subject to various payroll taxes. The store and land underneath are assessed property taxes. All of these taxes are also added to the cost of the produce.

Proponents of the Fair Tax, discussed in chapter 20, suggest that hidden taxes add as much as 23% to the cost of every retail item. Whether true or not, it is clear that a significant increase in retail costs results from taxes levied on businesses that are, in turn, added to the retail cost of everything.

When this family pays their utility bill and their telephone bill, they pay taxes. When they register their cars and renew their drivers' licenses, they pay taxes. When they pay insurance premiums, they pay a tax. Despite paying a high gasoline tax each time they fill their vehicle, to be used by the federal highway fund, should they drive one of the many interstate toll roads, they pay another tax.

Section V – The Whole Nine Yards

I believe it is fair to assert that, for every dollar earned by this couple, more than fifty cents ends up in government coffers, either directly or indirectly.

Our tax structure, anchored by the Internal Revenue Code, now includes so many interlocking layers of taxation that we pay taxes on taxes. Most Americans simply have no idea what their total tax burden is. They cannot know because many of the taxes they actually pay are hidden, indirect taxes. But the total tax paid is significant—and growing larger. And it is not growing equally among all taxpayers.

Would you like me to freshen up your drink or have you had enough?

Section VI

There Must Be a Better Way

Overview

> The nation should have a tax system that looks like someone designed it on purpose.
> William Simon, Secretary of the Treasury

> Unless we wish to hamper the people in their right to earn a living,
> we must have tax reform.
> President Calvin Coolidge

> We must simplify our tax system, make it more fair.
> President Ronald Reagan

History demonstrates that many different taxes can be levied. Taxes on economic factors other than income exist now and have been used previously, in the United States and in many other countries. And this multiplicity of taxes has been sufficient to enable governments to function for centuries.

These statements should dispel any argument that our government cannot raise needed revenue by imposing only a consumption tax or an income tax. A variety of factors determine the ability to raise sufficient revenues, not the least of which is how much government spends. Regardless, when developing a tax system, the basic questions remain the same: what gets taxed, who pays the tax, how much is the tax, and how is it collected?

This section considers alternatives to our existing federal income tax structure. It is assumed that a tax policy based solely on excise taxes, user fees, duties, or tariffs cannot produce sufficient revenue and thus must include a consumption tax or income tax or some combination of the two.

Although I limit the alternatives presented to only three, I recognize that other valid ideas may exist. Each of the three has merits and drawbacks, so I do not rule out any as a possibility. During the past ten or more years, two of the alternatives have been proposed in Congress and have received significant support. While the solution may be uncertain, we must select from one of these or develop and implement another. What is certain is that we cannot maintain the status quo.

The three specific alternatives presented are these:

- **Fair Tax**—This proposal suggests replacing all existing federal taxes—income, trust, estate, payroll, and gift taxes—with a consumption tax. As proposed, this would comprise a national sales tax.
- **Flat Tax**—This plan is based on retaining an individual income tax that employs a single tax rate for all taxpayers and eliminating or reducing other types of federal taxes.
- **Tax Do-Over**—Finally, I offer a plan that is fundamentally different than the current system, based solely on individual gross receipts. This plan

Section VI – There Must Be A Better Way

would also eliminate corporate and individual income taxes, trust, estate, payroll, and gift taxes.

Before investigating these alternatives, it is necessary to understand two tax models: consumption tax and income tax. If we are to consider a tax on *income* or *consumption*, we must agree on the definition of those two words. Taken literally, an income tax is levied on money that is made while a consumption tax is assessed on money actually spent.

Merriam-Webster defines *income* as "a gain or recurrent benefit usually measured in money that derives from capital or labor." Simply, total income should equal the value of all payments, goods, and services received, measured in money, earned by working or investing, whether spent (consumed) or held (saved or invested).

Merriam-Webster defines *consumption* as "the utilization of economic goods in the satisfaction of wants or in the process of production resulting chiefly in their destruction, deterioration, or transformation."

In economics, consumption is commonly defined as the use of goods and services by households. Mainstream economists largely consider consumption to be the final purpose of economic activity. Therefore, a consumption tax would tax money actually spent, whether that money came from income or savings.

Consumption taxes generally fall into one of three basic types: sales taxes, value added taxes (VAT), or excise taxes. Although they have similarities, the most notable being that the tax is assessed and collected at the time goods are transferred—sold—or a service is performed, they have important differences. In chapter 20, I only consider the Fair Tax (sales tax) and VAT.

The F-Word

In chapters 21 and 22, I describe two different tax systems based on an income tax. Chapter 21 examines a flat tax while chapter 22 describes a tax do-over, based on an individual gross receipts tax.

Before parsing the merits and flaws of any alternative, it must be acknowledged that proponents of any tax system are inclined to exaggerate perceived strengths of their proposal. On the other hand, they tend to obfuscate apparent strengths of any counter arguments or highlight weaknesses in those arguments. Someone less kind might suggest that opponents on either side of the debate lie. The reality of human nature is that everyone employs these practices. Have you read any personal profiles on the multitude of social media websites? Do you think any have been embellished?

During the 2008 Obama-McCain presidential election, an article titled "Scare Talk on Taxes" was written that underscores this tendency. Nothing pejorative about that title, I suppose, with no intent to sway the mind of the reader before presenting all of the facts.

In the article, the writer reasonably suggested, "There are legitimate arguments over what government's role should be…and how that tax burden should be allocated." He went on to write, "Given the rise in income inequality, we believe it is fairer than ever to ask those with more to pay more."

Whether one agrees or disagrees, those comments seem fair and reasonable. If that were the end of the writer's comments, that assessment might be correct. But the article had a political undercurrent and was a not-so-subtle attempt to discredit McCain's views and prior comments.

The article closed with the comment, "The toxic legacy of the arguments made by Mr. McCain and others is that it has become almost

Section VI – There Must Be A Better Way

impossible to have this discussion in a rational, fiscally responsible way." I guess not. If one or the other side characterizes arguments made by the other as "toxic," it is hard to visualize a rational discussion following.

It would be nice if we could just get to the truth. In the song "Honesty," Billy Joel sings, "Honesty is hardly ever heard, and mostly what I need from you." So true! Wouldn't it be refreshing if, just once, we heard the same truth about tax reform proposals from our elected officials that is required in a courtroom—the truth, the whole truth, and nothing but the truth?

My purpose is to present a reasonable, unbiased summary of consumption tax options as well as alternative income tax plans. While I believe that a complete overhaul, a do-over, of our tax code is needed, I acknowledge that many options exist, including the Fair Tax and flat tax, which have valid arguments for and against their implementation.

Who knows? Maybe we will all be pleasantly surprised one day and awaken to discover that our tax code has finally been modified so that it makes some sense. In 2012, H.R. 6169 was introduced in Congress as a "bill to provide for expedited consideration of a bill providing for comprehensive tax reform." Wait! What? Well, perhaps we can take heart that our elected representatives are taking steps to address this problem. At least Congress considered a bill to compel consideration of a bill.

Sarcasm aside, for the past several years, two measures have been repeatedly introduced in Congress advocating implementation of the flat tax or Fair Tax. One is H.R. 1040, designated as the Flat Tax Act. Its stated intention is "to amend the Internal Revenue Code of 1986 to provide taxpayers a flat tax alternative to the current income tax system."

The second is H.R. 25. Its most recent version was named the Fair Tax Act of 2013. In its preamble, the two objectives of the bill were stated: "Repeals the income tax, employment tax, and estate and gift tax. Imposes a national sales tax on the use or consumption in the United States of taxable property or services."

Neither of these proposals has moved beyond committee consideration. Despite this inaction, I remain unwavering in my view that we must do something, and I hold steadfast to my belief that we can.

In 2010, President Obama created a bipartisan commission charged with addressing our nation's fiscal challenges. That commission is commonly known as the Simpson-Bowles Commission, named after the two cochairmen. My view on the necessity of action echoes the conclusions stated in their final report.

In *The Moment of Truth—The Simpson-Bowles Report*, the commission asserted:

> The tax code is rife with inefficiencies, loopholes, incentives, tax earmarks, and baffling complexity. We need to lower tax rates, broaden the base, simplify the tax code, and bring down the deficit. We need to reform the corporate tax system to make America the best place to start and grow a business and create jobs.

The commission said fixing our tax code was a must and believed this could be accomplished. It held that the American people would accept no less. In the preamble to its final report, the commission wrote this (excerpted):

> Throughout our nation's history, Americans have found the courage to do right by our children's

Section VI – There Must Be A Better Way

> future. Deep down, every American knows we face a moment of truth once again. We cannot play games or put off hard choices any longer…families across the country have huddled around kitchen tables, making tough choices…They expect and deserve their leaders to do the same…Together, we have reached these unavoidable conclusions: The problem is real. The solution will be painful. There is no easy way out…it is long past time for America's leaders to put up or shut up. We believe that far from penalizing their leaders for making the tough choices, Americans will punish politicians for backing down.

In the Introduction, I parodied Morton's Fork. Facing a choice, particularly one with only hard or distasteful options, is often described using a fork analogy. My generation came of age with Johnny Carson, longtime host of *The Tonight Show*. He frequently used a skit that involved a map on which a piece of flatware was affixed. The map showed a winding road coming to split, literally depicting a fork in the road.

America is at that proverbial fork in the road regarding tax reform. We are running out of time. Failure to act now will result in a failure of this democracy.

The situation we now face was aptly described by Winston Churchill.

> [N]ow that it is thoroughly out of hand we apply too late the remedies which then might have effected a cure…Want of foresight, unwillingness to act when action would be simple and effective, lack of clear thinking, confusion of counsel until the emergency comes, until self-preservation strikes its jarring

gong—these are the features which constitute the endless repetition of history.

We do not know whether we have waited too long to fix a known problem. Clearly the repair would have been easier had it been addressed earlier, and the damage to our economy, to our culture, and to our freedom would have been less. Regardless, we can wait no longer.

This final section offers a summary overview of alternative tax systems. Pick one, or pick none and develop your own, but do something. I paraphrase one comment taken from the Simpson-Bowles report—what follows is not intended to provide all the answers but is offered as a starting point for a serious national conversation.

If you do not like any of the alternatives offered, the commission's suggestion for that was, "Follow what we call the Becerra Rule: Don't shoot down an idea without offering a better idea in its place."

I might offer one other suggestion. Why not pour yourself a stiff drink?

Chapter 20

Buy Now and Pay

> The sales tax seems to be more politically acceptable than the income tax.
> Professor Raymond C. Scheppach

> The last guy to push a VAT isn't working here anymore.
> Hon. Byron Dorgan, Senator

> I admit that if the point of taxation is progressivity or so-called fairness and redistribution, then my plan will not be your cup of tea.
> Hon. Richard Lugar, Senator

> It is a signal advantage of taxes on articles of consumption, that they contain in their own nature a security against excess.
> Alexander Hamilton, Founding Father

I definitely have to get out the whetstone for that tool in the shed because I have never understood the frequently used marketing slogan, "buy now and save." To me, it is more correctly stated as "buy now and spend." Regardless, it now looks as if some tax theorists have adopted this same approach. They argue in favor of a tax on purchases. Buy now—pay the tax—now!

In plain English, advocates suggest replacing income taxes with a tax on consumption. Excluding duties, excise taxes, and tariffs, two specific types of consumption taxes are used across the globe—sales tax and value added tax (VAT).

Sales tax is usually levied at the time a retail sale occurs—that is, the sale of a good or service to the ultimate end user. In effect, a sales tax is designed to be assessed only once in a product sales cycle.

Presently, most state and local governments within the United States rely on sales tax receipts as a primary source of revenue. While differences exist from one state to another, necessities such as food and medicines are often exempted from these taxes.

Unlike sales tax, VAT is levied at every point of exchange in the life cycle of a product. Double taxation is avoided because a business deducts the tax actually paid from its gross income as a cost of goods, just as it deducts the price paid for raw materials. Presently, Canada and most European countries rely on a VAT for a significant share of tax revenues.

Of the two common types of broadly used consumption taxes, the Fair Tax calls for the implementation of a national sales tax. This alternative has been the subject of a best-selling book, *The FairTax Book*, and the topic of numerous blogs and radio talk shows. Prior to publication of *The F-Word*, a feature film, *UnFair: The Movie*, was also released supporting the Fair Tax. My impression of the movie, however, is that it was more focused on eliminating the IRS than advocating tax reform.

Section VI – There Must Be A Better Way

Clearly, implementing the Fair Tax proposal would bring about a major shift from our current system, based primarily on income taxes, to one that would only tax consumption. Said differently, the United States would tax what everyone—Americans, immigrants, legal and illegal, and visitors to America—spends as opposed to what they earn.

Dubbed the Fair Tax, the name was not chosen at random. In an era of political spin, this name serves two purposes. First, it avoids the term "sales tax," which generally meets political and popular resistance due to the commonly held understanding that a sales tax is a regressive tax. Second, this name pejoratively asserts that this tax is *fair* and thus implies that all other taxes must be *unfair*. Like beauty, however, fairness is in the eye of the beholder, or, more pointedly in this matter, in the pocketbook of the taxpayer.

To summarize, the Fair Tax is proposed as a single-rate, national sales tax on all final consumption retail sales for both goods and services. The only proposed exception is that tuition for higher education would not be taxed. As proposed in Congress, the tax would be administered by the states, although administrative specifics are not well defined.

Many elected officials and average citizens argue in support of such a tax. It is clear, however, even to its proponents, that if this tax were simply added to the existing tax structure, implementation of this proposal would be extraordinarily regressive. It is difficult, if not impossible, to imagine what items could be excluded from this tax so that it would not place a higher tax burden on low- and middle-income families. Therefore, as a core component of this proposal, the Fair Tax would replace personal and corporate income taxes, as well as payroll, trust, estate, and gift taxes.

The F-Word

Because the Fair Tax would be the sole federal tax, opponents argue that it should be properly titled a "national sales tax" and, as such, would be too regressive. By using this argument, they try to focus the debate on the name rather than on the merits. Those opposed to this plan rightly recognize that a national sales tax, at least previously, has been politically unpopular. Before we kick this proposal to the curb, it merits serious consideration.

As stated previously, implementation of this proposal moves America away from a tax system based primarily on an income tax to one based solely on a consumption tax. In the interest of making an accurate comparison, I remind you that our income tax system already contains elements of a consumption tax.

As a household climbs up the income ladder, members begin to consume less of the income received. Money is saved and invested as well as consumed. The current tax code exempts much of the income that is not consumed from income tax. Think retirement accounts, medical savings accounts, educational savings accounts, and the like. The real impact on taxpayers using such accounts is that they are only paying income tax on approximate dollars they use for consumption.

Thus for lower-income households, our existing income tax code is a de facto consumption tax. It can be reasonably argued that such households are taxed threefold. Remember, we have to peel an onion to get to its true nature.

Although a primary argument against a sales tax is that it is regressive, many professionals recognize that our current system includes a number of provisions that have a regressive effect. For this discussion, I refer only to those households with earned income above the federal EITC threshold. For households below the EITC threshold, it is possible that they effectively pay neither federal

Section VI – There Must Be A Better Way

income taxes nor payroll taxes, although they may pay consumption taxes (sales tax).

Remember the definitions of income and consumption. For lower-income households, income generally means earned income, of which nearly every dollar is consumed. As a result, low-income taxpayers pay payroll taxes on their entire earnings; they pay income taxes on every dollar earned and, finally, they pay sales and excise taxes on most items purchased with what is left. One, two, three strikes, they're out.

Magnifying the regressive nature of the existing federal tax structure is the fact that Social Security tax is not assessed against income above the Social Security wage base—set at $117,000 for 2014. Said differently, a wage earner whose income falls below the threshold pays a higher percentage of income than wage earners who earn more than the threshold amount.

To counter arguments critical of the Fair Tax as overly regressive, advocates reply that the plan provides for payment of annual prebates. Each household would receive an advance tax rebate based on a preset amount—for example, the current poverty threshold. Therefore, households below a defined income level would effectively pay no federal tax. That system could be easily worked out. In fact, the idea of tax expenditures is already embedded in our present tax code. This concept would not be significantly different from the existing earned income tax credit.

It is not obvious how this prebate would function in actual practice. It is suggested that all individuals with a valid Social Security card would receive an advance prebate payment each month. How those payments would be distributed is less apparent.

In this respect, it is not clear whether this prebate constitutes a negative income tax, against which conservatives have long argued, suggesting it serves as a disincentive to work. I have not determined whether the proposed prebate would be provided to households that have no earned income. If it did, then it would operate similarly to a negative income tax.

Those on the right have generally supported the EITC because eligibility depends on working, on earning income. No less a conservative than President Reagan strongly supported the EITC as an incentive to work.

Advocates also argue that this plan would be fairer than an income tax because all members of society would be required to pay taxes. They claim that the current tax structure excludes significant income due to the amount of wages earned by illegal immigrants, often paid in cash. Under the Fair Tax, they suggest everyone would be required to pay tax when they purchase goods and services, regardless of source of income. Although true that these individuals would be compelled to pay tax, one of two other results might also occur.

Either (1) this tax system would enable the government to more easily identify illegal immigrants, or (2) illegal immigrants would pay the tax but would not file to receive a prebate—out of fear of identification. Because an undocumented immigrant would have to file some type of document to receive the prebate, that action might facilitate detection and possible deportation.

Because the majority of illegal immigrants most often live on the lowest rungs of the socioeconomic ladder, the second result would effectively place a higher tax burden—a regressive tax—on these individuals. Some proponents may view these two possibilities as unintended windfalls of the Fair Tax. I will leave it to you to determine if these are intended or unintended consequences.

Section VI – There Must Be A Better Way

This book is not meant as an analysis of our immigration policy. It is true that our immigration laws are broken—literally and figuratively—which is an apt description of the system and of the legal impact of those entering America illegally. Regardless, using the tax code to fix this problem is just one more example of how not to build a tax code.

Regardless, the argument that "all members of society would be required to pay taxes" doesn't hold up to close scrutiny. Households with income below the prebate threshold, whatever it may be, will, in effect, pay no Fair Tax.

Another benefit of the Fair Tax, as posited by its proponents, is a significant reduction in compliance costs, both on the government and on the taxpayer. In fact, the most vocal advocates suggest this proposal would eliminate the Internal Revenue Service. The logic is that the tax system would be administered by the states.

It is difficult for me to conclude that the creation of a separate division within the department of taxation in each of the fifty states would lead to a reduced cost on government—lower costs for the federal government, perhaps. However, I think a significant decline in compliance costs paid by taxpayers is a reasonable conclusion—a nontrivial benefit. Further, even if the Fair Tax is administered by the federal government, it is likely that compliance costs would be less than those currently borne by taxpayers and the government.

To the contrary, opposing voices say this system would be riddled with fraud and abuse. In fact, they suggest attempts to avoid paying this tax would create an entire black market for goods. However, remember the existing tax gap under our current structure. It is hard to imagine such a sizable gap existing under the Fair Tax.

The F-Word

It is reasonable to suggest that some abuse would exist just as it has always existed, regardless of the form of taxation. Sales tax can be subject to abuse as some buyers try to convince sellers that the purchase should be exempt from sales tax. Conversely, sellers often try to compel payment in cash, thereby avoiding the requirement to record the sale and as a result fail to collect the tax. And, as with any system, taxpayer attempts to avoid paying tax will require some type of administrative infrastructure to minimize revenue loss, to identify perpetrators, and to recover lost tax revenue.

Finally, proponents argue that a tax on consumption would, as a practical result, produce increased savings, thus adding to available capital for the economy as a whole. In principle, I accept this as a truism. I also accept as true that the lower one's income, the greater proportion one is compelled to use for consumption. Hence, even with the proposed prebate, this tax is necessarily regressive.

Advocates argue that tax revenue would increase because the tax base would be expanded, an assumption I accept as self-evident. Some who oppose the Fair Tax suggest that the government could not raise sufficient revenues under such a system. I reject that argument, indeed any argument that sufficient revenue could not be raised under any consumption or income tax system.

Throughout history, short of revolution, governments have always been able to raise necessary funds. Doing so simply requires the political will to add new taxes, raise tax rates, or expand the tax base. The corollary to that premise is that the same political will is necessary to back away from the feed trough, thereby lowering the demand for tax revenues.

Implementation of this plan is more a political question than an economic one. One only has to look at our current deficit to make

Section VI – There Must Be A Better Way

the case that a progressive marginal income tax system, combined with a regressive payroll tax system, is unable to raise sufficient revenue to meet our level of government spending.

Although the Fair Tax implements an entirely new federal tax, it is proposed to supplant, not add to, existing federal taxes. Nonetheless, I question both the tangible revenue effect of the Fair Tax and its impact on low- and middle-income taxpayers. Despite the prebate, is the Fair Tax regressive in principle? Would it add to the persistent budget shortfalls?

We have sufficient data to enable a reasonable estimate of the tax base under the Fair Tax. It is a simple measure to then develop a tax rate that collects sufficient revenues. The Fair Tax is proposed at a rate of 23% of the purchase price for all retail purchases of goods and services. Other than tuition payments, no purchase would be exempt.

Every family, regardless of income level, would receive a prebate. The amount received would equal the tax paid on spending, up to the poverty level, effectively excluding families below the poverty level from paying the tax. Those at the highest income levels would pay something less than 23% of their total income. The impact on middle-class families depends on individual circumstances.

More or Less

Using simple examples, let's examine some possible outcomes. For a household in the lowest income bracket, assuming they spent (consumed) all of their income, if total income multiplied by the Fair Tax rate resulted in an amount less than the prebate, they would in effect pay no tax. In fact, similar to households that now receive the refundable EITC, many of these households might incur a negative Fair Tax rate. In short, they might receive a

The F-Word

payment from the government larger than the tax paid. All other households in the lowest income bracket would incur a net tax burden equal to the total tax paid less the prebate.

What would the effect be on a household in the lower-middle-income bracket? For argument, say the annual prebate is set at $5,482. If an average family of four reports annual household income of $62,100, it is likely that substantially all income would be spent on consumption. Applying the 23% tax rate, this taxpayer would pay about $14,283 in Fair Tax. After deducting the prebate, the net tax liability equals $8,801, resulting in an effective tax rate of 14.2% compared to income. That seems reasonable.

Let's compare this result to our existing structure, excluding *all* tax preferences, credits, or deductions, other than the standard deduction and personal exemptions, which provide an exemption similar to that of the Fair Tax prebate. A family with income of $62,100 incurs a federal income tax bill of $4,256. Comparing apples to apples, if all income is from wages, this taxpayer also pays FICA tax of $4,590 for a total federal tax bill of $8,846. In effect, this taxpayer saves about $205 under the Fair Tax plan. Not much but any savings seems fair and reasonable at lower levels of income.

What happens to taxpayers on a higher rung of the income ladder? Let's assume double the income. Using the same assumptions and math produces the following result. With earned income totaling $124,200 per year, it is less likely this family would spend all income on consumption. It is probable that some percentage of income would be saved or invested, so let's assume the family saves 10% of its income, spending $112,100. At the 23% Fair Tax rate, total Fair Tax would be $25,709. After prebate, the tax paid equates to $20,228 for an effective tax rate approximating 16%. Again, this result seems rational and equitable.

Section VI – There Must Be A Better Way

Making the same comparison as before, using current income tax rates and including payroll taxes, the results are interesting. Again, allowing only the standard deduction and personal exemption allowances, this taxpayer incurs a federal income tax liability totaling $15,964. Assuming all income is wage income, payroll taxes would approximate $9,501. Adding the two, total current federal taxes are $25,465—$5,238 more than the Fair Tax. Additionally, if all of this income is wage income, the government also loses payroll taxes paid by the employer. Total lost revenue exceeds $14,000.

As an aside, if this taxpayer saves a higher percentage of income, savings would increase and the revenue lost would be even greater.

Both of the households used in these two examples realize a savings under the Fair Tax. Because they fall within middle-income levels, this might be a fair approach. But keep in mind, less tax revenue is realized from each household.

To complete the comparison, let's consider a household much higher up on the socioeconomic ladder, say, someone making $2 million a year. Let's suppose this family lives a luxurious lifestyle and only saves 15% of that income. For consistency, let's assume all income is from earnings. Under the Fair Tax plan, this taxpayer incurs a federal tax bill after prebate of $385,518, effectively paying 19% of his income in federal tax. Under current tax law, this taxpayer would pay combined federal taxes of $808,063—including the additional Medicare tax—including $734,815 in income tax and $57,498 in payroll tax, reflecting tax savings of $422,545.

Just as in the two previous examples, this household also realized a tax savings under Fair Tax. These three examples are summarized in table 25.

317

	Low-income Taxpayer		Middle-income Taxpayer		High-income Taxpayer	
	Fair Tax	Current Tax	Fair Tax	Current Tax	Fair Tax	Current Tax
Total Income	$62,100	$62,100	$124,200	$124,200	$2,000,000	$2,000,000
Taxable Income		$34,300		$96,400		$1,987,800
Income Tax		$4,256		$15,964		$734,815
Payroll Taxes		$4,751		$9,501		$57,498
Additional Medicare Tax		$0		$0		$15,750
Total Federal Tax		$9,007		$25,465		$808,063
Savings Rate	0%		10%		15%	
Fair Tax [1]	$14,283		$25,709		$391,000	
Prebate [2]	$5,482		$5,482		$5,482	
Net Fair Tax	$8,801		$20,228		$385,518	
Fair Tax Savings	$ 205		$ 5,238		$ 422,545	

Table 25 - Comparison of Fair Tax with total federal tax based on the 2013 Internal Revenue Code. Each taxpayer is married with two children, filing jointly, with two wage earners earning equal income.

[1] This table uses 23% as the Fair Tax Rate.

[2] The prebate uses the 2013 poverty threshold ($23,834) for a family of four published by the US Census Bureau.

In each of these examples, the effect of the Fair Tax on an individual taxpayer was explored. But what about the impact on businesses? Remember, the Fair Tax replaces corporate income and payroll taxes as well as individual income tax.

Let's compare taxes paid by a hypothetical company under Fair Tax with total tax paid under current tax laws. In 2013, our imaginary company had revenues of $6.1 million, producing net income of $306,000. Federal income tax on this profit approximated $97,500. Compensation paid to employees totaled $1.2 million, with an employer payroll tax liability of $81,000. The total amount paid in federal taxes was $178,500.

Under Fair Tax, this company pays neither payroll nor income taxes. Fair Tax would not be charged against business inputs (costs of goods sold), but the company would pay tax on any items purchased to be consumed by the business. These could include items such as fixed assets, office supplies, and the like. Assume the costs for those purchases came to $400,000 for the year. The Fair Tax

Section VI – There Must Be A Better Way

assessed on that amount equals $92,000. Am I mistaken or does this result in significant tax savings? This company possibly saves as much as $86,500.

I can go on, but you get the picture. For those taxpayers whose income falls under the prebate threshold, the impact of federal tax laws remains much the same as it is now. They effectively do not pay any federal taxes—income or payroll or Fair Tax. While it seems all taxpayers, business or individual, get a tax break under the Fair Tax, those at the very highest level of income get the largest break, at least in absolute dollars if not as a percentage of their income.

Why is that? The answer is simple. Our current tax structure, forgetting all preferences, deductions, credits, and capital gains treatment, provides for a maximum individual tax rate of 39.6% and a maximum corporate tax of 35%. To the contrary, the Fair Tax caps the tax rate at 23%, whether you earn and spend one dollar, a million dollars, or a hundred million dollars. Anyone who argues that the wealthiest would not receive the largest tax reduction is just not being totally honest.

Regardless of the impact on individual taxpayers, this approach raises more questions than it answers given the concern regarding budget deficits. With the tax savings depicted at all levels of household income, a logical conclusion is that the rate would have to be increased dramatically to raise required revenue. I am as much in favor of tax relief as the next person, but we have to begin balancing our budget, or at least pretend that we intend to.

Proponents argue that additional money would come from three factors. First, the plan would produce a reduction in compliance costs, such as the time and money spent in preparing and filing burdensome tax forms. Second, voluntary compliance would be significantly increased as all sales would be taxed. Finally, the tax base would be expanded because income previously unreported is generally consumed, hence would now be subject to tax, producing tax revenue. Essentially, those currently avoiding income tax by working in a cash economy would be added to the tax rolls.

I think each of these arguments is valid. Whether such efficiency savings, added to revenues derived from widening the tax base, are enough to offset the revenue lost as a result of the lower absolute tax paid by virtually all taxpayers is a critical question. I think not, but I will leave that debate to the economists.

Where Fair Art Thou?

Finally, let's assess the name "fair." As suggested, interpretation of what that word means under any tax code is likely in the eye—more likely wallet—of each taxpayer. Nonetheless, in order to have a reasonable discussion, we have to have a common point of reference—an agreed-upon definition.

One view might be that fairness requires every person to pay some federal tax. That does not happen now as families with earned income below the EITC threshold pay neither income nor payroll taxes. Nor, however, would everyone pay federal tax under the Fair Tax as currently proposed. Families whose income falls below the threshold used to calculate the prebate also would not pay any tax. Under this definition, even this tax is not fair.

A second opinion of what is fair might be that everyone pays the same percentage. If so, one is compelled to ask, "Percentage of what?" It is hard for me to use the word *fair* to describe a system under which a family of four, with a household income of $50,000, pays an additional 23% for the purchase of a loaf of bread, for clothes for the children, while a wealthy investor pays 23% for the

Section VI – There Must Be A Better Way

purchase of a 178-foot yacht. Yes, the price tag for that yacht would produce tax revenue in the millions, even tens of millions of dollars. But, remember, this wealthy sailor is likely paying something less than 23% of his total income in taxes. Over time he can continue to accumulate more and more wealth. It may even be likely that accumulation would accelerate.

A final interpretation of fairness could be that, as taxpayers move up the economic scale, they incur a higher tax bill in actual dollars. In truth, the Fair Tax, just as almost any income or consumption tax system, marginal, flat, or otherwise, produces that result. Those who make and spend more would pay a higher tax bill in actual dollars. Whether applying this criterion is the best way to determine whether the result is fair or not, I leave to you.

Restating my earlier conclusion, those on the lowest end realize little or no change while those on the highest end realize the greatest savings, both in actual dollars and as a percentage of income. A middle-income family may incur a higher or lower tax bill as a percentage of its income depending on circumstances and actual level of consumption.

I make one final point about the cost paid by an individual household for ordinary household goods. Advocates of the Fair Tax assert that the price we all pay today is higher than it has to be because of the embedded cost of business taxes—income, payroll, and others. I agree completely with that assertion. They further state that, under the Fair Tax, retail prices would drop by that amount. About that claim, I am less certain.

Those in support of the Fair Tax posit that the actual retail price paid for an item under a Fair Tax system, including the tax, would be essentially equivalent to the price paid today. Despite the fact that 23% would be added as a sales tax, they hold that retail prices would initially drop by that same amount. Although I agree with the basic premise, it is not clear to me that businesses would implement a one-to-one price reduction.

For more information on this plan, I suggest you read *The Fair Tax Book*, written by Neal Boortz and Congressman John Linder. As of the writing of *The F-Word*, the text of H.R. 2525, titled the Fair Tax Act of 1999, submitted by Congressman Linder on July 14, 1999, could be found at https://www.congress.gov/bill/106th-congress/house-bill/2525/text.

An alternative consumption tax, the value added tax (VAT), is currently in use in much of the rest of the developed world, including Canada and virtually every European country. However, this method has not gained a lot of traction in the United States. Adding a VAT has been suggested on a few occasions, most notably by Representative Paul Ryan in early versions of "Roadmap for America's Future," in which he proposed an 8.5% VAT, rebranded as a business consumption tax.

A VAT differs from a typical sales tax in that a VAT exists at each step of a product life cycle. Raw goods are taxed when purchased by a manufacturer; inventory is taxed when purchased by a wholesaler. Inventory is taxed yet again when purchased by a retailer. Finally, a retail sale to a consumer is also then taxed. Most proponents suggest a VAT should be adopted for three key reasons.

First, implementation would be relatively easy. Most businesses already have the infrastructure necessary to calculate and collect tax at the point of sale. Just as with the Fair Tax, compliance costs on businesses would be nominal, in fact lower than at present. Second, this tax would expand the tax base. All sales would be subject to tax, whether or not the source of the income is currently taxable. Finally, advocates suggest a VAT is pro-growth because it

Section VI – There Must Be A Better Way

does not tax capital, and with the revenues generated, it could lead to a reduction of other taxes.

Other arguments in favor of a VAT include these: (1) implementation would meet with little or no taxpayer resistance; and (2) the tax could raise hundreds of billions of dollars, even at a tax rate of 10%. To put this in perspective, some European Union countries mandate a rate of at least 15%, while some have set a rate as high as 20%. As an indirect tax, it falls under that out-of-sight, out-of-mind idea. Because individual taxpayers would not have to file anything, they would be less aware of this new tax burden.

However, there has been little serious dialogue on VAT in the United States. As such, it is hard to argue either for or against implementation of a VAT, at least with any specificity. Regardless, any proposal that would just add VAT to the existing tax system raises some serious questions about fairness.

Unless a VAT plan includes some rebate, prebate, or a deduction for VAT from federal income tax liability, adding this tax to the existing structure would be extraordinarily regressive. At a rate of 10%, a family of four, renting a home, with a household income of $50,000, all received as wage income, would, in effect, pay aggregate federal taxes in the neighborhood of $10,000 or 20% of their income (7.65% FICA, 10% VAT, 2.3% income tax).

Some critics of a VAT argue it would levy a double tax on businesses. First, this contention presupposes that business would remain subject to corporate income taxes. Second, it fails to take into consideration that most VAT systems allow companies to deduct tax paid as a cost of goods, thus eliminating double taxation.

As suggested, there can be no question that a VAT opens a vast new tax base. There can be little reservation that implementation would be relatively easy. Given the already complex nature of our tax code, simply adding a new tax type only muddies the waters further. Considering the vertical and horizontal inequity of our existing structure, adding a new tax that is assessed on the first dollar of income—a family has to eat—magnifies that problem.

It is possible that a VAT could be integrated with the Fair Tax proposal. In other words, take the provisions of the Fair Tax, including an individual prebate, and then assess a VAT as opposed to a sales tax.

There are good and cogent arguments for changing from a tax on income to one based on consumption. But make no mistake, this transformation would result in the ability of those on the highest rungs of the income/wealth ladder to continue to increase that wealth. While that may be a good thing, the fact that it would occur should be considered before implementing such a plan.

Are you paying for your drinks as you go or do you want to run a tab?

Chapter 21

One Size Fits All

> Call it the free choice flat tax, and it's an idea whose time has come.
> Hon. Newt Gingrich, Speaker, House of Representatives
>
> Ultimately, I would love to see a flat tax.
> Hon. Eric Cantor, Congressman
>
> A single tax rate puts all citizens in the same relationship with their government.
> Grover Norquist, President, Americans for Tax Reform

I am always somewhat skeptical when I read a sign on a clothing rack that claims "one size fits all!" I don't know about anyone else, but when I try on an article advertised as such, I never look as good as the model in the photograph. Despite the fact that I never look that good, even wearing a tailor-made suit, the truth is that one size never really fits all.

It may fit many; it may even fit most; or it may fit everyone who falls in a certain subset of body types; but it will never truly fit all.

The F-Word

Likewise, it seems to me that one tax rate does not fit all taxpayers. But many believe this idea offers the best remedy to the dilemma caused by the current, confused tax structure. Others doubt that claim, including tax attorney Kelly Phillips Erb, a *Forbes* contributing author, who wrote, "A flat tax doesn't solve our problems, it just introduces new ones."

It may be that this approach would produce the most equitable result, or generate the most revenue, or would be the simplest to implement. As long as a majority of taxpayers understand the actual criteria used to determine whether this is the best approach, then I say let's try it on for size.

Using the idea of one size fits all, a flat tax has been proposed as an alternative to the present-day system. In its simplest form, a flat income tax system levies the same tax rate on all taxpayers regardless of the amount of income earned. Before dismissing this idea out of hand, consider that the first attempt in the United States at implementing an income tax provided for a 3% single-rate tax structure (5% for citizens living abroad).

Even under America's first income tax, however, the method used was not truly one rate for all. Those who earned income above a certain threshold—set at $800 by the Revenue Act of 1862—were assessed income tax at 3%. Those whose income fell below that threshold incurred no income tax liability. So much for one rate!

Although controversial, supporters argue that a flat tax is fairer than a marginal-rate system. They suggest that it encourages enterprise and hard work, leading to wealth creation, because taxpayers who earn more are not penalized by paying higher marginal tax rates. They contend that a progressive tax rate punishes effort, risk taking, and entrepreneurship, which slows or blocks economic growth. The flat tax avoids this outcome by taxing every dollar at the same rate.

Section VI – There Must Be A Better Way

Opponents argue that a flat tax places an undue burden on the lower- and middle-income classes by removing deductions and expanding the tax base to include every level of income. They contend that this method is regressive and shifts the tax load onto those who are least able to pay. Perhaps, but before we can say true or false with any certainty, an agreement on the definition of *burden* must be reached.

If by burden, challengers mean the total tax paid in dollars, then those in the top quintile of income will, just as they now do, almost certainly carry the heaviest burden. If what is meant is the percentage of income paid, a final, comprehensive plan, including a tax rate, must be presented in order to assess that argument.

Although specific proposals have been submitted in Congress, within the current tax debate, the idea of a flat tax is not as developed as the Fair Tax. However, most versions include the reduction or elimination of many, if not all, tax preferences and the creation of a single tax rate for all levels of income. One key point is that most flat tax proposals fail to address payroll taxes. For those on the lowest rungs of the socioeconomic ladder, however, some adaptations of a flat tax allow for a threshold below which a taxpayer would incur no income tax liability.

A flat income tax is currently in use in seven states, with the fixed tax rate varying from a low of 3% in Illinois to a high of 5.3% in Massachusetts. A discussion of state tax systems will have to wait for another time. However, comparing a national flat rate income tax with flat taxes used by states is difficult.

Individual states establish tax rates that they believe will encourage business owners to relocate from other states. The intended result of lowering the top income tax rate to a lower flat tax rate is to attract and encourage business investment and bring in high-income individuals. This is believed to increase overall tax revenue and enhance economic stability. This consideration is generally irrelevant at the federal level.

Advocates argue that adopting a flat tax addresses the major concern about the existing tax system: complexity. They believe that eliminating deductions, tax credits, and multiple tax brackets will simplify the tax code, easing the compliance burden. I agree with this argument in concept but reserve ultimate determination based on the final proposal. I have seen too many reforms that fail to deliver on the promise to simplify the tax system.

Proponents of a flat tax make another key argument. Because income from investment, including dividends, interest on savings, or capital gains, would not be taxed under the system as proposed, they claim the suggested approach eliminates double taxation by only taxing earned income. This is seen as increasing the fairness and simplicity of the system as well as encouraging investment. Most opponents counter that exempting interest, dividends, and capital gains would create a society in which the working class would, in effect, support the idle rich.

Challengers of a flat tax argue that progressive, marginal-rate tax systems are fair because they tax disposable income (income minus expenses). While that may be true conceptually, this argument brings the entire complexity of the existing tax structure into the discussion. Which expenses are deducted from income can be a slippery slope. The foundation of the marginal-rate approach is the belief that those earning more should pay higher taxes because they have more disposable income and therefore a greater ability to pay.

Let's leave philosophical and theoretical arguments aside and take a pragmatic look at the impact of a flat tax using our three previous income examples, again using some simple math.

Section VI – There Must Be A Better Way

Unlike the Fair Tax plan, which includes a specific rate, proponents of a flat tax have suggested several rates. Herman Cain, one-time Republican presidential candidate, suggested a blended plan (9-9-9) which included a flat 9% individual income tax rate, a flat 9% corporate income tax rate, and a 9% sales tax rate. Governor Rick Perry, who also sought the Republican presidential nomination, suggested an optional flat rate of 20%, allowing taxpayers to opt out of the existing tax structure and pay the fixed rate. As an aside, it is not clear to me how either of these two proposals would significantly simplify our existing tax structure.

Less is More

In the last chapter, I compared the total tax burden produced under the Fair Tax with the current federal tax burden, including payroll tax, for three levels of income. Now, let's contrast the tax liability assessed under the current system with one produced by a flat tax system. For this analysis, I use a tax rate of 19% and a standard deduction of $32,496, both as proposed in H.R. 1040. These comparisons assume all income is wage income and there is no change to existing FICA taxes.

Under the flat tax, a taxpayer earning $62,100 pays income tax of $5,625 and payroll taxes of $4,751 to produce a combined federal tax liability of $10,375 (an effective tax rate of 17%). Under current law, this same taxpayer would pay income tax of $4,256 and payroll taxes of $4,751. These two produce a total federal tax liability of $9,007. Thus, under the flat tax proposal, this taxpayer would realize a tax increase of $1,369.

Now consider a taxpayer earning $124,200. Under the flat tax plan, income tax and payroll tax would be $17,424 and $9,501, respectively. Total taxes paid come to $26,925 for an effective tax rate of 22%. Under current law, this same taxpayer would pay federal income tax approximating $15,964 and payroll taxes of $9,501. The combined total is $25,465, reflecting a tax increase of $1,460.

What is the impact of the flat tax plan on a taxpayer at an even higher level of income—for example, $2 million? Using the assumptions stated before, he would pay a flat tax bill of $373,826 plus $57,498 in payroll taxes. Total federal taxes equal $431,324 for an effective tax rate of 22%. Under current law, this taxpayer would pay income tax of about $750,000 and payroll taxes of $73,248—including additional Medicare tax—for a total tax liability of $808,063. Under current law, this taxpayer would incur an effective federal tax rate equal to 40%. Under this flat tax, this taxpayer would realize $376,739 in tax savings.

These three flat tax comparisons are summarized in table 26.

	Low-income Taxpayer		Middle-income Taxpayer		High-income Taxpayer	
	Flat Tax	Current Tax	Flat Tax	Current Tax	Flat Tax	Current Tax
Total Income	$62,100	$62,100	$124,200	$124,200	$2,000,000	$2,000,000
Taxable Income [1]	$29,604	$34,300	$91,704	$96,400	$1,967,504	$1,987,800
Income Tax [2]	$5,625	$4,256	$17,424	$15,964	$373,826	$734,815
Payroll Taxes [3]	$4,751	$4,751	$9,501	$9,501	$57,498	$57,498
Additional Medicare Tax [3]		$0		$0		$15,750
Total Federal Tax	$10,375	$9,007	$26,925	$25,465	$431,324	$808,063
Flat Tax Savings / (Increase)	$ (1,369)		$ (1,460)		$ 376,739	

Table 26 - Comparison of a flat tax with total federal tax based on the 2013 Internal Revenue Code. Each taxpayer is married with two children, filing jointly, with two wage earners earning equal income.

[1] This table uses a standard deduction of $32,496 for the flat tax as proposed in H.R. 1040.

[2] The flat tax rate is 19% as proposed in H.R. 1040.

[3] The flat tax proposal does not address payroll taxes. This table assumes no change to FICA taxes including the additional medicare tax.

As you can readily see, total federal taxes on families with lower-middle incomes increase, taxes on the wealthiest decrease, while the tax burden for middle-income taxpayers generally increases. The tax burden increases until income rises above a level that triggers a marginal tax rate under current law that is higher than the established flat rate.

From that point, taxpayers realize a savings, both in terms of the percentage of income paid as well as absolute dollars. The fact is that the flat tax lowers the taxes paid in real dollars for the very highest incomes. That may or may not be economically desirable, but it is a fact. Regardless, it is difficult to consider that result to be fair, or even reasonable.

The idea of one tax rate, applied against all income, does offer a less complex tax system. Elimination of the various preferences and credits creates a less ambiguous, less random tax structure. Furthermore, elimination of deductions expands the tax base by bringing income into the tax base that is currently excluded.

While it is virtually impossible to assess the impact on individual taxpayers until a specific plan is presented in a final form, simple logic suggests that a flat tax makes our tax system more regressive.

Petite, small, medium, large, or extra large—getting the right size is important. Even distillers understand the benefit of offering different sizes, making pints, half-pints, fifths, quarts, and half gallons available to consumers.

Chapter 22

Tax Do-Over

> If we don't do something to simplify the tax system,
> we're going to end up
> with a national police force of
> internal revenue agents.
> Hon. Leon Panetta, Congressman

> A tax loophole is something that benefits the other guy.
> If it benefits you, it is tax reform.
> Hon. Russell B. Long, Senator

> Tax reform is taking the taxes off things that have been taxed in the past
> and putting taxes on things that haven't been taxed before.
> Art Buchwald, Syndicated Journalist and Pundit

In *Indiana Jones and the Last Crusade,* we hear the Grail Knight comment, "He chose poorly." He further advises Indiana Jones, "You must choose. But choose wisely." Everything about America's tax code tells me that, up until now, we have likewise chosen poorly.

The F-Word

The Taxpayer Advocate has reported to Congress, "In many instances the problems we identify grew up over time and bring about consequences that no one would deliberately design. These problems are 'errors' in the Internal Revenue Code that beg to be corrected."

A third possibility—tax reform—including provisions similar to some proposed in the Fair Tax or flat tax alternatives, yet fundamentally different, can also be considered in response to the mandate to improve our tax structure. I recognize that the phrase "tax reform" is worn from overuse and has even become trite, at least in political rhetoric. Everyone advocates for it, but no one undertakes any meaningful effort to bring about real change.

However, I propose a plan that encompasses real tax reform, real tax simplification, a complete do-over. For those of you who golf, I say let's take a mulligan; for tennis players, the existing system is ruled a let. The dice are cocked; roll again.

The *Macmillan English Dictionary* defines do-over accurately: "to do something again from the beginning, especially because you did it badly the first time." Okay, we did it badly the first time. Let's start over, but let's just do it better this time. We have historically chosen poorly, so let's now choose wisely.

More than a dozen TV reality shows are premised on the idea of a complete makeover. These shows transform restaurants, people, cars, and homes. Participants lose weight; they find or lose life partners; home and business owners reenter utterly different buildings. I suggest we take that same approach with our tax system.

One of these shows is *Extreme Makeover: Home Edition*. It is my belief that we should include that word *extreme* in our tax reform effort! The tax reform needed for America is not reform that adds a new

Section VI – There Must Be A Better Way

tax or tax rate, but that creates a completely new tax system. If we refuse to accept the inequities and inefficiencies of the current system, we must create a new and different tax system.

I believe it is time to develop a complete, coherent reform proposal based on philosophically sound fundamental principles—a complete do-over. Passage of yet another tax reform bill, however well intentioned, that merely tinkers with tax brackets, toys with tax credits, and does nothing to adequately address the inequities caused by the growing complexity of the tax code will again result in total failure.

It has been suggested that insanity is best demonstrated by taking the same approach and expecting different results. Placing yet more Band-Aids on the snafu legislation known as the Internal Revenue Code has not worked previously and will not work now. Continued attempts to do so burden our combined resources and try our collective patience. I believe that the IRC must be completely overhauled. I suggest a bonfire.

Bonfire aside, I am not alone in taking this position. This assessment is so commonly accepted that expressing it here states the obvious. Almost everyone, regardless of political persuasion, agrees that our tax code needs to be fundamentally changed.

Although implementing the FairTax would result in just such an extreme change to our federal tax system, I suggest we develop a system that bases federal tax on individual gross receipts—not income—and not consumption. This would serve as the core of the federal tax system.

Whether you support or oppose the basic premise of the existing structure—a tax on income—our current system levies several different, overlapping taxes. These include corporate and individual income, trust, gift, estate, and payroll taxes. The basic idea behind a complete makeover is that all these taxes would be replaced with a single, individual gross receipts tax.

I am not trying to hide my intent. This could just as easily be called an income tax, as long as income is defined to include everything of economic value received. In *Wealth of Nations*, Adam Smith hinted at the idea that a tax based on income is the best. In his first maxim he said,

> The subjects of every state ought to contribute… as nearly as possible…in proportion to the revenue which they respectively enjoy under the protection of the state.

Note the word *revenue*. I believe he was suggesting that the tax burden should be tied to the economic benefit gained from living under the government's protection. Whether that was his intent, I believe that is fundamentally the best, the fairest way to share the tax burden.

The key elements of this strategy are these:

- Implement an individual gross receipts tax as the primary federal tax.
  ○ Tax individual receipts, not family or household receipts.
- Implement one tax rate.
  ○ Receipts below the exclusion threshold would not be taxed.
  ○ Develop a linear function—not brackets—increasing the tax incurred as receipts increase, to the single fixed rate.
- Eliminate corporate income taxes.
  ○ Eliminate the entire not-for profit program (at least within the tax code).

SECTION VI – THERE MUST BE A BETTER WAY

- Eliminate payroll taxes.
  - Eliminate business payroll taxes.
  - Eliminate employee payroll taxes.
- Eliminate gift taxes.
  - Include any money received by gift in gross receipts.
- Eliminate estate taxes.
  - Include any money received by inheritance in gross receipts.
- Eliminate trust taxes.
  - Include any money received from a trust in gross receipts.
- Eliminate all income deductions, tax preferences, and tax credits.
  - Allow a deduction for expenses incurred to produce income.
- Create a single threshold deduction for all taxpayers.
  - Combine the standard deduction and individual exemption.
  - Eliminate all other deductions.
- Tax all receipts the same regardless of source.
- Index the tax rate and the exclusion deduction for inflation.
- Expand and improve automatic withholding.
- Expand and improve transaction reporting.

Create One Federal Tax—On Individuals

The core of this proposal is the creation of one basic federal tax: a tax on individual gross receipts. Any resemblance to the existing tax code is limited to the fact that *income* is included in gross receipts and the government would tax *individuals*. But, under this proposal, these two words mean something markedly different from their meaning under our current tax code.

The F-Word

Pay particular attention to the word *individual*. This system is proposed as a true tax on individuals. Not on families. Not on heads of household or households, but on individuals. Insofar as possible in today's culture, this approach gets the federal government out of the business of fostering or developing American families.

It's none of the government's damn business if two people marry or whether they form a family at all, regardless of the adult configuration of that family. It's also none of the government's business whether one or both adults work or if they have no children or many children, or whether those children seek higher education. None of this matters under my proposed tax reform.

Taxpayers would no longer parse "number of nights" or "over half the year" or "over half the cost." Whether a person is a "qualifying child," "qualifying person," or a "qualifying relative" would not be subject to debate. No more would we struggle to determine if we paid half the cost of care of a dependent. We would not decide to buy or hold something based on our prediction of changes to the tax code, nor would we incur a financial penalty compared to our neighbor as a result of making a purchase decision a day earlier or later.

No longer would the government care, at least under the tax code, whether a taxpayer bought a house or rented, whether a child received a scholarship or did not, or whether a homeowner bought energy-efficient windows. It would not care whether, due to an emergency, a taxpayer borrowed from money set aside for retirement or simply withdrew those funds. The government would no longer be concerned whether someone closed on a house on December 22 or two weeks later. Remember our two brothers?

This plan proposes a tax on all gross receipts as it allows no deductions for savings. To critics who might contend that this plan

Section VI – There Must Be A Better Way

discourages savings or investment, my reply is that the natural human desire to protect, to grow, would serve as the impetus to do either or both.

Regardless, I would counter that our government should get out of the business of dictating behavior via our tax code. And, I might ask, does it even work? What are personal, corporate, and government debt levels today? Although numerous preferences for saving exist under the present tax code, many economists are critical of savings rates in the United States.

Gross receipts would be defined something like the following:

> Gross receipts means the beneficial receipt of anything of value whether in money or property, from any source whatever, whether legal or illegal under federal law or state law in the state in which the action occurred, including the following:
>
> compensation for services, including salaries, wages, bonuses, fees, commissions, and fringe benefits; property or services received in a barter exchange; gross income derived from business (total receipts less all reasonable and necessary costs incurred to generate such receipts); gain from the sale or exchange of real or personal property; interest; rents; royalties; dividends; scholarships and grants; alimony and separate maintenance payments; annuities; pensions; income from discharge of indebtedness (unless discharged under bankruptcy laws of the United States); distributed share of partnership gross income; income in respect of a decedent; payments or transfers from an interest in an estate or trust; and, payments or transfers,

whether in currency, property or rights to either, received by gift or inheritance.

Based on the cash method of accounting, all gross receipts would be taxed the same, regardless of the source or type of receipt. A dollar received would be just that, a dollar received. The confusion, the discussion over different kinds of income—earned versus unearned, compensation compared to investment, passive or active—would cease to exist.

It might be reasonable to consider initial investment risk as a separate issue and possibly one that should receive special treatment. But any consideration would be limited to funds used at the start-up of an enterprise. Profit from buying and selling stock and receipt of dividends due to the ownership of stock would be treated as ordinary receipts.

Undistributed income from partnerships or other business entities would not be taxed. Money withdrawn from retirement accounts, or from any savings or investment account, would not be taxed, but earnings paid on those accounts, including interest and dividends, would be taxed.

Possible exclusions from gross receipts include income earned by those in uniform serving in a combat theater, transfers between spouses, and insurance payments for economic loss. Other insurance receipts—life insurance proceeds, lost income, and so forth—would be included in gross receipts.

Eliminate Business Taxes

A second critical element of this streamlined tax strategy is the elimination of corporate income tax. Opponents of this suggestion might argue that the rich would get away with financial murder.

Section VI – There Must Be A Better Way

Concerned about this eventuality, you might intellectually discard out of hand a single tax system based on individual gross receipts tax. But read on.

Not only does elimination of business income tax encourage investment, it reduces compliance costs—dramatically. It eliminates the entire need for not-for-profit sections of the tax code. Following this do-over, contributions to not-for-profit agencies would not be deductible and those agencies would not report income or pay tax.

In the event you are imagining Carnegie, Vanderbilt, and Rockefeller getting rich off their investments, remember that much of corporate America is owned by individuals, through brokerage accounts and other investment accounts. Although this proposal eliminates the countless tax preferences associated with contributions to various savings plans, history tells us that people will save and invest. Shares of corporate America will continue to be held by millions of Americans. The result: if a company makes money, so do those who invest in that company.

Furthermore, capital gains would be taxed at the same rate as all other receipts under this proposal. Although this plan would eliminate gift and estate tax, all gifts and inheritances would be included in gross receipts by the recipients. Thus, the passing of wealth is not given a free ride. This treatment may mitigate earlier concerns.

Eliminate Payroll Taxes

A third basic component of this plan is the elimination of the payroll tax on individuals and businesses. First, by statute, payroll taxes are assessed only on income below a wage base, which is, by definition, a regressive tax. Second, whether we wish to accept the idea or not, the reality of a Social Security Trust Fund simply does not exist. At best, the system is a large-scale government Ponzi scheme, whereby money paid by current workers is used to pay benefits for current retirees. At worst, it constitutes a hoax perpetrated against all current and future wage earners.

In case you believe this to be a condemnation of Social Security, let me again assure you that I am not suggesting we do away with a government retirement subsidy. I acknowledge that caring for our elderly has become a norm in American culture, regardless of the source of funds. But how we pay for this safety net no longer matches our romantic notion of what Social Security was once thought to be.

Simplicity, Clarity—Certainty

The fourth core concept of this do-over is the elimination of all adjustments to individual gross receipts, all deductions, all tax preferences, and all tax credits. The one exception to this statement is that ordinary and reasonable expenses incurred to produce income would be deductible.

As an aside, I do not think tickets to a luxury box at Mile High Stadium are either "ordinary" or "reasonable." Why should a machinist in Pulaski, Tennessee, who has to pay for a beer with his buddies on Sunday while watching the Tennessee Titans, subsidize senior executives in Denver watching Peyton Manning sling a football all over the field?

However, in recognition of a basic subsistence-level requirement, this plan allows one deduction from gross receipts. The two basic exclusions now provided—the standard deduction and personal exemption—would be merged to create a single income exclusion, perhaps based on the individual poverty level. Further, it

Section VI – There Must Be A Better Way

would be reasonable to consider a different exclusion amount for a taxpayer with a disability, or those above a certain age.

I can hear the arguments. Wait, this would give a husband and wife a double exemption. Yes, if both have income, that's true. Under the existing code, a single taxpayer is allowed $10,000 for the standard deduction and personal exemption. A married couple is allowed $20,000. Not a lot of difference in these two approaches.

Because the cost of maintaining one household is generally less than that needed to maintain two households, this provision might indirectly encourage taxpayers to live together. To the extent that those taxpayers have children, a secondary consequence of encouraging joint domicile is, I think, a good thing. Under the present code, some provisions actually discourage parents from staying together. Think about the chapter on the EITC.

In this vein, opponents might argue that it takes a lot of money to raise children, and that limiting a deduction to some set amount for a taxpayer does not take that into account. I would respond that our tax code should neither reward nor penalize individuals in their procreation decisions. An individual or couple should make their own choice about whether to have children and accept the responsibility and consequences of that choice.

Reflect for a moment on our existing methodology. We establish a number of progressive tax rates, but then we exclude some income from any taxation. We further mandate different rates for other types of income. Worried whether this results in an unfair distribution of the tax burden, we direct that income tax be calculated first one way, then another. And if this has not yet driven us to drink, we ask that a separate tax be levied on the net income derived from certain types of activities previously excluded.

Finally, out of apprehension that we have taxed people too much, we develop a series of overlapping credits to return taxes to the taxpayer. This madness would all go the way of the passenger pigeon and dodo bird.

Any amounts specified in this plan would be indexed for inflation. Finally, this plan would expand and simplify reporting and withholding methods now in use. Any money paid by brokers, banks, trusts, probate attorneys, and others would be subject to mandatory withholding and reporting.

This approach addresses the most serious problem of our current system, complexity, yet creates a fair tax system based on Smith's idea of taxes paid "in proportion to their respective abilities," defined as in proportion to the revenue they enjoy. Elimination of complexity has the added benefit of reducing costs of compliance, both to the government and to the taxpayer. That simplicity, together with increased withholding and reporting, should serve to significantly reduce the tax gap.

More importantly, a simplified system, similar to one created under this proposal, will restore fairness, transparency, and integrity to our tax code. The system created by this do-over is based on a rational philosophy and provides the certainty Adam Smith demanded.

Conventional wisdom discourages use of the phrase, "things can't get any worse." At the risk of talking about a no-hitter in the dugout, I suggest things cannot possibly be any worse than our current Internal Revenue system. Pencils and erasers are

Section VI – There Must Be A Better Way

no longer acceptable. It's time to buy an industrial-grade paper shredder.

We need to get out the paint cans, the makeup, and the exercise machines. We need to consider liposuction and Botox treatments. What America needs is an extreme tax do-over.

What I need is a drink.

Chapter 23

The Last Word

> Is there anyone here present
> who knows any lawful reason...
> If so, please speak now, or forever hold your peace.
> Traditional Wedding Ceremony

> If we desire respect for the law, we must first make
> the law respectable.
> Hon. Louis Brandeis, Associate Justice of the
> Supreme Court

> When the situation was manageable,
> it was neglected.
> Winston Churchill

I started out to describe just how #%#*@ (read *F* word) our tax code is. Has the existence and seriousness of the problem become clear? Are you angry yet? Befuddled? Apathetic? Or are you again opening the bourbon?

As Warden Norton asks in *The Shawshank Redemption*, "You understand me? Catching my drift? Or am I being obtuse?" Or, like our

The F-Word

tax code itself, has this discourse only complicated the issue and confused you?

Neither this chapter nor this book can be the final word on our tax code. Nor can any other speech, research paper, committee report, or book. We cannot have—we must not have—a final word on this matter until such time as Americans finally get real, meaningful, and lasting tax reform. Only then can we close the book on this subject.

This book is, out of necessity, incomplete. There is so much of the code left unaddressed. With the exception of a few outliers, my focus has been individual federal income tax. But I could have added so many more chapters that illustrate equally well the pervasive insanity of our tax structure.

How about a section titled "Don't Look a Gift Horse in the Mouth?" For example, Subtitle B of the Internal Revenue Code, titled Estate and Gift Taxes, levies a tax on a person for giving a present. Mind you, it is more likely than not that whatever is given has derived from income on which federal income tax has already been paid. Fear not, however, as there are numerous and sundry annual thresholds, lifetime deductions, and direct gift exclusions that exempt much of this from taxes. Makes sense to me!

What about a chapter titled, "Trust Me," based on Chapter 1—Subchapter J of the IRC, titled Estates, Trusts, Beneficiaries, and Decedents, which establishes taxes on various types of trusts. It describes in exquisite—others might say tortured—detail, taxes assessed against a trust that only distributes income. This section further explains different taxes levied against trusts that distribute the assets, or the body of the trust—referred to as the corpus—in addition to income. Sounds like something out of a Frankenstein movie—some half-crazed scientist dragging a cart through darkened streets handing out unwanted body parts.

Section VI – There Must Be A Better Way

The idea that "I'm not in it for the money" would also fill one or more chapters. The concept of not-for-profit has taken on a life of its own. Most Americans are familiar with the designation 501(c)(3). But how many are aware that, at present, there are at least fifteen separate 501(c) categories? Seems we have a couple of adult 501s in the back room making little 501s as fast as they can.

Consider this! The NFL, PGA, NHL, and NBA are defined as "not-for-profit" under our tax code. It was reported that Major League Baseball opted out of this status only due to executive salary reporting requirements. Has anyone looked closely at the revenues produced by those organizations? Does anyone believe they are "not in it for the money"? Really?

In chapter 11, I asked if a homeowner can deduct the cost of installing a swimming pool as an allowable medical expense. The answer will no longer surprise you. It depends.

To qualify as a deductible medical expense, the cost must be incurred for prevention or alleviation of a physical or mental defect or illness. If the expense is only for recreational purposes or for general health or well-being, it can't be deducted. The cost of installing a swimming pool so your kids can cool off during the summer is not deductible.

However, if the pool is necessary to alleviate a specific illness, such as arthritis, based on a doctor's orders, the cost is deductible. The amount that may be deducted for a medically necessary improvement to real property is equal to the cost that exceeds the increase in the value of the property. Additionally, all maintenance costs—chemicals, repairs, utilities, cleaning services, and so forth—are also deductible. Now the children can splash around and cool off in a partially subsidized, in-ground, doctor-ordered pool in the privacy of their backyard.

The F-Word

Regardless of the insanity of our tax code, deciding to write this book was not easy. I felt like a concerned relative at a wedding when those in attendance are asked that well-known question quoted earlier. I worried, should I write this book or just hold my peace?

First, I worried whether I could write the words necessary to clearly and completely explain the challenge we face. Second, I recognized that the Internal Revenue Code is among the least interesting topics imaginable. I felt that writing an engrossing, compelling book about something this complex, and at the same time so boring, was possibly an insurmountable task. As I considered these two factors, Voltaire's admonishment echoed in my ears, "It is far better to be silent than merely to increase the quantity of bad books." It may turn out that I should have taken note.

Third, I have observed that our political temperament, evidenced by public debate, has seemingly adopted a predisposition against engaging in important dialogue that stays focused on an issue without becoming personal and vitriolic. *Argumentum ad hominem* (against the man) has become a political blood sport. Although I want you to come away frustrated with the status quo and angry at elected officials who do nothing other than recite platitudes, I do not want you to infer that I am critical of any specific individual, even that generic IRS agent.

I know that I have expressed some strong criticism in this book. If it appears that I have directed any against a particular person, I apologize. My intent was to direct my criticism against the existing tax code and the implementation of that code. I attempted to mirror the approach taken by Thomas Paine in writing "Common Sense": "The author hath studiously avoided every thing which is personal among ourselves. Compliments as well as censure to individuals make no part thereof."

Section VI – There Must Be A Better Way

Fourth, I understand the entrenched barrier to real tax reform. Although everyone voices support for tax reform in principle, that support disappears in the face of reality. Remember Senator Long's description of reform: "A tax loophole is something that benefits the other guy. If it benefits you, it is tax reform."

We scorn the Internal Revenue Service. We bemoan our tax structure. We ridicule poorly disguised political agendas wrapped in the cloak of tax reform. Despite these reactions we stand by idly. As free citizens we have to take a different direction. Our tax code is at the heart of our laws, our economy, and our culture—in my view, too much so. Given the consensus of our criticism, we should pay special attention to Justice Brandeis's warning: "If we desire respect for the law, we must first make the law respectable."

While I was writing this book, my wife asked me what it would take to actually change the tax code. My first inclination was to say, "A miracle." I actually said that, while I thought it is possible to really reform our tax code, I thought it not likely. The problem, I offered, is not whether we can effect change, but that we needed someone who would bell the cat.

The exact origin of the phrase "bell the cat" is the subject of urban myth and some disagreement. It is believed to come from a parable that tells the story of a group of mice threatened by a hungry cat. The mice gathered to discuss how they could avoid the obvious danger. As the story goes, one mouse suggested they place a bell around the cat's neck to warn them of his approach. Although all of the mice thought this was a great idea, when the question was asked, "Who will bell the cat?" none stepped forward.

This fable points out two problems. The first is that any plan must weigh the desirability of the outcome against the potential risks of implementation. The second is finding someone who will step forward to execute the plan—someone who will "bell the cat".

Yes, change is difficult but not impossible. It requires a leader with the courage of his or her convictions. Bringing real change to our tax code requires political leadership and political will. Today, America suffers from a dearth of both. We need a leader who will bell the cat.

In 2005, President Bush appointed the President's Advisory Panel on Federal Tax Reform—yet one more in a long line of committees established to study our tax code and make recommendations for improvement. Just as committees appointed before and since, this committee had nothing positive to say about our tax code. It offered two possible solutions. In the cover letter to its final report, the committee warned, "The effort to reform the tax code is noble in its purpose, but it requires political willpower. Many stand waiting to defend their breaks, deductions, and loopholes, and to defeat our efforts."

Intelligent and informed citizens may disagree with the committee's conclusions and recommendations, but it was spot-on with its admonition.

Today, it is safe to say that American politicians will not act without "polling numbers." They must be convinced that a majority of Americans believe—or at least a majority of their constituents, or at least a majority of those constituents they believe will likely vote, oh hell, you get the idea—that tax reform is necessary. We must convince them.

One comment, attributed to the philosopher Edmund Burke, among others, suggests, "All that is necessary for the triumph of evil is that good men do nothing." Regardless of its origins, this

Section VI – There Must Be A Better Way

sentiment accurately describes the situation we face as a country. If we continue to stand by idly, nothing good will result.

I believe that the problems with our tax system, while staggering, can be fixed. However, the cure requires the same commitment, perhaps demonstrated through different methods, that was exhibited more than 250 years ago by a group of patriots who were willing to stake their fortunes, their freedom, and quite possibly their lives. Change requires a willingness to step into the fray, expressed by British philosopher John Stuart Mill, "The person who has nothing for which he is willing to fight...has no chance of being free unless made and kept so by the exertions of better men than himself."

So, if this problem is to be fixed, the impetus must come from us, the American people. It does not require that we risk our lives, our fortunes, or our sacred honor, only that we clearly communicate to our elected leaders that their political fortune is tied to their total, undivided commitment to this effort.

I understand that solving this problem will be difficult. But it is not impossible. The alternative is to continue to ignore the problem. We can take the easy path and choose to do nothing, or choose to simply tinker with the current law. Either approach serves America poorly. In my opinion, both lead to a lessening of the freedom we have enjoyed as Americans.

Short of armed aggression against our country, I believe this matter to be so grave that it should take priority over all other political considerations. In this respect, I echo the sentiment expressed by the National Taxpayer Advocate, the official charged with the responsibility to evaluate US tax policy from the perspective of the American taxpayers. In her 2001 report to Congress, she wrote:

> I realize that many...believe that there is no... political reward for achieving tax simplification, or, more importantly, tax rationalization. I maintain that this nation can ill afford to ignore the increasing burden...and irrationality of our tax system.

It seems to me that her statement constitutes a strongly worded plea—perhaps even, an ominous warning. If you think there is nothing to be done, or that nothing can be done, think again. Americans' shared hesitation can best be dispelled by the truism offered by Margaret Mead: "Never doubt that a small group of thoughtful, committed citizens can change the world; indeed, it's the only thing that ever has."

In movies of all genres, when someone is faced with a hard task, or a tough choice, someone typically offers them some strong whiskey. It may be hard to join in the fight, to help light that bonfire. So here, have a shot of bourbon. And, just as Don Corleone urged Tom Hagen in *The Godfather*, I say, "And now you've had your drink."

Extra, Extra: Read All about It

Before World War II, most major markets had a morning and an afternoon newspaper. Some cities had more than one of each or both. During that era, when newspapers were the primary news-delivery vehicle, if something big happened during the day, the publisher would print an "extra" edition.

When that so-called "extra" came out, newsboys sold them to passersby yelling, "Extra! Extra! Read all about it!" to call attention to the fact that something significant had happened. This was the equivalent of today's network and cable TV networks interrupting regularly scheduled programming with a "breaking news" flash.

What follows here is extra, not because something big has happened just now, but because this material provides perspective for what has happened throughout our history.

Although different kinds of taxes have long been in use, the prevailing use of income taxes is relatively new. In the seventeenth and eighteenth centuries, tariffs were the chief sources of revenue for most countries including the fledgling United States. But, with the passage of the Revenue Act of 1913, federal income tax quickly became the primary revenue source for the United States, far outdistancing all other tax revenues.

The F-Word

How did we get to this point? Without a historical perspective, it might be difficult to determine—to *know*—exactly how we got here.

Professor Morris Massey coined the phrase, "What You Are Is Where You Were When." That phrase offers an appropriate explanation of our tax code. The Internal Revenue Code is a by-product of the events, laws, and opinions from our past. This book has described what the IRC is. What follows is a description of when it was what it was—a chronological listing of the major events and changes to our tax code that brought us to our current federal tax structure.

This time line illustrates that the United States has had a flat income tax, that we have treated capital gains just like all other income, and that the lowest rate has been very low (1%) and the highest rate very high (94%). It shows that the tax laws have been used to drive behavior, even more so recently. It clearly demonstrates the frequency of changes to our tax code. (Author's note: Of necessity, this list is not all-inclusive. I have selected those events that I felt were most critical in getting us to the point we now find ourselves.)

What It Is and When It Was

June 1215, Magna Carta: The "Great Charter" is signed by King John of England, providing for specific liberties and limiting feudal payments (taxes) to the crown. It influenced early American colonists and the formation of our Constitution.

March 1733, Molasses Act: Parliament imposes a tax of six pence per gallon on imports of molasses, not to raise revenue, but to regulate trade by making British products cheaper. This was the first British tax affecting the American colonies.

Extra, Extra: Read All About It

April 1764, Sugar Act: This act, also known as the American Revenue Act or the American Duties Act, cuts in half the previous tax on molasses. Unlike the prior act, this measure is enforced, causing an almost immediate decline in the rum industry in the colonies. This is Parliament's first attempt to specifically tax the American colonies.

September 1764, Currency Act: Because there were no gold or silver mines, the colonies could only get hard currency through trade with Great Britain. Parliament, favoring "hard currency" based on the pound sterling, passed this act to gain control of currency in the colonies. The worsening trade deficit set the stage for opposition to the Stamp Act.

March 1765, Stamp Act: Parliament passes the first direct tax on the American colonies, requiring colonists to pay a tax on every piece of printed paper used, by demanding that printed materials be produced on stamped paper made in London. Response to this tax led to the first act of open rebellion and the first joint colonial Congress.

March 1766, Stamp Act repealed: American colonialists begin to raise the issue of taxation without representation. In response to increasing American resistance to British taxes, Parliament repeals the Stamp Act.

June 1767, Revenue Act of 1767: This act, known as the first of the Townshend Acts, levies a duty on imports—an indirect, or external tax—because Parliament believed the colonies only objected to the Stamp Act because it was a direct, or internal tax. This law rekindles hostilities, which rise to a revolutionary extent when a crowd mobbed the British customs office.

May 1773, Tea Act: Parliament passes a measure to prop up the foundering East India Company, which was burdened with nine thousand tons of unsold tea. This act triggers the final spark to the revolutionary movement, leading to the Revolutionary War.

December 1773, Boston Tea Party: In defiance of the Tea Act, colonists stage a political protest that became known as the Boston Tea Party, destroying an entire shipment of tea held on three ships anchored in the Boston Harbor.

July 1776, Declaration of Independence: Now referring to themselves as the thirteen united States of America, the assembled Congress approves independence from Great Britain. One of the grievances cited was "For imposing Taxes on us without our Consent."

November 1777, Articles of Confederation: The Continental Congress adopts the Articles of Confederation, creating the first union of the colonies. The Congress was not given any taxing authority under the Articles, but, instead, Article 8 directed that "the taxes…shall be laid and levied by the…legislatures of the several States."

September 1787, US Constitution: The failure of the confederation leads to a new Constitutional Convention. Delegates to the Constitutional Convention sign the new Constitution. Article I, Section 8, gives to the Congress the "Power To lay and collect Taxes, Duties, Imposts and Excises."

March 1791, The Whiskey Act: The newly formed federal government imposes the first tax on a domestic product—distilled spirits. Because whiskey was by far the most popular distilled beverage, the excise became known as the "whiskey tax." This act led to the first public resistance to the federal government. It would not be the last.

Extra, Extra: Read All About It

December 1791, Bill of Rights: The House and Senate approve twelve articles of amendment to the Constitution. Articles three through twelve are ratified by the states and become part of the Constitution. These ten are collectively called the Bill of Rights.

July 1794, Whiskey Rebellion: The protest to the Whiskey Tax, led by distillers in western Pennsylvania, which began in 1791, comes to a head. Using military force, the federal government demonstrates the will and ability to enforce its laws.

November 1832, Ordinance of Nullification: South Carolina passes its Ordinance of Nullification, declaring that the federal Tariffs of 1828 (known as the Tariff of Abominations) and 1832 were unconstitutional and therefore null and void within the state. Growing tension between the North and South would lead to the Civil War.

August 1861, Revenue Act of 1861: Costs of the Civil War lead to new and higher taxes. Congress introduces a federal income tax "levied, collected, and paid, upon the annual income of every person...whether such income is derived from any...source whatever." This act creates the first income tax in the United States—a flat tax.

July 1862, Revenue Act of 1862: Because the Revenue Act of 1861 is largely ineffective, Congress passes a new measure, modifying the income tax rates set in 1861 and creating the first progressive income tax. The new law establishes the office of the Commissioner of Internal Revenue, predecessor of the Internal Revenue Service.

June 1864, Internal Revenue Act of 1864: The war increases demand for revenue, and Congress passes another income tax law. This adds a third tax bracket and increases tax rates established in 1862. For the first time, this law imposes a tax on "every person residing in the United States…and any citizen of the United States *residing abroad.*"

June 1873, Internal Revenue Act of 1864 expires: Viewed by most Americans as an emergency wartime measure only, the law is allowed to expire. This is the first and last time an income tax law would "go gentle into that good night."

January 1881, *Springer v. United States*: Although the Internal Revenue Act of 1864 is no longer in effect, the Supreme Court renders a decision in a suit filed several years before, upholding the constitutionality of the income tax imposed under that statute. Though unsuccessful, *Springer* was the first of many court challenges to income taxes.

August 1894, Revenue Act of 1894: This act, also known as the Wilson-Gorman Tariff Act, was proposed by Democrats in favor of free trade to lower tariffs. To make up lost revenue, this law levies a 2% income tax on incomes over $4,000, affecting less than 10% of all households. This act is important because it imposes the first peacetime income tax and leads to a second constitutional challenge.

April 1895, *Pollock v. Farmers' Loan and Trust Co.*: The Supreme Court rules that the income tax levied by Wilson-Gorman is unconstitutional because a tax on income from real estate is a direct tax. In the earlier *Springer* case, the court held income tax to be constitutional because the suit was based on tax assessed against wages, which the court held was an indirect tax. *Pollock* leads to the Sixteenth Amendment allowing income tax.

July 1909: Congress approves an article of amendment to the Constitution and refers it to the states for ratification. This action serves as a lesson in the adage "be careful what you wish for."

Extra, Extra: Read All About It

Believing that a sufficient number of states would not ratify the article, Republicans supported approval precisely to stave off an income tax.

February 1913, Sixteenth Amendment: The requisite number of states ratify the article of amendment, making the Sixteenth Amendment part of the US Constitution and exempting income taxes from the constitutional requirement to apportion direct taxes.

October 1913, Revenue Act of 1913: Also known as the Underwood Tariff, the first tax bill passed under the Sixteenth Amendment reimposes the federal income tax. This law provides progressive tax rates, including seven brackets. All income was subject to a 1% normal rate.

September 1916, Revenue Act of 1916: Congress passes a second income tax measure, raising the lowest tax rate from 1% to 2% and the top rate to 15% on taxpayers with incomes above $2 million. The act institutes the federal estate tax.

October 1917, War Revenue Act of 1917: WWI creates a stronger demand for revenue, and the War Revenue Act is approved, greatly increasing federal income tax rates (raising the top rate from 15% to 67%) and lowering exemptions. Tax revenue collected in 1917 is greater than the total tax revenue collected for all prior years.

February 1919, Revenue Act of 1918: Congress approves (yes, it is actually signed into law in 1919) another tax law, again raising tax rates. The due date for filing a return is pushed forward from March 1 to March 15.

November 1921, Revenue Act of 1921: Arguing that significant tax reduction was necessary in order to spur economic expansion, a

Republican-led Congress passes the first-ever tax reduction, lowering the top individual tax rate from 73% to 58%. A preferential treatment for capital gains is introduced for the first time.

June 1924, Revenue Act of 1924: This law, also known as the Mellon tax bill, cuts federal tax rates, lowering the bottom rate assessed on income under $4,000 from 1.5% to 1.125%. This law establishes the US Board of Tax Appeals, later renamed the United States Tax Court.

February 1926, Revenue Act of 1926: The Republican Congress again lowers overall taxes, reducing inheritance and personal income taxes and eliminating the gift tax. This act ended previously permitted public access to federal income tax returns.

May 1928, Revenue Act of 1928: Congress passes a law that changes a number of tax policies, including a 12% rate on net corporate income. Sec. 605 offers a conundrum. "In case a regulation...is amended by a subsequent regulation...such subsequent regulation...may...be applied without retroactive effect." What does that mean?

October 1929, Black Monday: Stock markets crash worldwide, including those in the United States, ushering in the Great Depression. Congress, with the urging of President Harding, passes the ill-advised Smoot-Hawley Tariff Act, which leads to a calamitous decrease in world trade.

June 1932, Revenue Act of 1932: A failing economy generates far less tax revenue, forcing Congress to raise income tax rates across the board. The rate on top incomes rose from 25% to 63%, the estate tax was doubled, and corporate taxes increased by 15%.

May 1934, Revenue Act of 1934: Roosevelt continues his policy of increasing taxes on the wealthy, leading to enactment of this law that raises individual income tax rates on higher incomes. The top individual income tax rate remained at 63%.

August 1935, Revenue Act of 1935: This law, popularized as the "Soak the Rich" tax, introduces the "Wealth Tax," once again raising tax rates on higher income. The top marginal tax rate is set at 75%, a rate previously seen only during time of war.

August 1935, Social Security Act: President Roosevelt realizes his most revolutionary New Deal initiative: passage of the first social welfare legislation to make caring for the elderly a national responsibility. Payroll taxes are levied on both employers and employees.

June 1936, Revenue Act of 1936: Congress, in an effort to tax the income and wealth of those who use of the vagueness of the tax code to avoid paying tax, changes many tax provisions. It establishes an "undistributed profits tax" on US corporations and a tax on "unjust enrichment."

February 1939, Internal Revenue Code of 1939: Published as volume 53, part I, of the United States Statutes at Large and as title 26 of the United States Code, the tax statutes were recodified as the Internal Revenue Code.

June 1940, Revenue Act of 1940: WWII increases the demand for revenue, which was met with higher income tax rates. After examining alternative methods of effecting increases, including raising rates, lowering exemptions, or imposing so-called super taxes, the act embodied a program of super-taxes and went through Congress in less than a month.

October 1940, Second Revenue Act of 1940: After passing the Revenue Act of 1940, Congress considers a second tax measure to prevent war profiteering. With strong support from both sides,

Congress enacts an excess-profits tax, retroactive to the start of the year, and increased the top corporate tax rate from 33% to 35%.

September 1941, Revenue Act of 1941: Waging war requires money—lots of it—and WWII was no exception. The tax system was in the process of conversion to a total war footing as tax rates skyrocketed and the number of taxpayers increased. Traditional taxation objectives of fairness and simplicity became harder than ever to achieve as this measure continues an inexorable march to higher individual, corporate, and excise rates.

October 1942, Revenue Act of 1942: Congress introduces a novel new tax, the "Victory Tax," which applies to every American, and levies a 5% tax above the normal taxes and surtaxes on all income over $624. Tax rolls swell from two million taxpayers in 1932 to almost fifty million.

February 1943, Revenue Act of 1943: Looking at every possible revenue source, Congress increases federal excise taxes on, among other things, alcohol, jewelry, telephones, and admissions to entertainment events. The law raised the excess profits tax rate to 95% but lowered the Victory Tax to 3%. It was the first revenue measure passed without the president's approval as the measure was passed over the president's veto.

June 1943, Current Tax Payment Act of 1943: Congress reintroduces the withholding requirement for federal income tax. Tax withholding, initially required in the Revenue Act of 1862, was included in the Tariff Act of 1913 but repealed in 1916. America's income tax system becomes a "pay-as-you-go" system.

May 1944, Individual Income Tax Act of 1944: Unaware that the end of the war is approaching, Congress again raises individual income tax rates. The Victory Tax, lowered to 3% in 1943, is repealed.

November 1945, Revenue Act of 1945: For the first time since 1929, Congress passes major tax reduction legislation. This law repeals the excess profits tax and reduces individual income and corporate tax rates. The top individual rate dropped from a wartime high of 94% to 86.45%.

April 1948, Revenue Act of 1948: Congress approves this law over President Truman's veto. The law again reduces individual income tax rates, by 5 to 13%. For the first time, this law permitted married couples to split their incomes for tax purposes.

September 1950, Revenue Act of 1950: Congress reverses the postwar trend of lower taxes and eliminates some reductions from the 1945 and 1948 tax acts. This law addresses the not-for-profit provisions of the law and introduces the unrelated business income tax.

October 1951, Revenue Act of 1951: Congress temporarily increases individual and corporate income tax rates and modifies capital gains treatment. The 1951 act introduces the "head of household" filing status.

August 1954, Internal Revenue Act of 1954: Congress passes the first comprehensive revision of the federal income tax system since its origin in 1913. The due date for filing individual tax returns is moved from March 15 to April 15. It is significant, however, not for the changes to the tax code, but for the process by which reform was achieved.

October 1962, Revenue Act of 1962: Congress amends the Internal Revenue Code of 1954 to provide an investment credit. This measure institutes dividend and interest reporting requirements for financial institutions.

February 1964, Revenue Act of 1964: This law is also known as the Tax Reduction Act. Congress passes a bipartisan tax bill to cut individual income tax rates across the board by 20%. Initial estimates predicted lower revenue; however, revenue increased in 1964 and 1965.

June 1968, Revenue and Expenditure Control Act of 1968: This measure creates a temporary 10% income tax surcharge on both individuals and corporations through June 30, 1969. The Hon. Wilbur Mills, Chairman of the House Ways and Means Committee uses his influence to try to curb deficit spending.

December 1969, Tax Reform Act of 1969: Congress changes, yet again, many tax code provisions, including the addition of a new tax schedule for single taxpayers. Unfavorably described by Senator Curtis of Nebraska as an attempt to "cut off the dog's tail an inch at a time", this measure establishes individual and corporate minimum taxes, a precursor to the current alternative minimum tax.

December 1971, Revenue Act of 1971: Congress reinstates the investment tax credit and increases the minimum standard deduction. This law establishes the framework for public funding of presidential campaigns. Beginning in 1973, individual taxpayers could designate $1 for the Presidential Election Campaign Fund.

March 1975, Tax Reduction Act of 1975: Congress passes a number of measures to lower individual taxes. This law begins the "tinkering" that now permeates our tax laws, providing a 10% rebate of 1974 tax and added a temporary $30 general tax credit. Passed while returns were being filed for 1974, this law mandated a lump-sum refund of 1974 taxes.

Extra, Extra: Read All About It

October 1976, Tax Reform Act of 1976: Congress again includes several ways to lower the tax burden, extending the general tax credit and increasing deductions. This act increased the holding period for long-term capital gains from six months to one year.

May 1977, Tax Reduction and Simplification Act of 1977: Congress temporarily extends the general tax credit. This law replaces the percentage standard deduction and minimum standard deduction with a single standard deduction; hence, for the first time, *simplification* is used in a tax title.

November 1978, Revenue Act of 1978: Congress reduces individual income taxes, increases the personal exemption, and increases the standard deduction for joint returns. The act establishes flexible spending accounts and adds section 401(k) to the tax code.

August 1981, Economic Recovery Tax Act (ERTA) of 1981: This measure is also known as the first of the Reagan tax cuts or the "Kemp-Roth Tax Cut." It lowers the marginal income tax rates by 23% over three years. For the first time, tax rates were indexed for inflation.

September 1982, Tax Equity and Fiscal Responsibility Act of 1982: This measure, known as TEFRA, rescinds certain provisions of the Kemp-Roth act. This law has been described by critics as "the largest tax increase in American history." The Senate increased tax provisions from the version passed by the House, leading to a lawsuit because the Senate violated Article 1, Section 7 of the Constitution that states, "All bills for raising Revenue shall originate in the House of Representatives."

July 1984, Deficit Reduction Act of 1984: This law was originally part of the stalled Tax Reform Act of 1983. It was adjusted and reintroduced as the Tax Reform Act of 1984. After passing the

House, it was merged with the Senate version into its final form. This law restricted income averaging.

April 1986, Consolidated Omnibus Budget Reconciliation Act of 1985 (or COBRA) deals with a variety of issues: Contrary to instinct, *reconciliation* refers to a legislative process, not an accounting procedure. The act mandates continuing health care coverage for eligible employees if a qualifying event causes loss of coverage.

October 1986, Tax Reform Act of 1986 (TRA): Congress, at the insistence of President Reagan, simplifies the tax code to lower rates and broaden the tax base. As of 2012, this act was the most recent major simplification of the tax code and the subject of a best-selling book, *Showdown at Gucci Gulch.*

October 1988, Technical and Miscellaneous Revenue Act of 1988: Despite the major simplification of the tax code in 1986, this bill makes a number of corrections to that law. For the first time, taxpayer rights are codified under the Omnibus Taxpayer Bill of Rights —Part I: Taxpayer Rights. It requires the Secretary of the Treasury to set forth the rights and obligations of a taxpayer and of the Internal Revenue Service in nontechnical terms.

November 1990, Omnibus Budget Reconciliation Act of 1990: Congress passes a measure specifically designed to reduce the federal budget deficit and establish the "pay-as-you-go" mandates for discretionary spending and taxes, Signed by President Bush, this law violates his pledge given when he first ran for president for "no new taxes," creating an election issue during his second presidential campaign.

August 1993, Omnibus Budget Reconciliation Act of 1993: This law, unofficially referred to as the Deficit Reduction Act, raises the top individual and corporate tax rates. It took a significant step to address the Social Security crisis by eliminating the wage cap for

Medicare taxes and increasing the percentage of Social Security benefits subject to tax.

July 1996, Taxpayer Bill of Rights 2: In the wake of numerous complaints about IRS methods, Congress again addresses taxpayer rights. Among other things, this law creates the Office of the Taxpayer Advocate.

August 1997, Taxpayer Relief Act of 1997: Congress lowers several federal taxes and introduces a new child tax credit. This act establishes Roth IRAs.

July 1998, Internal Revenue Service Restructuring and Reform Act of 1998: This law, also known as Taxpayer Bill of Rights III, resulted from hearings held by the Congress in 1996 and 1997. This act dealt almost exclusively with the structure and methods of the Internal Revenue Service.

June 2001, Economic Growth and Tax Relief Reconciliation Act of 2001: This act, known as EGTRRA, but more commonly referred to the "Bush tax cuts," made sweeping reductions to federal income taxes. One report claimed it would eliminate the national debt by 2010. How is that working out?

March 2002, Job Creation and Worker Assistance Act of 2002: Congress passes a measure designed to provide tax incentives for economic recovery. It addresses potential shortfalls in the Social Security Trust Fund: "the Secretary shall transfer...from the general revenues...an amount sufficient so as to ensure...[Social Security] trust funds are not reduced."

May 2003, Jobs and Growth Tax Relief Reconciliation Act of 2003: Congress accelerates provisions of EGTRRA and further reduces tax on investment income from dividends and capital gains. This law moves the economy to the fiscal cliff and initiates annual debates over the expiration of tax cuts as nearly all of the cuts were set to expire after 2010.

October 2004, American Jobs Creation Act: Primarily focused on tariffs, this tax act repealed the export tax incentive (ETI), which had been declared illegal by the World Trade Organization and had sparked retaliatory tariffs by the European Union.

May 2006, Tax Increase Prevention and Reconciliation Act of 2005: This law prevents several tax provisions from expiring in the near future. The bill extends the reduced tax rates on capital gains and dividends and extends the alternative minimum tax reduction.

December 2006, Tax Relief and Health Care Act of 2006: This law affects a number of provisions, including health savings accounts. In its preamble, the law reads, "to extend expiring provisions," but it actually extended many provisions *retroactively*. How is that possible?

February 2008, Economic Stimulus Act of 2008: Congress provides several kinds of economic stimuli to boost the US economy and to avert a recession. For those of you who can remember the last of 2008, how did this measure work out? For the second time, Congress provides a rebate for the prior year's tax liability.

July 2008, Housing and Economic Recovery Act of 2008: The act was designed primarily to address the subprime mortgage crisis. It establishes the first-time homebuyer credit, given to eligible taxpayers in the form of an interest-free fifteen-year loan.

February 2009, American Recovery and Reinvestment Act of 2009: This law, commonly referred to as the Stimulus or the Recovery Act, was enacted to immediately save and create jobs. The law retroactively eliminated repayment of the first-time homebuyer credit but only for purchases made in 2009.

November 2009, Worker, Homeownership, and Business Assistance Act: This measure, originally passed by the House as the Unemployment Compensation Extension Act of 2009, gave an extra thirteen weeks of unemployment benefits to jobless workers in states with high unemployment rates. The Senate version gave an extra twenty weeks, but also gave an extra fourteen weeks to states with lower unemployment. The law extended the first-time homebuyer credit until April 2010, provided a tax credit for current homeowners, and increased the income limits to qualify for the credit.

March 2010, Patient Protection and Affordable Care Act: This controversial measure is commonly called the Affordable Care Act (ACA) or Obamacare. This law attempts to make universal health care part of American culture. For the first time, the tax code penalizes actions—inaction actually—not specifically related to tax events (filing returns, paying taxes, withdrawing savings prematurely, and so forth).

March 2010, Health Care and Education Reconciliation Act: Serving as an object lesson in not getting it right the first time, this measure, which amends certain provisions of the ACA, was signed only seven days after the ACA. Essentially the result of political maneuvering, passage of this law relies on the reconciliation process to get amendments originally added to the ACA passed that could not get by a Republican filibuster.

December 2010, Tax Relief, Unemployment Insurance Reauthorization, and Job Creation Act of 2010: This bill, also known as the 2010 Tax Relief Act, provides a two-year reprieve of sunset provisions of Bush tax cuts. This law also provides a one-year reduction in the FICA payroll tax.

January 2012, American Taxpayer Relief Act of 2012: Congress partially resolves the looming fiscal cliff by addressing certain provisions of the Bush tax cuts. This law makes permanent the lowest rate set by the Bush tax cuts and allows the highest tax rate to revert to the pre-Bush tax-cut level.

June 2012, *National Federation of Independent Business v. Sebelius*: The United States Supreme Court upholds the constitutionality of the ACA's individual mandate as an exercise of Congress's taxing power. The court held that states cannot be forced to participate in the ACA's Medicaid expansion under penalty of losing their current Medicaid funding. This may lead to the demise of the ACA.

www.ingramcontent.com/pod-product-compliance
Lightning Source LLC
Chambersburg PA
CBHW020723180526
45163CB00001B/84